TO:

Best Interest of the Children

A Father's Struggle to Stay Relevant in His Children's Lives Following Divorce

Book I

a novel by

Thomas Doll

The story in this book is based on real events.

Details and names have been changed to maintain anonymity.

ISBN 979-8-9909056-0-3

Written by Thomas Doll

Cover design by Jamie Doll

Published by Thomas Doll LLC

To my mother, Mildred Marie, and my father, Walter Bernard

… of course.

Foreword   *by Walter VanBuren*

Not far from his former married home, Tommy, my oldest son, rented a tiny second floor apartment. He didn't have much left by then – his ex-wife had taken almost everything – just his clothing, a bed, and his golf clubs. But I helped him carry in what he had. On the staircase, I glanced down at him hefting the heavy end of the load and my heart ached at what I saw: an unconfident young man, a shell of his former self really. I hated to see him suffer, and I wished I could do more than just help him move furniture.

After we finished with our work, he grabbed two beers out of the fridge. He drank more than I liked him to, but I accepted the beer and took a seat with him on the living room floor. It was there that we had our one and only conversation about divorce.

"You know, Tommy," I said after taking a swallow. "I think this is the right thing to do."

"What?" he asked with a smirk. "Having a beer?"

"Not that, knucklehead. I mean your divorce. Under the circumstances, I don't see how you could do anything else."

"Do you think maybe I didn't try hard enough to stay married, Pop?" he asked sincerely.

"That's just it, Tom, you *did* try hard. I give you credit for that. Kathy's own father once told me he didn't know how you were able to put up with her as long as you have." I shook my head. "I'm not saying I'm happy with your divorce, mind you, but I think I'd be doing the same thing if I were in your spot."

He looked surprised. "Pfft," he returned quickly. "No you wouldn't, Dad. I know you better than that. You would tough it out forever." He then softened up and added, "It does help me to hear you say what you said though. Thank you for that."

He was right, I reflected, *I would never have left his mother, no matter how crazy she had become. Marriage is forever – God said so. It doesn't have to be any more complicated than that.*

But Tommy doesn't hold the same faith that his mother and I do – that's why decisions like whether to divorce or not are so difficult for him. He puts it all on his own shoulders; rationalizing too much to suit me and using his head too much. But I know his heart is in the right place, and most importantly, I know he is a good father. I want him to at least know that I know that.

He finally spoke up after a long silence, his voice doleful and barely audible. "I know this is hard on you and Mom, Pop, and I'm not at all sure I've done the best thing. But I can't change it now. I can only try, as hard as I can, to make things good again ... can you forgive me?"

I nodded my head once, then studied his face looking for a better way to help him with his guilt. I wanted to show him that forgiveness was not necessary, to tell him it was okay. But I only nodded a few more times – it was the best I could do – and I think he knew what I meant.

~

Chapter 1   *Fountainhead*

August 1966

"Please come to Tom's going away party," the invitation read. It was a bit confusing since my best friend and I had the same first name. I, Tom VanBuren, was a short, hyper, sandy-haired kid, and Tom Grensylvian a tall, funny, overly smart guy with a deep announcer's voice and pimples.

I found it surprising that Kathy had known Tom G. in school, but not me. Royal Oak High was large enough that nobody got to know everybody, of course. But still, a shorter-than-me blue-eyed blonde totally escaping my notice?

"Who's that?" I asked with a jab of an elbow.

Tom looked up from the record player to see what my eyes were locked onto. "Oh, that's just Kathleen Scapaticci," he said. "She's a year behind us. You must know her."

"No, I don't," I said back.

I had seen the legs first – nice legs, not too skinny – descending the basement stairs. Then the little red skirt, the tight red sweater, and the blonde hair and blue eyes. Blondes in red were my weakness.

"I don't know her," I repeated. "Never seen her in my entire life. What's she doing here?"

Tom G., a full head taller than me, glanced down his educated nose as if I were rather stupid. "Like everybody else, bright fellow," he said, "she's here to see me off to war. It may be her last chance to get a piece of me before I'm dead, you know. You can tell by looking at her how much she wants me." He grinned like a dork. "I may just let her."

I gave him my best disgusted look and whispered, "I'm going to tell Rose you said that."

4

"Ha! She'd only laugh at you," he responded. "She knows I'd never be untrue to her."

"You mean she knows no other girl would ever touch you, don't you?"

"Either way, wise guy, the effect is the same.... By the way, did I tell you Rose said before I leave tomorrow that she and I can maybe get lovey-dovey, if you know what I mean?"

I looked away for a moment to hide my amusement and to check out the girl in red, then back to my friend. "You mean you *asked* her?"

"Of course, I asked her," he said, looking a little worried then. "Don't you ask Sandy?"

"Heck no, there are things she and I have not yet experienced, but I never thought to ask her permission.... It just happens when it happens."

"Well," he parried, "maybe you should."

"Hello soldier boy," a blonde voice in red interrupted.

My buddy seemed happy for a chance to change the subject. "Well, hello there, Kathleen," he said. "Welcome to my last day on Earth. It's good to see you. Thanks for coming." He bent forward and extended his cheek to his pretty guest. She gave him a little peck, and then he straightened up and smiled at me.

"See?" he said with a puffed-up chest. "They can't keep their hands off me."

"I can see that," I responded. "Why don't you ask her if you can ..."

"Never mind," he quickly interjected to cut me short.

We heard the clicking of the record changer behind us and the *Righteous Brothers* began their very deep and very mellow famous verse:

You never close your eyes anymore when I kiss your lips.

5

And there's no tenderness like before in your fingertips.

My good friend Tom G. bowed deeply to the young lady in red and gestured toward me. "Kathleen Scapaticci, do you by chance know my brainless friend here?"

*****

The next day Tom left for his first day in the United States Army. He had decided to just let his country draft him, so he pretty much knew he'd be going directly to Vietnam as an infantryman. It was something I didn't want to happen to me.

Kathy and I hit it off well the first evening we met. It turns out, like many other young Detroiters in those days, we were both into muscle cars. I owned a '66 Chevelle SS396 convertible, which wasn't that uncommon for an 18-year-old high school graduate in the lofty position of a mechanical detailer at Gemco Electric. But I was surprised to hear that such a little pipsqueak of a girl drove a real beast of a car; a '65 Pontiac GTO, 4 speed, 389 with Tri-power and Positraction. No power steering or brakes, of course, because that would drain too much horsepower.

"Do you have enough strength to push in that heavy duty 11-inch racing clutch with those skinny legs of yours?" I asked.

"I can manage the clutch just fine," she answered, feigning a kick to my shins to prove it. "And any time you want, we can head out to Woodward Avenue, and I'll show you just how wimpy your Chevrolet is!"

Pretending to rub the sting from her vicious kick, I suggested that because it was such a nice warm evening, instead of racing, we might better enjoy a quiet drive with the top down in my wimpy Chevrolet. She agreed.

Kathy and I lived less than a mile apart in a working-class suburb just north of Detroit: me in a house with 8 siblings and her with 4. Both households were very crowded, I suppose, but we didn't really notice it.

6

The main difference between our families was that mine had no discernible heritage and hers did. The Scapaticcis, you see, were not just Americans like everyone else I knew, they were also Italian. Her father and grandparents had immigrated from somewhere near Rome and had carried with them many of the ways of the old country. Up until then I had never experienced anything like it.

I was quickly accepted into that group of friendly and enjoyable people. Not that my own family members weren't friendly and enjoyable – they were. The Scapaticcis were different from the VanBurens, however, in a hundred ways that were not lost on me. Not necessarily better, but very different. They don't shake your hand, for instance, they hug you, and everyone drinks wine at dinner, even the kids.

Another difference is in their eating habits. They feast on big beautiful Italian food every single day. They taught me the phrase, *viviamo per mangiare – we live to eat.*

Kathy's mother, I swear, spends her entire life in the two kitchens of their modest house. One kitchen is on the main floor, as usual; the other, much larger, is in the basement. Pasta is made from scratch. Sausages, cheeses, and peppers of every sort are hung up to dry. A kettle of incredibly aromatic tomato sauce, usually with half a pork loin inside, is always bubbling on the stove top. Every bite created in those kitchens is utterly succulent and designed to be savored. They don't just eat on Helene Street in Royal Oak, they cherish their food.

Most of the meals I enjoyed at their table, I had never even heard of before – items such as peas and veal, gnocchi, and sticky chicken. And they have pizzazz that hitherto I had not known possible. More than even my new girlfriend, eating at the Scapaticcis brought me great pleasure, and every one of my new friends – parents, grandparents, aunts and uncles, siblings and cousins – seemed to take great delight in watching the new kid eat.

It had been a few months of delightful new experiences for me before I found a way to adequately express my sentiments. It was in the heat of passion, halfway secluded from others, on the landing of the staircase between the two kitchens, that I first mumbled, "I love you" to Kathleen Scapaticci. But, in all honesty, it was long before then when I fell in love with that fine Italian gang.

*****

To lessen the chance of being thrown into the broiling conflict of Vietnam, I did what my buddy Tom G. had *not* – I joined the Navy before the Army could get me. And I creatively worked my way into guaranteed stateside duty with a one-year delay before leaving. That was plenty of time for Kathy and me to get married and for her to get pregnant, in that very order.

~

Chapter 2   *Kristen*

August 6, 1968

I stood absently gazing out the 12th floor window. I could easily see the surrounding Minnesota neighborhood: slanted rooftops, moving cars, people walking, and millions of trees. The day was bright with only a little white fluffiness against the pastel blue and yellow sky. The room I stood in was completely quiet – too quiet to suit me normally – but then I hardly noticed.

I was 20 years old – still too young to drink – and my wife was still only 19. It didn't occur to either of us that it may have been a bit early in our lives to be married and expecting a child. I hadn't yet learned how to earn a proper living, and Kathy, doing her best to set up a household, didn't even know how to cook yet. But as young people tend to do, we didn't dwell much on our relative naivete.

After Navy boot camp I was shipped to a location about as far from the oceans as one could get. The seeming paradox was not lost on the two of us, but we were happy with the assignment. The twin cities of St. Paul/Minneapolis were not too far from home, and we thought it a lovely place to be.

The fight against communism escalated, and Americans were dying in Vietnam at an alarming rate. But even though I was in the military, politics and war were hardly ever the topics of discussion. The war, we were happy to notice, was happening someplace else.

Also, someplace else for us were the hippie movement, the race riots we had left behind in Detroit, and the sexual revolution we had never bothered with. Our lives were just not much affected by those things. We only wanted to be married, have babies, work, and have fun. And we weren't about to wait for any of it.

My young Italian wife had gained quite a bit of weight during pregnancy, or maybe it just looked like it to me because she was so small otherwise. During our stay at the married housing on base she developed what seemed to be an insatiable desire for ice cream. She had doctor's orders to control her intake, of course, but being the independent thinker she is, she didn't always listen.

Unfortunately for the dairy industry, our little world was small enough that Kathy sometimes got tattled on by my fellow sailors and/or their wives. She and her oversized stomach would be spotted standing in line at the Velvet Freeze or sitting in the park with a half-gallon of chocolate marshmallow fudge swirl and a tablespoon. When confronted by me, usually in bed with her big, beautiful belly being lovingly stroked, she would eventually resolve to try a little bit harder to be good.

Abruptly, a tall middle-aged nurse brought me out of my daydream as she entered the quiet expecting fathers' waiting room and, rather sternly, called out my name.

"Yes?" I said, turning from my Minnesota vista.

"Would you come this way please, Mr. VanBuren?"

I had been beginning to wonder if I was in the right place or not, having been waiting for more than three hours. With the soon-to-be mother ready to go into the delivery room, I was escorted to my present location and told to have a seat. I was the only dad in the waiting room all that time, and no further direction of any kind came my way.

The big moment, however, seemed to be at hand, and for the first time that day I felt a little shaky. I didn't immediately take a step, but the lady spun around and left the room without me.

She had said my name, so she must have meant me. I pushed open the door and looked both ways. There she was on the right amongst other women dressed in white … maybe. I hurried to catch up.

I followed the blur rushing down the hallways turning once, then twice, not at all convinced I was on the right trail. The lady never looked back; she just kept forging ahead, dodging sick people and other nurses bustling to and fro. It was so frantic and noisy!

Everything must be alright with Kathy, I reasoned, or the nurse would have said so. But she hadn't smiled and hadn't said *congratulations you have a boy* like I had expected. Kathy and her mom and most everyone else also expected a boy. Some thought a girl would be nice too, of course.

The lady suddenly stopped at a pair of swinging doors with a sign that read "Do Not Enter." She put her hands on the doors as if she were about to push through, but first looked over her shoulder. She caught my eye and smiled, apparently pleased she hadn't lost me. I pulled up short, but my momentum caused me to bump into her a little.

"Oh, I'm sorry," I said loudly.

She shot me a teasing scowl and held an index finger to her lips in the universal "quiet please" signal. Then she backed through the doors with a grin.

We entered what seemed to be an entirely new world, leaving behind the crowd, the bright lights, and the noise. The lady went ahead slowly from that point. The hallway was wide and nearly empty. Baby powder was the dominant bouquet.

Soon she stopped next to a wheeled contraption of some sort, a plastic box on a pushcart with cords and things attached.

"Here you go," she said quietly with a gesture to the device.

"Here I go what?" I thought, glancing into the container.

Inside I saw a delicate creature's little round face, eyes softly closed, wrapped tightly in pink up to her tiny chin.

Her tiny chin! I noted ... *my daughter's chin.*

Oh, my God, I realized. *My daughter!*

All else in the world faded away as I mouthed the words in astonishment. *"This is my daughter."*

My knees weakened at the thought of it all, apparently not having understood until that very moment what I had done – what my wife and I had done. What I had expected to see or feel, I cannot say, but the first sight of that infant – that very infant – engulfed my being with wonderment like a 10-story wave overcoming an unexpecting surfer.

I watched the blanket rise and lower with each tiny breath. Pulsing aqua spider webs behind translucent eyelids echoed a steady heartbeat. Wisps of nearly invisible angel hair veiled her precious forehead.

In those few seconds emotions built inside of me that seemed no man prior could possibly have felt – bursting love and the overwhelming need to forever nourish and protect. There, what shone before me, changed the meaning of my life for all time. It was as if I had just been born myself. Elation overflowed my heart and tears released down my cheeks.

I stared, wide eyed and mouth agape, for who knows how long, powerless to do anything else, when a warm motherly hand gently touched my shoulder. The nurse and I then watched together, intently, and patiently, as the child slowly, slowly blinked open her pale blue eyes and, I swear, smiled directly at me. At that marvelous happening I spoke then the very first words of my life as a father.

"Hello, Kristen."

~

Chapter 3   *Minnesota*

March 1970

My tour of duty in the United States Navy was coming to an end. I had gained valuable training as an electronics technician, and the overall experience had not been unpleasant, but both Kathy and I were anxious to get the military behind us. There were no thoughts of reenlistment.

Almost the entire two years and three months I was stationed at the Twin Cities Naval Air Station, I had also worked an off-base, part-time job selling mobile homes in the city of North St. Paul. It was an opportunity I stumbled upon quite by accident my first week in town, and it turned out I was a good salesman. I had no problem putting in the hours, and I earned some nice commission checks. Consequently, when it came to things such as cars and money in our pockets, we lived comparatively abundant lives. In fact, life all around Minnesota was quite good for us.

Kristen was 19 months old; the most beautiful kid on base, of course, if not on the entire Earth. And she loved her daddy, which was all I really cared about. She was so smart! She could sing "Twinkle Twinkle Little Star" in its entirety without reading the words. Kathy learned how to cook, somewhat like an Italian too, although her skill came with enormous phone bills to her mother in Detroit. Just as it had been in Michigan, the three of us spent a good deal of our lives in the kitchen area.

About the only dampness we felt in our lives in those days, the only real disagreements we had, were when discussing life after the Navy. Where were we going to live following my discharge on April 8th? I voted for staying in Minnesota; we liked the town, and I had a good job already waiting for me.

"Why not stay here?" I often asked.

"Because all my family is in Michigan, that's why," Kathy answered one day while draining hot water from a large pot of pasta.

Steam filled the kitchen of our new 12-foot-wide mobile home and collected on the ceiling. "And you know full well how I feel about it ... I want to go home!"

Busy at the kitchen table trying to put together a toy buggy for Kristen while she took a nap, I had little chance of finishing the construction before the child was three years old.

"Yeah, I know how you feel, honey," I said, trying to match the correct nut to an axle. "But ..."

"But nothing, Tom," she cut me off. "And don't start with me now. Jim and Candy will be here soon, and I don't want us to be fighting in front of them."

"They're used to this topic, Kath," I replied, "and they've decided *not* to go back to North Dakota, you know."

"Yeah, I know. So what?" she answered, stirring her tomato sauce. "That's no reason for us to do the same."

"But it's a similar situation, Kathy. Jim has no prospect for work back home, just like I don't have work in Detroit."

"BS Tom! You can go back to work as a draftsman. Don't give me that!"

"I don't know that at all, Kathleen," I said, shaking my head, my voice rising. "Even if I could get my old job back, I'd only be earning half as much money as I can earn here."

"We don't need money!" she insisted, flailing her hands in front of herself. "How many times do I have to tell you? My parents want us to live with them; and I don't want to talk about this anymore!"

"But we *have* to talk about it, *dammit!*" I yelled, rapping my pliers on the Formica tabletop. "We've got to be out of here in two weeks, and you know we can't live forever with your parents. They can't afford to feed us, and they shouldn't have to anyway. *I* must support us, not them, and not you. And I don't have a job in Detroit."

"Well, you'll just have to *find* one then, buddy. That's your problem. When you married me, you didn't say anything like this. We

14

are not staying in this godforsaken place a minute longer than we must!"

I laughed and got up from my chair to emphasize my point. "Oh, don't pretend you don't like Minnesota, Kath," I said, wagging a finger at her. "I know better."

"I don't like it so much I want to stay here," she shot back, whipping the sauce around with more force than necessary, splattering the stove. "It's way too cold here."

"It's hardly colder than Detroit," I returned. "Just a little bit more snow, that's all. And we've gotten used to it."

She stopped stirring and glared at me like I was crazy. "I've not gotten used to 10-foot-deep snow, Tom, and neither has Kristen! She hates it!"

"Oh, don't be silly," I smirked. "You don't have to exaggerate, Kath. You know darn well you've never seen snow deeper than 9 feet."

Not thinking I was funny, she scowled and turned back to her cooking.

"Besides," I went on, "Kristen never told you she doesn't like the snow. Heck, she never wants to come indoors. And that house for rent on Lake Phalen has a nice little sledding hill in the park next to it that she and the dog will just love. And ..."

"Cut it out Tom. I'm not listening. You know how important it is for me to go home. Why can't you just give that to me?"

Wanting to slow down the arguing, I took a deep breath and approached my wife from behind at the stove, slipping my hands around her waist inside her apron. She didn't resist.

"Oh, honey," I said, trying to turn on my salesman's charm. "I know what being near your family means to you. I'd like to be near my family as well. But mostly I'm just thinking about us – you and me and Kristen ... and more kids in the future, I hope. You know I want 12 more."

15

"We're not having 12 more kids, goofball," she said, warming to my touch.

"Okay," I agreed. "Half that would be fine, but whatever it is, I've got to provide for us the best I can … and I know I can make a good living right here in snow town."

I felt her body tense up a bit, but she stayed in place, so I continued my pitch. "I'm not saying we should commit to staying here forever, honey. I'm just saying we have good reason to give it a try. It could be very good for us, you know, and if we leave now, we'll never know how it might have turned out."

I moved my roving hands around and pushed in closer from behind. She returned the favor.

"Why don't we commit to a one-year lease on that Lake Phalen house, sweetheart," I went on as our spooning continued. "If after that time you still want to go back to Michigan, heck, I'd agree to it then, no problem. What do you say to that?"

She shrugged me away and turned to face me. "I'd say you're out of your mind, mister. It's okay being here while you're in the Navy, but as soon as that's over, I want to go home. I don't have to wait a year to know what I want!"

I stood back a step and asked, "What about what I want, Kath? Doesn't that count for anything?"

"You can do what you want, Tom," she said without rancor. "I won't stop you."

Not exactly sure what she meant by that last remark, I folded my arms. "Does that mean you'll accept my decision as man of the house?"

Her hands set firmly on her hips told me the answer was no, and that the discussion was about to end.

"I did not say that" she replied clearly. "But our guests will be here in 10 minutes, and you haven't given Kristen her bath yet, so get that buggy off the table and get moving. And find something else to talk about!"

*****

April 1970

Eventually, Kathleen relented. She didn't exactly say, *you are my husband, and of course I'll live wherever you choose for us to live,* but she signed the lease with me, and that was enough. In one afternoon, we moved out of the Navy housing and into what was for me an entirely new, interesting world.

I was excited with our new home and fenced-in yard near the lake, and so were Kristen and our highly active little puppy, Missy. Both the child and best friend happily ran their little legs off round and round. Springtime in that part of the world was something special. Sunshine and warm air, and the subsequent thawing of the land after such a long deep freeze was enough to put everyone in good spirits. Everyone, that is, except for my wife.

Six weeks passed without seeing brightness in my wife's ordinarily cute expression, not even while being romantic or while eating, both of which were normally stimulating for her. And not even when she played with Kristen, or when I would act like a clown trying to uplift her. She just refused to be cheerful.

One night as I crawled into bed after working late, she pretended to be asleep. I nuzzled up tight behind her, but she did not acknowledge my presence. I kissed her neck, and still got no response. Finally, then, I pinched her behind, and got the yelp I was looking for.

"What's wrong with you?" she grumped, slapping my hand without turning. "Can't you see I'm sleeping?"

"No, you're not," I answered playfully. "I saw the bedroom light go out as I pulled up the drive; you can't fool me."

"Why are you so late?" she asked in monotone, still without turning.

"Oooooooh," I sang. "So, you've missed me, have you?"

17

Unmoved by my teasing, she did not twitch a muscle or make a sound. So, I squeezed in tighter. "Don't you love me anymore, sweetheart?"

At that she abruptly tossed my arms aside and rolled to face me. "It's not that, Tom," she barked. "It's just that I'm home alone all day long with a two-year-old, bored stiff. I've nothing to do and I don't know anyone. And then you don't come home when you're supposed to. I know you finished work an hour ago because I called there. What have you been doing?"

I leaned back on my pillow and grinned. "Well," I said with pleasure, "that's the most life I've seen out of you in a long while. Welcome home earthling. You know you look sexy when you're angry. Wanna fool around?"

"No, I don't wanna fool around, fool," she insisted, folding her arms. "Are you going to tell me what you've been up to?"

I sat up. "If you must know, honey, I'll tell you. But I'm warning you, when I do, you're gonna feel badly for suspecting some wrongdoing here."

"I'll take my chances," she said, the scowl still present.

I saw the blankets at the end of the bed pulsating as if she were tapping her foot on the floor waiting impatiently for my confession. "Well, it's like this," I began, "remember the Fort Snelling marketplace down by the base?"

"Yeah, what about it?"

"Well, I know they're open till 10 o'clock, you see, cuz I used to buy beer there."

"Yeah, so?"

"So, I drove out there after work to buy a case of beer."

"What? And your buying beer instead of coming home is supposed to make me feel bad?"

I laughed. "Well, I also happened to remember they sell Minnehaha ice cream, and I picked up four quarts of that too."

Her eyes widened. "You didn't!"

"Oh, yes, I did! *Now* do you feel bad?"

"You bought me ice cream so I would feel bad?"

"I didn't say I bought it for you."

"Oh, you're such an asshole!" she said with a huge smile, throwing back the covers and flying out of the room.

"Save some for me!" I called after her.

Sometime later, I watched my wife dig the last dollop of chocolate goo from the first quart of Minnehaha's Best. "So, what do you think of me now, honey?" I asked.

She smiled and licked her spoon. "That was very nice of you," she conceded, "but next time call me first so I don't worry."

"Okay, okay," I agreed. "But I don't think you were so worried about me as much as you were just feeling neglected."

"Yeah, that too," she said quickly, seeming happy I pointed that out. "So, what are you going to do about it?"

I folded my hands behind my head and leaned back in my chair. "Well, I do have an idea," I said. "Why don't you take the baby and fly home for a nice long visit with your family?"

Obviously surprised by my suggestion, she didn't respond right away, perhaps trying to sort out my intentions. When she did speak, she asked, "And leave you here alone?"

"Yeah, why not? I'll be okay."

"Because you can't so much as make a sandwich for yourself. What are you going to eat?"

"I'll manage."

"Why don't you come with us, Tom?"

I sat forward and put my elbows on the table. "You know I have to work, but you don't have to. We can afford the airfare, and I know you miss your family, and they'd like to see Kristen, I'm sure.

19

Aaaaaand," I added proudly, "maybe that'll help you feel a little less neglected."

Her eyes narrowed in suspicion as she glared condemningly at me, the vibes pressing me back in my seat again. "I think you just want to play golf with Tony Meijer again, don't you?" she accused.

Normally, I wouldn't take such silly remarks to heart, but as of late that type of talk was becoming commonplace, so I responded with some seriousness.

"Come on, Kath. You don't have to be so cynical all the time. I hope I don't have to send my wife out of town just so I can play a round of golf in peace."

I bit my lip and held up a hand. "But if you feel like you can't let me out of your sight, Kathleen, that's alright. I don't like to prepare my own food, that's for sure. And, come to think of it, I have no idea how to use the washing machine, so ..."

"No, no, no, Tom!" She stopped me. "I trust you, don't worry. I was acting a fool." She smiled broadly then and bubbled, "and I would love, love, love to go home!" She got up from her chair, ran around the table, and plopped herself into my lap, smothering me with hugs and kisses.

~

Chapter 4   *Airport*

June 1, 1970

Misty-eyed at Northwest Orient Airlines Gate 24C, I stood waving goodbye to my two loves: Kathleen Anabella and Kristen Kathleen VanBuren. I had been separated from my wife before, for a month, when I first went active duty, but with my daughter this was the first time. I wondered if she understood at all how this was affecting her daddy? *Naaaaaa,* I decided. *How could she?*

Kristen looked to be a miniature of her mother: the same fly-away sandy hair, rosy cheeks, and sparkling blue eyes. God, I was going to miss them!

The baby girl held tight to her mother's coat tail, being led down the loading ramp. She looked back at the last second, frantically throwing kisses my way with her little arm extending from her brand-new pale-yellow spring coat.

In her own pale-yellow spring coat, Kathy looked back also, but with her hands filled with carry-on luggage, all she could do was smile.

It had been 10 days since we decided the two of them should go without me back to Michigan for an extended stay. Not wanting to define exactly when they would return, Kathy insisted on buying one-way tickets.

"Probably just for two or three weeks," she said.

"That's okay with me," I told her. "Stay until you're ready to come home, or until you miss me too much, whichever comes first. But don't worry about me, honey. I can eat Frosted Mini Wheats seven days a week, and I'll figure out how to use the washing machine, no problem."

I stood by the glass wall, hands in my pockets, until the big plane blended in with a hundred others just like it on the tarmac and rolled out of sight. No other plane moved into the vacated space. I took a deep breath and wondered out loud: "So now what?"

*****

The first three weeks went by quickly, and the experience hadn't been that awful for me. During that time, I tried to take advantage of not having a wife to answer to; I played golf as much as I could, put a lot of miles on my motorcycle, and even spent a little happy hour time in the bars after work. The freedom was refreshing.

Before too long I discovered I should rinse out my cereal bowl following each use, so the spoiling sugared milk left inside would not draw ants to the kitchen sink. Also, I hired a cleaning lady I found in the newspaper to come over once a week and clean the place and do laundry. I'd not tell Kathy about that, of course.

Every three or four days I phoned Michigan, usually after dinner. Kathy would describe to me in detail every item that had been on the Scapaticci table that evening. "I hope you're watching your mother this time around, Kath, so maybe you can learn something," I would remark. Then I would tell her the different ways I learned to serve shredded wheat with milk, and how I couldn't wait to share it with her.

Except for *Twinkle Twinkle Little Star,* Kristen wasn't yet speaking in complete sentences, but that didn't stop her and me from having great conversations. I always wanted to know what she had been up to, and she always wanted to know about her puppy. The key for me to hang up happy was to hear the word *daddy* as many times as possible. The magic sound of "Daddy, Daddy, Daddy!" emanating from my little princess always made me melt.

"Oh, we're not coming home for two or three more weeks, Tom," Kathy said one evening after a question from me. "My brother wants Kristen and me to spend some time with him and Yvette at their new home in Hillman. It's about 20 miles from Alpena. He's going to come down here and get us next week or the week after."

Crestfallen and just a little peeved, I was speechless.

"Tom?" she said. "Did you hear me?"

"Yeah, I heard you, Kath," I finally spoke up. "I ... I'm just a little surprised."

"You don't mind, do you?"

I took a deep breath, having not seen this coming. "Well yes," I said. "I do mind a little. I don't like being alone like this, you know."

"But you said ... "

"Yeah, I know what I said, honey, but man, it's been a month already. I didn't expect you to be gone this long, and I don't want Kristen to forget what the heck I look like, you know."

"She knows what you look like, goofy," she easily dismissed. "Don't worry, she talks about you all the time. But I want her to know the rest of her family too. Ron and Yvette have hardly ever even seen her, and I want to see their new house, and Ronny bought a new charter boat and he's going to take us all out on Lake Huron and ... "

"Okay, okay, honey," I interrupted. "It's okay with me. I want you to go, really. It sounds great. Maybe you can fly back here directly from Alpena though. Is there an airport there?"

"There's not a big airport, Tom, I know that. But it's only four and a half hours from there to Detroit Metro, so Ronny can take us there anytime we want, and we can fly right home and be back with you in nothing flat. Okay, lover?"

*****

"Okay, lover?" Those words and the way they were spoken to me ran through my mind many times over, usually as I lay in bed, alone, night after night. Her tone felt so condescending, or patronizing, or something. I didn't know how to describe it. But it was a new attitude coming from my wife, and I wondered what it meant.

On top of that, the novelty of being a bachelor for the first time in my life had more than worn off. I was not that good at it. I had played enough golf and drank enough beer with my buddies. Enough already! I wanted my family life back.

When I closed my eyes and thought about it, I could feel loving arms around my neck or a warm cheek to my cheek, but that only made things worse. I needed the real thing again, not just dreams. I could not understand at all why anyone would want to be single. I longed for a home-cooked meal, and a conversation about the day's events with someone who cared about what I did. And I missed my daughter for chrissake – her running and jumping into my arms, so glad to see me every time I walked in the door, even if it was 10 times in the same day.

"Jesus, Kath! I need someone to be happy to see me again!" I finally burst out some days later over the telephone. "I can't stand coming home to an empty house anymore, without a baby to greet me, and no one to talk to, and no one to eat or sleep with. You've been gone for 47 days. I hate it!"

"Boy, Tom," she said. "You've never seemed like you needed us so much before."

"Oh, I have so! This is nothing new for me. It's why I wanted to be married and have babies in the first place. It's what you wanted too, remember?"

I calmed down then, wanting to ask a question that had been haunting me. "What has happened, Kath? How come you can stand being away from me so long, so easily?"

She didn't respond right away, and I didn't say another word. It was a sales technique I had learned. Ask a leading question: "What's keeping you from taking this mobile home today, Mr. Smith?" And then shut up. Don't let him off the hook by speaking again before he answers. Unfortunately, the technique didn't work too well for me in this case.

Kathy just ignored my question, and after a long silent moment changed the subject completely. "My grandfather's 90th birthday party is next week at my Aunt Elsie's. Kristen is getting her hair cut just for the occasion. She loves to bounce on her great grandpa's knee."

*****

July 31, 1970

Following great grandpa's birthday party, I was determined to put my foot down and end this extended vacation baloney. I had had enough. Besides, Kristen's second birthday was coming up soon, and I had no intention of missing that.

"Alright, Kath," I started right in when she phoned me. "I've made up my mind. Your vacation is over. Next week is our daughter's birthday, and the three of us are going to celebrate it right here in good ole Minnesota – me, you, and Kristen. Got it? And I don't want to hear a single word otherwise. I don't care if the pope is coming to Michigan. Understand?"

"Well," she laughed. "Who'd you borrow balls from, Tony Meijer? Not Jimmy Quoiness, that's for sure!"

"You don't think I have a mind of my own?"

"It's not that, Tom. You don't have to be so defensive … and you know being bossy doesn't work with me."

"Is that right? Then what *does* work, Kath?"

"Well," she said in good cheer that caught me by surprise. "You don't have to force me, Tom. You know I can't bear to be away from you for long. You are my husband, after all. As it turns out, I've already made plans to come home. That's what I called to tell you about."

Not trusting what I was hearing, I pressed for details. "When's that, next Christmas?"

"On Kristen's birthday," she said with pride. "Thursday, at 2:55 pm, Northwest Flight Number 103. So there!"

*****

The rain was falling hard as I stood at the airport glass watching the planes move around the tarmac like pieces in a giant chess game. The flight was due from Detroit any minute. I felt a little self-conscious holding a teddy bear and a bouquet of flowers I'd just bought at the gift shop. Soon, a big Northwest airliner pulled up to the gate. "This must be the one," I said to the lady standing next to me. I couldn't help but be excited.

As the passengers poured out of the tunnel, I anxiously searched for two pale-yellow overcoats. I spotted my wife, lugging baggage with two hands. "Is she making the baby walk again?" I said to myself. "She'll get trampled."

Kathy caught sight of me, smiled and struggled to where I was waiting at the end of the tunnel, but no little cherub trailed behind her. "Aren't you going to help me, big fella?" she asked playfully, then set her bags down and took the flowers from me.

Alarmed, I peered around both sides of her yellow coat. "Where's Kristen?" I cried.

"Oh, I left her home with my mom and dad. Didn't I tell you?"

"No, you didn't tell me!" I yelped, then relaxed a bit and grinned. "You're kidding, right?"

Her shoulders dropped low, and she said without emotion, "I'm not kidding, Tom. I left her home."

"Oh, you did not!" I insisted. "Is she sleeping or something? You can't leave her there alone, you know!" Fighting then against the flow of people I squeezed around my wife to run back onto the plane.

"*Tom!*" she shouted, grabbing at me, but too slow. "I told you I didn't bring her."

After a few steps, the jolt of what she had said struck me. My face burning, I stopped and glared back at the woman in total disbelief.

"It's true, Tom," she said over the crowd noise. "I can't believe you're so upset."

Two fat guys in Bermuda shorts, perhaps having had too much to drink on the flight, bumped into me, passing in tandem. "Excuse us, please. Excuse us."

"You can't believe I'm upset!" I yelled at the top of my lungs, startling the hell out of the two fat guys. I then pushed through them and charged at my wife as if I were going to throttle her.

She didn't wince, but looked around furtively, then hissed, "Would you shut up! You're making a scene."

"What are you trying to pull here, Kath?" I demanded.

She thrust her hands onto her hips, crushing her flowers. "I'm trying to save our marriage, you jerk, that's what I'm trying to pull."

Flailing my arms without regard, I bellowed back, "What are you talking about, woman? What's wrong with our marriage?"

She stuck her chin out. "You knew damn well I wouldn't like it here, but you made me stay anyway!"

"But you agreed!" I screamed, shaking the teddy bear in her face.

More of the crowd trying to exit the plane made their way unhappily around us, staring, some probably wondering if they were about to witness a murder.

She shook her crumbled flowers at me in return. "You left me no choice!" she yelled. "And now I don't agree with staying here anymore. So there, dumbass!"

"Dumbass?" I blared incredulously. "You abandon our child – on her birthday, no less – and *I'm* the dumbass?"

"I didn't abandon anybody!" she blared back, making sure everyone around was watching. "I left her with my mom and dad, where she's very safe, and I flew halfway round the world to fetch her stupid father. Why are you so angry at me for that?"

Dumbstruck, I slapped my open palm to my forehead and dragged it heavily down to my chin. Closing my eyes then, I raised my face to the ceiling and said barely audibly, "How can you be doing this to me, Kathleen?"

27

"I'm not doing anything *to you*, buddy," was her immediate snotty response. "You've brought this upon yourself."

Not a drop of wifely compassion or consideration for me did she show. Not a hint of it.

"You should have known better," she vindictively added for good measure.

Rage, disbelief, and panic filled me all at the same time. My jaw clenched and my arms began to quiver. A growl of sorts emanated from deep inside my heaving chest.

She gave me a look I'd not seen in my life before; a look of fear so intense it bordered on terror. "You're scaring me, Tom."

"You should be scared, Kath," I spat out through my teeth. "You've done something very bad here." I shook a finger in her face. "I should make you pay for this right now, but that's not worth going to jail over! I'm just going to leave you here and I'm going back to Detroit as fast as I can to get my daughter." I swung around then and hurried away not caring if I ever saw that stupid woman again in my life.

"Wait, Tom!" She hollered and ran after me. "Where are you going?"

I had made it only a short distance down the busy aisle when she caught up to me. *"Wait, Tom, wait!"* she pleaded, grabbing my arm. "You don't understand."

I didn't stop moving, tearing her hands off me as I went. "Oh, I understand alright, Kath! Leave me alone!" I hurried my step to almost running, but she kept up, one or two paces behind.

"You can't just leave me here, bonehead!" she hollered, reaching for me. "I'm coming with you! You can't stop me! Don't think you're going to get away with this. Wait for me, dammit!"

The gate attendants and the passengers alike made a wide path for us as if we were an approaching ambulance. Then they watched in amazement as the commotion flew by.

The yellow fireball blared while trying to catch up with me. "You can't just go back to Detroit and pick up Kristen, dumbass! I'll call my parents; they won't let you! I'm your wife, damn it!" Her pitch rose higher and higher. "You can't leave me here!"

I knew she was talking, but I wasn't hearing it. I'd never been so livid. My only mission at that point was to get out of the building before I blew a gasket.

"If you think you'll get away with this, you've got another thing coming! I know where you live, asshole! I'll make your life miserable! I promise. If you don't think I won't ..."

As I churned through the marble corridor gaining some distance from the maniac in pursuit of me, I became aware of something in my right hand. I lifted the ragged teddy bear to my eyes and snarled, reminded of everything I was angry about. I spotted a trash can at the upcoming intersection where I intended to turn right. As I rounded the corner, I smashed the stuffed animal through the flap of the receptacle and never broke stride. Two seconds later I heard the flap rattle again, with what I assumed to be a bouquet of flowers.

"Will you slow down, for crying out loud!"

~

Chapter 5   *Decision*

August 1970

All the way to my car in the parking garage, Kathy maintained her position of no more than a few steps behind me, yapping endlessly in a screechy tone the entire distance. She grabbed the passenger door handle before I could start the car and drive off. "Open the door!" she demanded. "Before I call the police."

Reluctantly, I did, but I hardly waited for her to get in before I sped away.

Mercifully, once she arrived in the seat next to me, she shut up. In fact, more than a week passed before I heard her voice again. Kathy must have gone back to the airport the next day to retrieve her belongings; her carry-on bags she had left on the floor by Gate 24C and a large Pullman was waiting for her at baggage claim.

When I came home from work the next night – deliberately late, about 10 pm – the now empty luggage was in the mud room waiting to be put away. Kathy was busy setting up a house for herself in the living room. I ignored her and went to bed.

We simmered that way for the next few days. I gave up on my mindset of flying back to Detroit to get the baby. She was well cared for, I was sure of that, and I knew I had to work things out with my wife first. The problem was neither Kathy nor I wanted to take any steps to break the ice.

The next Friday, however, a full week after the airport incident, I was ready to make a move. I went home on time for a change, and I had a plan.

When I entered the back door, I knew instantly Kathy had been cooking. Beautiful, wonderful, fabulous Italian aroma filled the air, and I sighed. "Oh boy, I sure hope she's cooking for me." I started for the kitchen with a huge grin, then remembered I didn't want to be the first to speak. Stubbornly then, I walked past my wife without a word and went to the back of the house to shower.

As I was toweling off 20 minutes later, there was a soft knock on the bathroom door. "Dinner is on the table, Tom," she said.

Hot damn! I thought. *She's the first to speak.* Then, knowing I was being silly, but also being hungry as hell, I responded. "This doesn't mean I'm not mad at you anymore, Kath, but I'll be right out."

I sat down with my wife to a nice spread on the dining room table. The presentation was a bit grand for a weekday meal for two, but I assumed it was her way of offering peace. Through the first half of the meal little was said beyond the occasional "Would you pass the roasted peppers, please, or would you like some more wine?"

Then, I finally spoke up. "This is a fine meal, Kath. Thanks for doing this."

I got no response. She didn't even look at me. But I pressed on: "Does this mean you want to make-up, honey?"

She just took a bite of roast pork and looked out the window chewing it.

"Well, don't worry, tuffy, I don't want to make-up either," I fibbed. Then I sopped up some of my spaghetti sauce with a piece of homemade bread and bit off a chunk.

We finished the rest of our meal in relative silence, but I thought I understood what was going on in her head. She wouldn't have gone through the trouble of making this meal had she not wanted to patch things up. Heck, if she didn't have goodwill toward me, she wouldn't have come back here to "fetch" me in the first place. She would have just stayed in Michigan.

While I did not expect she was considering acquiescing on her position about living in Minnesota, she at least seemed ready to quit acting disdainful. I thought she was probably good and ready to have me back in her arms again, but I supposed she would continue to feign aloofness for a good while yet.

31

It was my plan to try to get us physically close again before attempting to talk out our differences. We would have a chance for meaningful dialogue if we first showed and felt some love for each other. Besides, and perhaps most importantly, I wanted to touch my wife again, and I thought she felt the same about me.

As she was clearing the table, I resolved to put my original plan into motion. Nonchalantly, I mentioned: "Tony asked us to go on a motorcycle trip this weekend with him and Connie."

She placed a stack of dirty plates into the kitchen sink, and without turning to me responded: "You know I don't like Tony."

Perhaps she was just offering up phony resistance. I was sure she didn't dislike Tony half as much as she pretended. Maybe I was gaining some traction.

"Yeah, I know," I answered, "but you like Connie well enough, and it may do you and me some good to be forced into sitting next to each other for two days on a bike. Besides, it would be fun."

Still not looking at me, she offered up her next lame objection. "Who will take care of Missy?"

Thinking then I had her, I covered the issue. "Mrs. Wilhite will, I bet. If we ask her."

"Mmpfff," she responded.

It wasn't exactly a yes, but she didn't say no.

*****

We left early the next morning. It was the first time we had touched each other in more than three months. After meeting up with Tony and Connie we headed east down the empty sunlit highway. The air was still cool; the fog slowly lifting from the nearby farmers' fields. The machine we sat upon thumped a strong beat into our souls. Mile after mile, hour after hour, I was conscious of my wife's arms around my waist, her legs tight to mine, her breasts pressed

32

against my back. It all felt very good to me. I wondered what she was feeling.

Before sunset, the four of us reached the middle of Wisconsin. We found a small country store, picked up some food and drink, and rode into the woods in search of a place to camp. Where the dirt path seemed to end, we parked the bikes and quickly gathered some fallen branches to build a fire before darkness set in. We ate, drank, and laughed around the fire for hours; worry never revealed itself.

Slowly but surely Kathy and I eased back into our comfort zones together. She assembled sandwiches for all of us with her typical Italian flair, then sat close to me on an old log to enjoy her meal.

I gave her a squeeze. "Thanks, Hon," I said, and really meant it. Then with a smile, I added: "Where'd you learn to cook like this?"

Heaven was bright with a billion sparkles against the blackness of a moonless night. The fire crackled and danced, and three bottles of wine made us giddy. All our troubles seemed to fade away.

In the clearing in the woods that night, lying in the warm grass next to glowing embers, covered only by a blanket of stars, we made love. It was not the frenzied passion of long separated lovers, nor was it gratuitous or obligating. It was something else –something better.

*****

The next morning, we took our time getting started. By the crack of noon, the four of us were sitting in Paul Bunyan's breakfast saloon drinking coffee and reading menus.

"I'm having one of each," Tony teased. "I'm starving."

"I'll have one Paul Bunyan with nothing on him," Connie quipped loudly with a smirk.

33

Tony looked with admiration at the tiny woman with the loud voice sitting next to him in the booth. "I bet you could handle his big ax alright, Connie – no problem!"

Kathy laughed heartily at her two friends, seeming to have forgotten she didn't like Tony.

Halfway through our huge meals, following a rare lull in the conversation, Connie stated, loudly as usual, "You know I really have fun with you guys. I sure hope you stay in Minnesota."

Kathy dropped her fork into her syrupy pancakes, then looked embarrassingly at Connie and said, "Shit, now look what I've done."

"Oh, I'm sorry," Connie said hastily. "Should I not have said that? Waitress! Can we get another fork over here, please? I'm sorry, Kath, really. Tom! What have you done to this poor child?"

"Me?" I questioned.

Kathy's chin started to quiver, then her water faucets turned on full blast. Connie and Tony both glared at me as if I were Attila the Hun.

"I didn't do anything," I protested. "Come on Kath, cut it out before I get arrested for beating my wife. We haven't discussed yet, Connie, whether we're staying here or going back to Michigan."

I picked up my wife's hand and cradled it. "We've got a lot to talk about, honey," I said softly. "Don't assume you're not going to get what you want."

"Really?" She turned to me, tears still flowing, but with a big smile. She gushed as if she'd just been picked *Queen for a Day.* "This is so wonderful Tom; I knew you would do the right thing. Our daughter is going to be so happy!"

"Slow down Kathy," I said, feeling myself getting in much deeper than I'd intended. "I didn't say yes. I just said you and I are going to talk about it, and don't be surprised if you win."

She stared at me, perhaps pretending to be confused, then asked the closing question. "Okay, we're going to talk about it. I get that. But I know you think *you* must make the final decision. So, when are you going to inform *me,* Tom?"

I looked helplessly to Tony, then to Connie, then to the waitress bringing a new fork, then back to my wife still staring at me sniffling. All of them were waiting for an answer. Nobody was about to let me off the hook by talking before I did. They were all trained salespersons too.

The silence was overpowering. I had to commit to something, and quickly. *I don't know* was not going to suffice. Finally, I took a deep breath and said the only thing I could think of.

"Three more days, Kath. I'll give you an answer on Wednesday."

*****

The next day at work, Tony called me into his office and greeted me with his usual warm charm. "We sure had a good time this weekend, didn't we, Tommy boy? Do you want to play golf this afternoon? I think it'll be slow enough around here today."

"Yeah, that would be great," I answered without enthusiasm.

Ignoring my lack of usual zeal at the mention of golf, Tony then came out with what was really on his mind. "Did you have any luck convincing that wife of yours that the two of you ought to stay here in Minnesota?"

"Well," I hesitated, "we really didn't talk much about it last night. We got home so late, you know. We pretty much just went to sleep." I grinned. "At least she slept in my bed for a change.

The stylishly dressed 30-year-old leaned way back in his chair and eased his hands behind his head of wavy blond hair. "You're not going to cave, Tom, are you?"

After a long embarrassing moment of silence, I sadly conceded. "I don't know, Ton', maybe. She'll never be happy here,

35

you know that. Besides, I don't even have enough money to fly to Detroit and retrieve our daughter."

"You need money?" he asked, sitting up quickly, and pulling a checkbook out of his desk. He quickly wrote it out and handed me a check for two thousand dollars. "Consider it a bonus," he said. "Is that enough?"

I looked carefully at the piece of paper in my hands, then to my boss' piercing blue eyes, then back to the paper. I knew what it would mean if I accepted it. For better or for worse, my decision would then be made.

I would be crazy to leave a job like this, I thought. *How lucky can a guy my age expect to be? I'll never find anything like this again, and Minnesota is a perfect place to raise a family.* I wondered if Kathy might think differently today after our nice weekend together. *Surely, I could persuade her*, I reasoned.

"Yes, this is enough, Tony," I finally said. "Thank you! Maybe we can pay the airfare for Kathy's parents to bring Kristen out here to us. Kathy will be grateful, I'm sure."

*****

I was wrong again, of course. Kathy was not grateful in the least bit, even though I intended to use the money for her family to visit us.

"You said you were going to take three days to make your decision!" she screamed at me. "And we were supposed to talk about it first. You *lied* to me."

"I did not lie, Kath; I meant exactly what I said. But things changed when Tony handed me this check. I had to decide right then and there, so I decided."

"Well, you can just give him that check back and unmake your decision, because I am not staying here, and neither are you!"

"I can't give it back; I already signed it."

36

I stepped over to the refrigerator and stuck the check behind a magnet, then eased back and tried to touch my frozen wife. But she shook me off.

"C'mon, Kath, lighten up," I said to her back. "Let's not fight like this. We know we love each other. Can't we just grow up and ..."

She spun around. "Not if you insist on doing this to me, Tom."

"I'm not saying we must live here forever, Kath. I'm just saying let's finish out the trial year we agreed on. We only have eight more months to go, for Pete's sake. We'll save up our money and if you still want to go back to Michigan after that time ... then we'll just go, I promise."

She stuck her chin out at me like she had done at the airport. "If you're so willing to go in eight months, Mr. Bigshot, why not just go now? I'm not going to change my mind, Tom."

"You might, Kath," I insisted in a calm tone. "If you'd just give it a chance."

"No, I won't," she stubbornly returned.

"You'll never know," I reasoned. "But in any case, we have a lease here that we can't get out of, and I'm making good money that we need. It'll go by fast, honey, you'll see."

"She stomped her foot on the dining room floor. "What gives you the right, damn it, to dictate to me where we're going to live?"

"I'm not dictating, Kathleen," I said, taken aback. "We're talking it over right now. I'm offering compromise and sensible solutions that benefit the both of us."

She put her hands on her hips. "And I suppose you expect me to just do everything you say because you're the man of the house?"

"Well," I answered, wobbling my head a bit. "If you want to go there, yes, there is that part of it. When a married couple can't agree on something important, you can't just flip a coin, can you? You know the man of the house has the responsibility to make the final call. We were taught that as Catholics and in pre-marriage classes, weren't we? They say God has given that burden to me. Do you think I'm going to tell *Him* I won't do it?

"But besides the religious part of it," I continued, "I'm the breadwinner in this family, by the wishes of us both. It's what we agreed on before we were married. I would work and you would have babies and take care of the house. That's the way our families had done it for centuries, and that's what we both wanted. We discussed it endlessly. I have to take the best job I can get, Kath, and our home has to be in the same general area as my job; how can we avoid that?"

She threw her arms up as if she were exasperated with a 6-year-old forgetting to wash behind his ears. "You can work in Michigan, dummy, and you know it!"

Frustrated with the same old tired arguments, I took my wife tenderly by the shoulders and looked deeply into her eyes. "You're not hearing me at all, honey, please listen carefully. I love you with all my heart. I love Kristen more than I thought possible, and I put our family above everything else. The three of us together is all I live for. I would never do anything to hurt us. You've got to trust me on that.

"My heart tells me to give you what you want, Kathleen," I continued, "only because you ask for it. But my mind tells me that's the wrong thing to do. We would be foolish not to give Minnesota a chance, particularly since we've already invested so much. Can't you just give this one little thing to me? It's only for eight months."

She stood limp in my hands, watching me, seeming to scrutinize my every word, but unwilling to relent, unwilling even to speak. Slowly I released her shoulders, careful she didn't collapse to the floor. Then I resumed my speech as she continued to stare.

"I can see we're never going to reach an agreement here, Kath. I'm sorry for that. I wish I didn't have to take a stand. But a decision must be made, and it falls on my shoulders to make it, and I choose for us to stay here. Let's get our daughter back as fast as we can and make the best life we can for all of us, together, right here in this house, at least for now; that's my final decision."

It seemed to take a few moments for her to realize that I was through speaking. She backed up a couple of steps then, but never took her eyes away from mine. Her expression changed slowly from anger and indignation to something more resembling resignation. Her jaw slackened and the creases seemed to fade from her forehead.

"It'll be okay, Kath," I said with a smile. "You'll see."

She turned then and marched back to the bedroom. A minute later she returned with sheets and blankets and went to work making up the sofa for her use.

"Alright, woman," I said with a chuckle, then gave her fanny a pat as she bent over her work. "You can act like a recalcitrant child if you insist, but feel free to come into my bed whenever you get cold."

~

Chapter 6   *Surrender*

My wife slept quietly on the sofa as I readied myself for work the next morning. The noises I made with my cereal bowl did not rouse her, and I resisted giving her a kiss goodbye. As I passed through the mudroom on the way out, the dog anxiously pleaded for my attention, knocking down Kathy's empty luggage, which still had not been put away.

"Don't worry, Missy," I said loudly for all to hear. "Mama will take care of you just as soon as I leave, I'm sure…. "Au revoir, my love," I called as I shut the back door behind me.

*****

I almost closed a deal that day on my first custom-built, double-wide mobile home. I spent hours with an elderly Swedish couple, Mr. and Mrs. Torgerson, going over floor plans and walking through models. It was our fourth such day. Mr. Torgerson had his checkbook out, ready to sign, when, unfortunately, his wife put her foot down.

"Don't write that check, Wilbur, until Thomas changes the order form to Harvest Gold appliances."

"Awwwww c'mon, Lizbeth," Wilber replied. "What the heck is wrong with avocado? We've had avocado for years now, and it always looks nice."

"I've told you, Wilber, I'm tired of avocado. We've been over this a million times already. When are you going to stop arguing with me?"

"I'm not arguing with you, Lizbeth. I just don't want us to make a mistake is all."

I sat back in my chair listening to the senseless repartee, wondering if this was the way Kathy and I were going to act in 40 years. I hoped not.

Finally, I interjected. "We can change the color of the kitchen, Mrs. Torgerson, right up to the day they build your new home. How about we turn the order in with the color choice blank for now? At least that'll get you on the schedule to be built."

"Oh no, Thomas! We'd better not do that. I don't trust my husband, you know."

"Well, that's a hell of a thing to say, Lizbeth, after all these years," Wilbur returned.

Their bickering continued all the way to the parking lot, where Mrs. Torgerson said, "We'll be back, Thomas, just as soon as I straighten out this stubborn husband of mine." The two of them waved goodbye and left.

"Call them tomorrow, Tom," Tony said a short time later. "Tell them because you're overcharging them so much, I said they can have two kitchens – one in each color."

"Yeah," I laughed. "That oughta do it. I can't wait to tell them that!"

Tony slapped me on the back. "Well, mister salesman," he said. "in all seriousness, whether you close this deal or not, I want you to know I think you're doing a bang-up job, and I'm glad you and Kathy decided to stick around here."

"Thanks, Tony," I returned with a smile. "I am too."

"It's 4 o'clock, Tommy boy, why don't you go home early and surprise that young wife of yours?"

My face lit up. "That's a good idea, boss. If you don't mind." I rubbed my hands together. "Maybe I can make her happy."

Tony raised an eyebrow and smirked. "Who do you think you are, mister, Paul Bunyan?"

With the top down and the radio blaring, I pulled my '67 Cutlass Supreme into the driveway. I noticed right away the garage door was open and Kathy's brand-new, German built Opel Kadet was missing. *She must be out shopping*, I figured. I hoped she was buying ingredients for tonight's dinner. *Maybe she'll want me to grill some steaks*, I thought.

As I stepped out of my car, I gave my Harley a longing glance. It was a perfect day for a ride around the lakes, and I was in a great mood. "Naaaa," I said aloud. "Not a good idea, Tommy boy."

I then pranced across the freshly mowed lawn toward the back door, feeling as light on my feet as I had in quite a while. Entering the mud room, Missy jumped all over me.

"Hey there, little girl," I said, bending down to roughhouse with her a bit. "Do you want to go outside or something?" I asked. Judging by her frantic actions, she obviously did.

"Do you promise not to climb the fence?"

Yeah sure, she answered. *No problem, boss. Just let me outta here before I wet my pants.*

"Alright, antsy," I said, opening the back door. "Here you go." She sprang out like a school kid at the recess bell. "Now don't get lost!" I called out after her.

The house smelled like Pine-Sol and Tide, no dirty clothes were in the laundry room, and everything was nice and clean. *So, I* thought, *Kathy's been busy*. Her makeshift bed on the living room sofa had been put away too. That was a good sign.

I went back to the bedroom to change my clothes. I was ready for shorts and a tee-shirt, and especially ready for a cold beer. The bed was freshly made with all the pillows in the right spots. I sat on the edge to take off my shoes, noticing pleasantly that Kathy was a better housekeeper than even the professional I had hired in her absence. Maybe I had married the right gal after all. It seemed life was good again.

My euphoria ended abruptly, however, when I reached for a hanger to put away the dress pants I had been wearing. The closet was half empty! And it didn't take me three seconds to figure out that all the missing items were Kathy's.

I dropped the hanger, rushed over to our shared bureau, and yanked open the two top drawers. They were both empty! "Shit!" I muttered, then looked up blankly, trying to recall what I had seen when I first came in the back door. I slammed the drawers shut, then ran through the house in my underwear and socks.

"Jesus," I whispered upon seeing no empty luggage on the mud room floor waiting to be put away. *She's packed up her car and is driving back to Detroit. But how can that be?* I was puzzled. *It's a 13-hour trip and she doesn't even have gas money.*

Upon realizing the bigger picture of what had happened, fear and anxiety swelled within me. I grabbed my head and wailed: *"Oh my God, my wife has left me!"*

I felt the cold tile floor through my thin, black socks, and chills running up my bare legs. I had no idea what to do next. Then it dawned on me – she may have left a note somewhere.

I frantically began to search the house. Nothing was on the dining room table or by the telephone. Nothing was on the kitchen counter or the windowsill above the sink. I looked then to the refrigerator where she sometimes posted such things and was instantly frozen into place. The magnet that I knew to hold my two-thousand-dollar bonus check was empty. *EMPTY!*

I stared in disbelief, not fathoming that the missing check might help explain a few things when the telephone rang. I ran and snatched it up.

"Hello!"

"Oh, hi Tom," she said casually. "So, you *are* home. I called your work. They said you left early, so I called that damn golf course of yours. You weren't there either, so I …"

43

"Where are you, Kathleen?" I interrupted loudly. "What are you doing?"

"Settle down, settle down," she exhorted. "What'd you expect me to do?"

"Where are you at?" I demanded again.

"I'm at the airport, Tom. My flight leaves in five minutes. I'm just calling to tell you my car is in the green lot if you want to come and get it. Row 14C."

"What are you doing!" I screamed.

"Quit yelling at me. I'm going home, that's what I'm doing.... I'm not mad at you, Tom. I understand why you've made the decision you've made. I just can't go along with it, that's all. I've got to go now though; they're calling my flight. We'll have to talk about this later."

I stood there with the receiver in my hand, mouth agape, absently facing the kitchen window. My mind was all but blank, not being able to process what was happening. Suddenly a movement in the distance caught my eye and brought me out of my daze. There she was, my dog, running free as the wind through the wooded park as if she owned the place, headed towards sky blue Lake Phalen.

*****

Tony grabbed the ticket at the entrance to the red long-term parking lot. "It's a good thing you remembered Kathy said something about the color, Tom," he said. "I would hate to have to drive through every inch of five four-story parking garages."

"Yeah, I suppose so," I agreed. "But I wonder if she wouldn't throw us off on purpose. She might delight in causing you and me to have to drive around for three days."

From the driver's seat of his blue Corvette, Tony looked at me in surprise. "You'd better hope your wife's not so devious, Tommy boy," he said. "You're not getting three days of search time out of me, you know."

44

As it turned out, it only took about two hours of searching before we finally spotted the small, orange Opal at the very end of the green parking lot. It had enough gas in it, luckily, and it started right up.

"Follow me to my house, Tony!" I shouted. "I know a shortcut."

*****

I called Detroit once or twice a day in the beginning, but besides getting a chance to talk with Kristen now and then, not much good came from the effort. Kathy thought she held the moral high ground, of course, and at first, she tried to reason with me. But when I proved to be just as stubborn as she was, her tactics became tougher.

"You know what, Tom?" she said sometime in the third week. "I'm sick of these stupid discussions. You know exactly what it takes to make things right with me, and I'm *sick, sick, sick* of talking about it."

"But we *have* to talk about it, Kath."

"No, we don't. And I'm not going to anymore. Until you come to your senses, don't even bother to call here again, because I won't talk to you.... Now I'm hanging up."

"Wait!" I shouted. "Let me talk to Kristen, please."

"No," she said firmly. "I'm not letting you talk to Kristen; she's mad at you too, you know."

Before I could argue with her further, the all-too familiar "click" happened again.

*****

The snot held to her word too, and she quit coming to the telephone when I called. While that did lead to some additional conversation between her mother and me, that didn't last long either. Apparently, Kathy had become hell to live with for everyone there and, of course, I was to blame.

"Kathy is going out of her mind," her mother would say, "and it's all your fault, and no, you can't talk to Kristen. What's wrong with you anyway?"

My work suffered too. I never did make the sale to the Torgersons, and my depression was more than noticeable to my boss.

"You were scheduled to start work at nine this morning, Tom," Tony said looking at his watch one day when I arrived at ten.

"Yeah," I answered." I am sorry, Tony, I've got no excuse. I just could not get myself going this morning."

He tapped his pen on his desktop, then asked sincerely: "Is there anything I can do to help out, Tom?"

I flashed him the best sly smile I could muster. "Another $2,000 would be nice, boss, but I wouldn't let you do that again."

He grinned but did not reach for his checkbook.

"No, I'll be alright, Ton'," I insisted then, holding up a hand. "But thanks for asking, and I promise I won't be late for work again."

*****

Six weeks into Kathy's abandonment of me (and that's exactly how I perceived it), I reduced my phone calls to the Scapaticci house to about once every three or four days. It wasn't that my desire to fix things had waned – it hadn't – but the effort had become an increasingly painful experience, and I never got to talk to my wife or daughter anyway.

I stood by the kitchen window on the park side of the house one evening, remnants of red sky fading away, as I dialed the telephone. I was expecting nothing different from that call when Kathleen surprised me by picking up the phone herself.

"Hello," she answered in a balmy voice.

"Well, hello, Kath," I said back pleasantly, genuinely happy to hear my wife's voice in good spirits. "How are you doing?"

Her mood seemed to shift dramatically at the hearing of my voice, and she responded in a calm monotone: "I'm pregnant, you bastard."

I blinked a few times and slowly sank into the chair by the phone. *How can this be?* I asked myself. *We haven't … we haven't …* then I remembered the motorcycle trip when we made love in the grass by the fire.

"Don't worry, Tom," she continued before I could find any words of my own. "This doesn't concern you."

I then heard only the sickening click.

*****

Thus, at the age of 22, when by rights, I thought, I should be entering the best of times, my life was in shambles. Everything I valued most, I did not have. What I had been fighting for suddenly seemed meaningless. And I could not bear to be away from my family another minute. I was ready to surrender.

In short order, I said goodbye to my boss – and what a great boss he had been – and gave him my motorcycle as a thank you. I talked my way out of our lease, sold Kathy's car, and packed up the rest of our belongings into a tow-behind U-Haul.

Only two weeks following Kathy's bombshell announcement, on a foggy midwestern morning, I pulled out of our Phalen Lake driveway for the last time. Heavily loaded, yet full of hope, Missy and

I headed east on the very same highway Kathy and I had motorcycled just a brief time before.

*****

October 22, 1970

Kathy was glad to see me – proud – as if there were never a doubt I would do the right thing. Kristen ran into my arms, hugging my neck like she would never let go. I squeezed back for a long while. We had been apart for four and a half months. I vowed to her right then and there to never let that happen again. We both cried.

The three of us lived upstairs in the little bungalow on Helene Street that Kathy's parents had owned and occupied forever. Missy did well in the backyard with Bootsy and Specksy, my father-in-law's hunting dogs.

I quickly found a job, and we were soon able to buy a small house in nearby Madison Heights. Things were not so bad after all, and I really did like being around our extended families again. Our lives had found some peace. Kathy's belly swelled with new life, and Kristen had both her mommy and daddy again. We soon forgot our past tribulations.

~

Chapter 7   *Amy*

April 30, 1971

The phone call came late on a Wednesday afternoon while I was working at the Cadillac Fence Company in Detroit. I had had the job then for about four months. My work involved engineering and sales, with most of my day spent on the drawing board, waiting on walk-in customers, and answering the telephones. The pay was not nearly as good as for selling mobile homes in Minnesota, but I liked the work and there seemed to be good potential for me there.

Kathy was eight and a half months pregnant by then, but we had no reason to expect a premature delivery. Second children never came early, we had heard. Everything had gone so smoothly with the first baby; there was little to be concerned about the second time around.

We had spent plenty of time preparing the nursery, mostly in blue, in anticipation of a junior me. While I was sure a boy would be wonderful, I had secretly hoped for another girl. I was so much in love with the little girl/daddy thing I had going on with Kristen, I would have welcomed a hundred more just like her, not caring if I ever had a son or not.

A rickety, old black man in his dirty overalls was standing on the other side of the counter from me, carefully drawing a plan of the fence project he was currently working on. I would then be able to make a list of materials needed for the job and give the order to the warehouse. Three more customers waited patiently in the line behind the old man. The phone rang sharply, taking my attention away from the work in front of me.

"Hello, Cadillac," I said into the mouthpiece.

"Tommy, it's me," the voice anxiously shot back.

"Ma?" I responded in surprise.

49

"I am at your house. Kathy is ready to have the baby," she said quickly, her voice cracking a bit.

What is my mother doing there? I wondered. *This was not in the plan. Why isn't Kathy calling me herself?*

"Are you sure?" I questioned the mother of nine.

"Yes, I'm sure," she answered, "and it's happening fast."

"But she hasn't even had any labor pains yet!" I said loudly.

"It does not always work that way, Tom. Sometimes the baby just comes fast, without warning, but she *is* having pains, and they are strong and remarkably close together."

Feeling panic, I stammered, "wh … wh … what should I do, Ma?"

"Come home right away!" she said firmly. "I will have her ready. As soon as you get here, you can take her to the hospital. Hurry!"

"Okay, goodbye," I said, dropping the phone.

Looking for a second at the startled man in front of me, I offered no explanation. I grabbed my keys and ran out of the store, shouting into my boss's office. "I've got to go, Joe!" I did not wait for an answer.

Chain-link fence had been unrolled in the parking lot behind my black Cutlass. Bill, the century-old yard man, looked up at me with questioning eyes, a bit of chewing tobacco at the corner of his mouth.

"I have to go fast, Bill," I said. "I'll help you roll this stuff back up."

"Just drive over it," he said, waving his arms. "It won't hurt nuttin."

I lived about 12 miles from work, and then another 8 miles back to the hospital in Southfield, and it was rush hour. The drive was going to take a long time, I knew. I wondered why my mother had not just taken Kathy to the hospital herself, or called an ambulance, but it was by then too late to suggest that.

The construction on Plymouth Road was interminable. I waited impatiently in the noise and the fumes as a traffic light at each intersection turned red at least four times before I could pass. Finally, I entered I-75 and headed north at about 20 mph. More than an hour after the phone call, then with the top down and the radio playing, I turned off Eleven Mile Road by the Dairy Queen onto Osman Street. Kids were everywhere on that warm spring afternoon, eating ice cream, on their bikes, and walking. By then any urgency had left my mind.

My mother's red Chevy station wagon sat in the driveway; the doors wide open. Ma and little Kristen were on the front lawn, frantically waving at me. I remembered then what I was up to.

"What took so damn long?" my mother implored as I ran up from the street. It was the first time I had ever heard her swear. I did not answer.

I stuck my head and shoulders in through the front door of the Chevy. There I saw my wife clutching her giant belly, her sweat-covered face contorted in pain and anger. Her head twisted to the left to look directly into my eyes, and she spat out with all the strength she had left: "You bastard!"

My mother pushed me into the driver's seat. "Get going!" she urged. "I'll call the hospital."

Back onto Eleven Mile Road heading west, I was plenty scared. Every couple of minutes, Kathy caught her breath long enough to scream at me that the baby was coming.

"It's going to drop on the floor, go faster!" But I could not go faster, traffic was at a crawl, cars were everywhere. *"Get out of the way!"* she bellowed to a big truck in front of us. *"Go faster, Tom!"*

"Should I stop, Kath? We'll never make it!" I cried. "I can help you on the side of the road."

"No, no, no, keep going! You don't know what to do, dumbass!"

I pulled into the empty oncoming lanes and passed a hundred cars waiting to make a left turn onto Southfield Road. I then made an illegal detour through a neighborhood which I hoped would save more precious minutes. It did.

"There's the hospital!" Kathy yelled. "Go into that driveway."

Racing up the drive and slamming on the brakes, I practically cast Kathy off the front seat. No one was waiting for us at the curb! Throwing the car into park, I jumped out to get help. *"Wait here!"*

I sprinted to the entrance; not a soul was in sight. The double sliding automatic doors did not open fast enough, and I crashed into the glass and bounced off hard. I had to wait a second to start running again, only to crash into a second set of slow-moving doors. Finally, ricocheting into the hospital lobby, I was met by the wide eyes of three elderly ladies sitting behind the front desk. "My wife is having a baby!" I wailed. Nobody moved or said a word.

"Right now, in the car," I shouted, pointing at the doors.

"Oh," one of the nice ladies calmly responded. "You'll have to drive around to the emergency entrance, sir. We cannot help you here."

Not bothering to try to convince them otherwise, I turned without question and ran back through the ridiculous doors. It took forever to find the emergency entrance, but when we finally made it there, hospital staff were waiting for us this time. *Maybe my mother had succeeded in warning them that we were in route*, I thought. They took my frantic and shaken wife quickly away.

Trembling, I managed to park the car and then stagger my way back to the entrance. It was only a few minutes of filling out papers before they took me back to the private room where I was told mother and child awaited.

I stopped in the doorway and saw my wife lying comfortably in her bed with an infant safely in her arms. A flashback poured through my mind from three years before in a Minnesota hospital hallway, when I had been completely overcome by the first sight of our precious daughter, Kristen. Knowing I was on the threshold of having that experience again was a thrill all by itself.

52

Slowly, I approached the bedside and leaned closely in. There, a serenely beautiful child softly breathed, peacefully sleeping. Kathy smiled brightly at me and whispered in a tired but cheerful voice.

"We have another girl, honey."

~

Chapter 8   *Friends*

May 1971

Amy Renee, with sandy hair and bright blue eyes, was a near clone of her big sister – in appearance that is, if not quite in personality. Like Kristen, she was happy, energetic, and a joy to be around. But early in her life she proved to be a bit of a problem. She never once slept the entire night through. Not once! My mother said she must be nocturnal, like an owl or a cat. The little pipsqueak woke up every single night around midnight and stayed up. She would want to eat, of course, but then she would want to horse around until dawn. The problem was, she did not want to horse around alone. She cried until someone – anyone – joined her.

That unusual schedule was not one the rest of us adapted well to, including poor Kristen. But we all did our best to accommodate little Amy. She left us no other option.

Kathy and I worked diligently to spruce up our little three-bedroom ranch. Built on a slab in a mismatched, tree-lined neighborhood, the homestead worked nicely for small gatherings and backyard picnics. We had plenty of visits from both the large Scapaticci clan and the even larger VanBuren gang. It was sure nice to be around our families on a regular basis again.

Eventually, our home was added to the list of approved locations for the famous Scapaticci card parties. Those events took place once or twice every week and rotated from house to house. More than any of us, Amy Joy, as she was nicknamed, appreciated those gatherings, as they took place at night.

My work at Cadillac Fence was decent; our daughters were beyond delightful, and best of all, Kathy and I had completely stopped arguing. Before long, I forgave my wife for forcing the move back to Michigan, and eventually I even thanked her for it.

At that point, Kathy felt our lives were idyllic, and for the most part I agreed with her. I was fully in love with what we had. But after a time, I began to yearn for some other things in life beyond hearth and home.

*****

By the summer of '72, we had been back in Michigan for nearly two years, but still I had not contacted any of my old friends - not even a single phone call. Kathy never said I shouldn't (that I remember) but I had the sense she wouldn't approve, so I never bothered with it. It was okay with me though. Between my job, maintaining the house, and all the kid chores, I did not have time for much else anyway.

But there was something eating at me that I just could not ignore any longer. There was a serious void in my life: an emptiness that a wife and little girls, no matter how wonderful, just did not seem to fill. I tried to stay away from it, I really did, but I was too weak, and as time went on the urgency grew. I needed it more and more each passing day. Finally, no matter the consequences, I became determined to have it. Kathy would not understand, of course, but I had to have it, and I had to have it fast. I absolutely, positively had to play golf!

Lucky for me, my dad, my uncle Herb, and my soon to be brother-in-law Mike, had to have it too. Our first chance came one Saturday afternoon in late August.

"Where do you think *you're* going?" Kathy asked, standing in the kitchen as I tried to pass through.

"Golfing, hon," I beamed excitedly in an obvious hurry. "I got off work early today for the first time ever, and we have a 2 o'clock tee time at Rackham. I can't wait! I wonder if I remember how to play. I peered into the laundry room. "Do you know where my blue shorts are?"

Kathy stiffened up, put her hands on her hips, and gave me a look I hadn't seen in quite a while. "Your first day off," she questioned, "and you're going golfing?"

55

"Yeah," I said. "When else can I go?"

"Well," she derided, "*never* would be all right with me. I thought you left that bad habit back in Minnesota."

It was the reaction I had hoped not to receive, but I was ready for it and responded calmly, trying to sound reasonable. "It's not so bad for you, Kathy, is it? I will be home by eight."

"Dinners at 7!" she spat out; her arms crossed. "You know that."

"Can't you hold dinner till 8?" I begged. "Or eat without me?"

"No way … if you only play 9 holes, you can easily make it home by 7. Even I know that."

"But they all want to play 18 holes," I whined. "It's my dad, uncle Herb, and Mike. I can't let them down."

"Oh boy, I knew it," she responded, shaking her head. "Your friends are more important to you than I am, aren't they?"

"Of course not, honey," I said compassionately, reaching out to touch her. "You know better than that."

She shook off my hand and scowled. It was the type of rejection I never took well, and I stiffened in reaction.

"If you love me, Tom," she said then, not caring that she sounded juvenile, "you'll do right by me and tell your stupid friends you can only play 9 holes."

At that point, my compassion had evaporated. "I'm not doing that, for chrissake!" I yelled, throwing up my hands. "This is the first time in *two years* I've done anything for fun, and you're not gonna wreck it for me."

"You better not talk to me like that, buster!" she screeched back, crocodile tears filling her angry eyes. "What about what you're wrecking for me?"

"You?" I bellowed. "What could I be wrecking for you? You didn't even know I was getting the afternoon off. You just cannot stand that I might enjoy something without you."

Frightened by my yelling and their mother's wails, both Kristen and Amy came running into the kitchen from the back of the house. "Mama! Mama!" Kristen cried, "What's wrong?"

Kathy crouched down and gathered the girls into her arms. "There, there, my little precious ones," she said. "Don't cry, mama's okay." She looked up at me and sneered. "Your daddy's just being a big meanie."

I looked to the heavens. "Oh my God," I said to no one. "It was a perfectly good day for all of us just five minutes ago, and now the world is ending."

*****

It was not easy escaping the house in one piece that day, but I finally did it. I found my blue shorts at the bottom of the hamper, put the wrinkled things on, and bolted out the front door. Kathy followed me onto the lawn, screaming and hollering, the kids hanging on her legs bawling their heads off.

"If you leave this house, you bastard, don't bother to come back!" she announced at the top of her lungs. Half the neighborhood watched the terrible scene in shock. I was so embarrassed.

I played golf that afternoon and shot a respectable score. But knowing what was waiting for me when I got home took most of the fun out of it. I didn't go home until much later than necessary, to protest, I guess.

The house was very still when I got back around 11 o'clock. I quietly undressed and slipped into bed with my wife, seemingly unnoticed. All stayed peaceful until an hour later when, right on cue, our younger child woke up crying. Kathy placed a foot into the small of my back and pushed me out of bed. Sometime later, when I returned with the fed and changed baby in my arms, the fireworks began.

57

"Why were you so late getting home from golf?" my wide-awake wife demanded.

"You told me not to bother coming home at all, Kath," I replied, setting Amy down in the middle of the bed. "I didn't know I had a curfew."

"A married man doesn't stay out all hours of the night, Tom. You need to pick better friends."

Insulted, I responded loudly, *"You don't approve of my father? Are you crazy?"*

"I didn't say that. Do not put words in my mouth."

"Well, you implied it. And I'd like to pick my own friends, if you don't mind."

"I didn't imply anything. If you are feeling guilty about how badly you're treating me, that's not my problem."

"Guilty? I am not feeling the least bit guilty. You are the one acting like an asshole, not me."

"Don't call me names! Did Mike teach you that, I suppose?"

"Teach me what? What are you talking about, woman?"

"Never mind. You still did not tell me why you didn't get home till 11 o'clock. I know it's too dark to golf after 10."

And so it went, round and around in circles, insults and accusations, questions and no answers, nonstop, until the sun came up. Little Amy Joy loved it.

*****

Kathy and I bickered that way for days, without a kind word between us, until one time after work the girls were playing in the backyard sandbox, affording us some privacy. I approached my wife as she busied herself over a pile of clean laundry. She wore a sleeveless cotton blouse, revealing soft pale skin. I said nothing, but rested a hand on her shoulder. She drew in a whisper of breath and quivered faintly. After a moment, she dropped the baby's tee-shirt she had been folding and turned quickly to wrap her arms around my neck.

"Oh, Tom," she said as she squeezed hard. "I don't want us to fight anymore. Hold me tight."

I did … and once again we discovered what *The Ronettes* meant when they sang, *The Best Part of Breaking-up is When You're Making up.*

The relative peace we reached, however, lasted only until the next Saturday evening when I announced I intended to play golf with my dad the next morning. Kathy and I sat together on the Italian provincial sofa we had bought before we were married, half interested in what was on the black and white TV. Both girls were already in bed.

"On Sunday?!" she screeched, loud enough to rattle the lampshade. "Doesn't your dad go to church?"

"Catholics can go to church on Saturday night now if they want, Kath," I answered. "Go figure."

"And your mother will let him leave her alone?"

"It was her idea actually," I said, reaching for my Miller High Life on the end table. "She doesn't smother him, you know. And she wants him to have some *man time.*" I laughed at the thought of my mother saying such a thing.

"Oh, you think that's funny?" my wife exploded. "Well, don't expect me to let you get your *man time* at my expense, buster. You are not about to leave me and two kids alone here tomorrow!"

"C'mon Kath," I said. "I need my *man time* too, you know." I probably shouldn't have giggled again, but I did. "It's not so bad, Kath," I went on after I composed myself. "We've got a 7:15 a.m. tee time at Arrowhead Golf Course. "You know I hate getting up early when I don't have to – we're all doing that just for you. We'll be home by noon. You and the girls will hardly be out of bed by then anyway.

We'll still have the entire day together. Would you like to go to the beach or something?"

"Beach? You have to cut the grass and fix my car tomorrow. You should be doing *that* in the morning instead of golfing, then we *could* go to the beach."

I took a long swig of my beer, let out a big "ahhhhh," and grinned at my fuming wife. Then said with way too much satisfaction, "But I gotta get my *man time.*"

Following that *man time* moment, Kathy not only got angry at me every time I wanted to do something with my friends, but she also got mad at my mother. And she got mad at my dad, Uncle Herb, and Mike, and anyone else who she perceived was taking me away from her.

Every time I did something without her, we would fight like devils for three days. This meant the whole family was miserable every Sunday, Monday, and Tuesday, because I went golfing every Sunday morning at 7:15. Kathy never got used to that, and she never once let me out of the house without pitching a fit. But I did not give in, either.

On about Wednesday of each week, I would usually find a bare shoulder of hers on which to lay a gentle hand, and we would become lovers again, if not friends. Then afterwards, thrilled with the making-up, exhausted, and liking each other again, we would talk.

"You know, honey," I would say, "every time we fight, we know it is not going to last forever. We know before long we are going to get over whatever it was, and we are going to end up like this, feeling good about each other again, and happy to be together.

"Yeah," she would sigh. "I do love you, Tom. I'm sorry for the things I do."

"And I love you too, Kath, and I'm sorry too. I don't want us to hurt this way anymore…. So, because we really do love each other, and we know we are always going to get to this point anyway, why don't we just skip the fighting part?"

"Okay," she would agree, kissing my face all over. "Let's just skip the fighting part and get right to this."

It was a fine idea, of course, but we never managed to skip the fighting. For months and months, the cycle went on – nasty arguing, always loud and hateful, and always in front of the girls – and then we would make-up. It was a cycle that one should know had to be broken – either stop the fighting or stop the making-up.

*****

Wednesday, February 14, 1973

I never missed celebrating Saint Valentine's Day with my mother. She was the sweetest of my sweethearts, and I loved the opportunity to tell her I felt so. Even when I was in the Navy, I may have been late on Mother's Day or a birthday or two, but I never missed Valentine's Day.

That day I stopped at my folks' Royal Oak home for a short lunchtime visit while making a sales call for my job. The kids were at school and Dad was at work. I walked in the side door with a huge bouquet of daisies and baby's breath in my hand.

"Oh Tommy," she said. "They are beautiful! Thank you so much." She smiled and went immediately to the cupboard to find a vase. "I thought you might come by today." The vases were on the top shelf, and at less than 5 feet tall, the lady could not come close to reaching one.

"Would you like me to get you a stepladder, little girl?" I teased.

At a trim 98 pounds, with a head full of dark thick hair, she did look more like an eighth grader than a 53-year-old mother of nine. She pointed deep into the cupboard and said with a grin, "Okay, *Wilt the Stilt*, get me that tall green vase way in the back there."

61

I laughed and pulled out a kitchen chair to stand on. "You would have to pick that one," I said, shaking my head. At only 5 foot 7 myself, I almost needed a step ladder too.

My mother worked at arranging the flowers in the vase as I watched from my seat at the kitchen table. I munched happily on a pile of cookies I had grabbed from the cooling rack on the stove.

Her dark brown eyes were focused on her task when she casually asked, "What are you going to do about this situation you're in, Tommy?"

Not sure what she was referring to, I asked in return, "What situation is that, Ma?"

"You and Kathy," she said while trimming the bottom of the daisy stems with a large pair of scissors, "fighting all the time … and in front of the girls."

I took a deep breath. "Gee Ma, I didn't know it was that obvious. You and I have never spoken of this before."

She fussed with the baby's breath, getting it mixed in with the daisies exactly right. "I've seen it happen more than once between you two, Tom, and your father has relayed to me some of the stories you told him."

I could feel my face turning red, embarrassed by the thought of my mother knowing the content of some of my stupid stories. I took a bite of the cookie and looked away. After a moment though, I turned back and admitted, "I guess I have told Dad some juicy stories, but really, Ma, Kathy and I are just bickering about a bunch of nothing."

She picked up the finished vase of flowers and carried it into the living room where she placed it atop the television set. "There," she beamed, looking over her shoulder. "Isn't it beautiful? Thank you again, Tommy."

She came back then into the kitchen, poured a glass of milk for me, and sat down at the table. "It doesn't sound like nothing to me," she said, resting a small hand over mine. "It sounds serious, actually."

I knew I could not con my mother, even if I wanted to, so I decided to just admit what I had to admit and take my medicine. "Yeah," I nodded, staring into my cookies. "It's pretty awful, really ... I hate it ... but I do not know what to do, Ma. We just cannot seem to stop." I lifted my eyes then to look directly into hers. "And, yes, we do it in front of the kids. They are always around us. I am sorry."

She playfully pushed my hand away. "Oh, you don't have to feel so guilty about it, son. I know Kathy's difficult. She and I don't get along famously either, you know. But tell me, what exactly is she so upset with you about all the time?"

"Well," I began hesitantly. "It's lots of different things, really. I think she just does not like me to enjoy life without her. Even at her own family gatherings, she will be the only female in the card room with all the men, hovering around, listening to the conversation, then dragging me out of there cuz it's my turn to change a diaper or something stupid."

"Well ... was it your turn?"

"Maybe ... I do not know ... but it is a lot more than just that. She does not say it, but she seems to not want me to have a single friend in the entire world except for her. If I like someone, or God forbid, they like me, then she will work to drive a wedge between us ... like she tried to do with you and Dad. It even carries over to Kristen and Amy anymore. If they show too much affection for me, Kathy gets jealous, I guess, and starts throwing out all sorts of nasty stuff about me as if I am not worthy of such affection. All lies, of course, but the girls do not know that. Before long we're all crying."

"Oh, that's just deranged, Tom," my mother said in disgust. "She needs professional help, don't you think?"

"Well, I do think that Ma. But if I suggest anything like that it only gets worse."

"How did it get this way, Tommy," she gently asked. "When did it start?"

"Well, for the first two years after we came back from Minnesota, I did not do anything without her, and everything was fine.

63

Then I started to play golf with Dad and things changed. But it is not just golf, Ma. You should have seen what happened when I stayed after work for our Christmas party last year. Holy cow! You would have thought World War III broke out."

She sat back in her chair. "I did hear that story, Tom," she said with a slight grin. "Your father told me. It is almost funny, but when I think about Kristen and Amy witnessing it, it breaks my heart. They are just little girls, so impressionable. She took a deep breath. On the other hand, that wife of yours is so incredibly unreasonable, I am glad you stuck to your guns on that one."

My face lit up. "Really?"

She nodded quickly. "You are married to her, yes, but you're still an individual, you know. A good deal of life happens without one's spouse. That's just the way it is. What is she so afraid of? She better grow up."

"Yeah," I spouted, encouraged to have my mother on my side. "I agree!" Then, like a helpless 10-year-old, I asked what I often asked, "So what do I do, Ma?"

The question was clear. How do I stick to my guns without upsetting my wife to the point of Armageddon?

My mother seemed to be trying to formulate some words of wisdom as she absently stood up and took away my half glass of milk and two remaining cookies. She dropped them off at the kitchen counter, then turned around and answered.

"I do not suggest you give into her inane demands, Tommy. She would just find other things to yell about. But you have to stop arguing in front of the girls. You have just got to."

"But that's just impossible Ma," I objected. "You don't know my wife."

"It's not impossible, Thomas Walter," she insisted. "I know Kathy is difficult, but she is the girl you married, and she's the mother of your children. You must find a way to fix things, or you two have no business being married."

My eyes widened. "What are you saying, Mother? If we cannot fix things, should we get divorced?"

"Of course not!" she shot back. "You cannot divorce, because you have children, if for no other reason. You know that."

I nodded my head sheepishly.

"But besides that," she pleaded, hands reaching. "What about you and your wife? Is there no love between you two anymore?"

She caught me off guard with that question. I did not expect a switch from concern for the kids, and this was not a subject my mother and I had ever discussed before. I too took my time answering. I was tempted to get up and take back my cookies and milk, but I resisted.

My mother sat back down beside me at the corner of the table and waited patiently for my answer. Patience was something she never ran short of.

Finally, I spoke. "Yes, there is love between me and Kathy, Ma ... about half the time ... and when it's good, it's exceptionally good. And not just the physical part either, although we are having no problems in that area."

I took a deep breath and slowly shook my head. "I do not know why those good feelings seem to slip away from us so easily ... but they do. Over and over again."

My mother did not respond to my words, other than to look sadly at me with her hands folded in front of her on the table. "So," I continued, "When we are not fighting, Kathy and I *do* talk about this stuff, Ma -- a lot. And the one thing we always conclude is that we know we love each other, and we desperately love our children. And no matter how tough it gets, we know we cannot ever abandon the commitments we have made. And we will not ... do not worry.

"But I also know our commitment to staying together is not enough. We must grow up – both of us – and we must do it fast, before too much damage is done. And we will, Ma, I promise. We will."

Chapter 9　*Rupture*

During the two years following my Valentine's Day visit to see my mother, Kathy and I made no progress toward keeping the word I had given to my dear mother. "We have to grow up," I had said, "and we will, Ma. I promise."

Oh, we went to counseling, and we tried to hone our individual philosophies about marriage and parenting, but our juvenile arguing about the same shallow issues never slowed down. We just added more topics. Next came the loss of the camaraderie of the Scapaticci family, which we had so very much enjoyed.

It started when Kathy's mom and dad followed Ron and Yvette up north to retire on the lake in Hillman four hours away from us instead of 10 minutes. Not long afterwards, Grandma and Grandpa Scapaticci, the aged and most delightful holders of the old Italian ways, both passed away. Then, for reasons not understood by me – or anyone – the aunts and uncles began to feud. Consequently, the friendships, the card parties, and the palatial feasting we had come to rely on all but ceased.

My wife's family presence – the impetus for our leaving Minnesota four years prior – was then entirely missing from our lives. The loss was a considerable shock to Kathy. Surprisingly, though, she did not ask that we follow her parents north. Instead, in a mostly destructive way, she clung ever tighter to me and the girls.

Kathy had always been controlling and possessive – I was attracted to that part of her in the beginning – but when she felt her extended family slipping from her a second time, she took those traits to new, unbearable levels. She wanted me and the girls for *only* herself and was not ashamed to say so. "I deserve your complete attention," she often spouted. "And I intend to have it."

She thought then to hold her perceived rivals at bay, which were all my family and those who showed affection for me or the girls. With increasing viciousness, she pushed everyone away. And God help me if I tried to do anything without her. As a result, despite our efforts to *grow up*, we clashed even more.

But still, even in the heat of battle, Kathy and I would always say we loved each other. And, as tense as life would get in those days, I always wanted to see my wife again. When I came home, maybe I would catch a smile from her, and we would make-up in bed that night. We always had that to look forward to.

*****

My younger sister Donna's husband, Mike Bowers, who had become my best friend, was a particular thorn in my wife's side. Mike, 6 foot 5 with over-long dark hair, was a happy-go-lucky gorilla of a guy who loved my company. Kathy, of course, hated him.

In March of '75, Mike suggested that because spring was taking so long to pop up in Detroit, he and I ought to head south in search of some fun. "We may not have to go very far to get out of the snow," he said, "but if we take turns driving, we could be in Florida in less than a day."

Having never even contemplated doing such a thing, I looked at him dubiously. But man, that did sound good.

"Think about it, Thomas," the big guy gushed with a huge grin, "We could be golfing tomorrow!"

Kathy would pitch a fit, I knew. But I agreed instantly to try to make it happen.

As predicted, my wife hated the idea. She screamed at the top of her lungs, "If you even just think of sticking me in this stupid house with two little kids for days on end, so you can go mucking about to who knows where, doing who knows what, with that idiot brother-in-law of yours, I'll scratch your beady eyes out!"

I knew she did not really think I had beady eyes, so I did not take her threat seriously, and my boss easily gave me the time off. Before the sun came up the next Thursday morning, like Tom Sawyer and Huck Finn down the Mississippi River on a raft packed with golf clubs and beer, Mike and I excitedly set out down I-75.

As it turned out we did not have to travel further than Kentucky to find warm air and green grass. That is where we stopped, and it was perfect. For four days straight we drank beer, played golf, and laughed our heads off. We talked about everything on Earth except our wives and children. My mother would have said it was quality *man time.*

After dropping Mike off about 11 o'clock that Sunday night, I drove slowly the rest of the way home, still not having thought about Kathy or the girls for more than two seconds. I was replaying in my mind the round of golf we had finished that afternoon, each hole, each shot. I was not thinking one way or the other about arriving home for the first time in days. I was still on vacation.

As I turned onto our street, I noticed the dark windows of the house and no car in the driveway. Instantly, I said to myself, "Oh good, nobody's home." I parked the car and began to unload my stuff when the realization of what I had just said hit me like a runaway cement truck. I stopped in my tracks and uttered aloud, "My God, what did I just say?"

Glancing again at the dark house, I wondered if I had just been reacting to the confrontation likely coming up with my wife, or was I truly dreading returning to my own home? In a daze I finished unloading, took a beer from the fridge, and plopped down at the kitchen table.

Up until that moment, no matter the situation, I had always wanted to see my wife again. This time I did not, and the thought of that was very unsettling. Hiding my face behind my hands, I closed my eyes and waited.

Not long afterwards, I heard a commotion at the side door. Both Kristen and little Amy, not bothering to remove their snow-covered hats, coats, or boots, ran excitedly into the house calling "Daddy! Daddy!" Scooping them into my arms, the three of us danced around the living room floor, laughing, and carrying on, so happy to be together again.

I looked then to Kathy putting her coat away in the front closet, hoping for a fun reception from her next. Instead, I received just a sneer and a "humph," as she turned and disappeared down the hallway. I tried to hide my disappointment, but my face was usually an open book.

The little girls exchanged concerned glances with each other. Then Kristen, a facilitator even at 6 years old, lit up with an excited smile and said, "It's okay, Daddy, now you can give us horsey back rides!"

Kathy did not say another word to me that night, which I accepted as a good thing. Unfortunately, by the next morning she had found her voice again. As I was dressing after my shower, she started in on me with her usual flair.

"After what you did," she said sitting up in bed, "I'm surprised you had the nerve to step foot into this house again."

I had not gotten enough sleep, had a big day ahead of me, and I was certain it was not a suitable time to have a conversation with a demon. Hoping she would go away if I ignored her, I quietly opened the top drawer of the chest and fiddled with the contents. But she pressed.

"How many sluts did you screw, Tom?" she demanded.

Pulling a tee shirt out of the drawer, I looked at her with disgust. "I wish you wouldn't talk like that within earshot of the girls, Kathleen."

"Oh, don't worry," she said calmly. "They know all about what you do. I told them. So … how many did you screw, Tom?"

"I'm not going to react to such stupid shit, woman," I shot back. "And I'm late for work, so please stop it."

She then spoke loudly, I thought, to purposely wake the kids. "Don't think you're going to cheat on me for four days, spending money we need for food, then you just get up and leave as if nothing happened."

I looked at her sadly and took a deep breath. "As usual, dear, you have everything wrong. But I am late for work, and I do not have time now to argue with you about it. We will have to talk later. I am leaving now, Kath, goodbye." I turned and left the room.

"Oh, no you don't!" she shouted, springing from the bed and pushing past me in the hallway.

Kristen and Amy, sleepy in their nightgowns, timidly poked their sandy heads out of their doorways to see what was going on. Ignoring the kids, Kathy rushed to the kitchen and grabbed my car keys hanging on a hook by the side door.

"You're not going anywhere!" she cried. "Don't you think you've done enough harm already?"

I was stuck. Short of force, I knew, there was no way I would get the keys out of her grasp. The girls ran to their mother's side, of course, and clutched at her legs.

"We agreed not to do this in front of the kids," I pointed out. "Remember?"

"You started it, Tom. I told you if you went on that phony golf trip with asshole Mike, I would never forgive you. But you went anyway."

I nodded my head slowly. "Yes, you did say that, and I went anyway. So, what now?"

"So, I hate you for it, and the girls know what a terrible father you are, and that you don't love them, and they hate you too."

I lowered my eyes to our daughters, still attached to their mother's legs. Amy bit her quivering lip but stared at me intently. Kristen turned her head completely away to avoid my eyes.

I had been in that spot too many times before; wanting to clutch the kids to my chest and protect them, but not daring to make a move for fear of their mother's reaction. Instead, I stooped down to their height and spoke as soothingly as I could. "Your mother is mistaken about the things she is saying, sweethearts. You know I

70

love you both, with all my heart." I put both hands over my chest and smiled. "And I know you love me too. I understand how it ..."

"Give it up, Tom," Kathy cut in. "Your smooth talking is not going to work this time. We know you are lying, and we made up our minds together that we do not want you in this house anymore. Please get out."

Slowly, I stood up. I had been in that situation many times; Kathy threatening to kick me out, and me knowing she really did not want me to go. No matter how distasteful it was, I had always kissed up to her when she got that way, never once calling her bluff. That time, however, things were different. I no longer knew what was best for the girls, and my confused feelings from the night before were still fresh in my mind.

"What would you like me to do, Kathy?" I asked softly.

"I told you," she barked, "Get the hell out of this house ... *right now!*"

Dejected, I hesitantly nodded my head again, then turned and stared out the kitchen window at snow flurries blowing aimlessly in the daybreak's muted sunshine. Turning back then to the devil's enraged face, I responded meekly, "Okay ... perhaps that is what's best." I held out my hand, palm up, "Give me my keys and I'll leave."

Kathy glanced down at what she still held in her hand, as if she had forgotten they were there. "No!" she said quickly.

"What do you mean, *no*?"

"No!" she cried louder. "You can't go!"

"You just told me to get out!"

"I do not care what I said. You cannot go!"

"I have to get to work, dumbbell!"

"No, you do not. I will not let you."

"You're out of your mind, woman!" I bellowed, throwing my arms in the air, and taking a menacing step toward her. *"Give me those damn keys!"*

71

"Noooooo!" she screeched. *"Don't hurt us!"*

"Aaaaaaaah!" Both Kristen and Amy let out shrieks of terror like I had never heard before. Kathy cowered, but gripped the keys tighter, daring me to try and take them, as the girls continued to scream.

Like a caged cat, I paced the floor looking for a way out. Then I spotted the answer hanging on the hooks by the side door – a second set of keys. Before Kathy could react, I had snatched the keys from the hook, was out the side door and speeding down the street in *her* car.

I had escaped the demon's trap once again, but that time, not unwounded. I sure did not know what to do next. Running away would help nothing, I was sure of that, but neither would staying.

Our children had been frightened – truly frightened – of me. Whether I or their mother was the cause of their fear did not matter, it was *me* they feared, and that cut deep.

Like a bad dream, as I drove the streets – not towards my job but just anywhere – the scene I had just cowardly ran from replayed itself in my mind. I could see my children, fear on their faces, clutching their mother's legs. I could hear their screams for help. And repeatedly, I could not save them.

*****

Late that evening, after I thought the girls would be asleep, I returned home. Before I entered the house, however, in case I were to become trapped again, I hid spare keys in the backyard. I prayed I would not need them.

The doors were unlocked, and the place was quiet. I tiptoed into each of the girls' bedrooms and tenderly kissed their warm cheeks. I wanted to wake them so much, but I dared not. Creeping then to the open doorway of my own bedroom, I stood silently, staring

72

into the darkness, not even sure that Kathy was inside. Before long, though, she spoke up.

"What are you doing?" she asked pleasantly.

"I don't know, Kath."

"Are you coming to bed?"

"No."

"Why not?"

"I can't take the chance."

I heard the ruffling of the covers. "I'm sorry, Tom," she said softly. "I'm *really* sorry."

I waited for a long moment to gather my nerves. "I believe you are, Kath," I finally responded. "But we cannot just make up this time like we always have. We must grow up ... or we must split up."

She reached over and switched on the table lamp next to the bed. A soft yellow light fell over her, sitting up perkily, wearing a small silk nightgown. "You're right, Tom," she said with a smile. "I know you're right." She padded the mattress with her palm. "Come to bed, honey, please? I need you. We can make things better again."

"That won't work anymore," I said, angry at her for doing the same old routine. "It just ... it just will not work. That is all there is to it. I am staying away from you, woman ... *forever!*"

Her eyes widened. "Forever?"

"Maybe," I said, taking a deep breath. "If that's what it takes. I am very afraid of you, Kathleen. I cannot tell you how badly today hurt me. And the girls. My God, we are killing our own children. Can't you see what we are doing to them?" I shook my head. "No ... we can't take the chance that what happened today will *ever* happen again."

Tears began to tumble down her cheeks. "It won't happen again, Tom," she pleaded. "I promise. It was all my fault. I know that."

"Your fault or mine, Kath, it does not matter. We have been through this a million times. It is insane for us to be together."

73

"No, it isn't!" she cried defiantly. "I do not believe that for a minute. We love each other. That's all that matters." She reached her arms out to me and softened her tone. "We can overcome anything together, honey. Come here … please … I need you."

"No Kath," I said with finality. "Too much damage has been done. I am going to sleep on the couch tonight … and the next night, and the next … and maybe forever."

~

Chapter 10   *Divide*

As threatened, I slept on the sofa that night, and remained in camp there for the next few weeks. Kristen and Amy never once questioned what I was doing. They seemed to like having easier access to me, especially on days I would try to sleep in. Every night my wife would ask me to come to bed with her, and every night I politely turned her down.

During my time of self-banishment from the bedroom, I thoroughly examined the question of whether Kathy and I should stay married or not. Like a lawyer searching for a preponderance of evidence, I clinically inspected all aspects of the situation: *Was it possible to save our marriage? If yes, was it desirable? If yes, was it wise to try?*

At marriage counseling and religious sessions in the past, Kathy and I had assessed our lives together in that very same manner. This time, however, I added topics of my own: *Was I willing to spend the rest of my life without friends? Did I love my wife anymore? Did I even like her?*

Having the matters of Kathy and me covered, I moved then to the more important subject – our offspring. *What was best for 6-year-old Kristen and 3-year-old Amy? Were they better off emotionally with their parents together or apart? If separated, could Kathy and I provide properly for their needs?*

If we stayed together, Kathy and I would no doubt battle in the girls' presence repeatedly. That, to me, was an unforgivable sin, and all by itself answered my questions. I concluded then, despite what God and my parents might have said, that, in our case at least, keeping the family together only for the children's sake was the *wrong* thing to do.

So it was then I unilaterally decided divorce was the only rational solution to the problem. I was certain it was the proper direction to take, and that it was the right time. But I did not expect it to be easy to convince my wife of that idea. Surely, she would counter any argument I made, and if she cried and begged, I was not at all sure I had the strength to resist her.

It took me quite a long time to get up the nerve to tell Kathy I wanted a divorce. Expecting a grueling and protracted fight, I arranged for my parents to take the girls for the evening. Being the chicken that I am, however, I did not tell my folks what I was up to.

Kathy was shocked, of course. At first, she did not even believe me. I spent the last two months living on the couch, and we had hardly spoken, but still, she did not see it coming.

"It can't possibly be so bad, can it, honey?" she said with a smile. "I told you I'd change if that's what you want."

"I don't want us to change anymore, Kathy," I responded calmly. "We are what we are ... and that's it."

"Okay then ... what do you want to work on?" was her only other thought.

"I don't want to work on anything, Kathleen," I said, quickly frustrated, starting my usual pacing around the living room floor. "We have been working on our marriage since we said *I do*. We have been to marriage training, marriage clinics, marriage counseling, parent training and parent counseling. We have had years of public and private debate with our folks, our siblings, our friends, our children, and the entire bloody neighborhood. Nothing ever changes, and you and I both know nothing ever will."

Kathy, sitting demurely on the sofa, hands on her lap, tried to show patience as I explained myself, but she could only take so much. Finally, working to her limit, she tossed her hands in the air and interrupted my speech with her standard line: "You always said, Tom, that love would keep us together ... and we love each other."

"No, Kathy," I returned promptly, having anticipated the point. "*You* always said that, not me. Love is just one ingredient needed. Everything else a marriage needs to be worthwhile ... we just don't have."

Panic built and tears formed in her big eyes. "Are you saying you don't love me?" she asked, her voice cracking.

I leaned forward, placing both hands above my kneecaps, and shook my head. "You're not listening Kath," I insisted in a low, reasoning voice. "This is no longer just about that."

"But I have to know!" she wailed. "Don't you love me?"

I straightened up then, expressionless, not wanting to answer the question; not even really knowing the answer.

Theatrically then, she threw herself to the ground and wrapped her arms around my legs. "Oh, Tom," she whimpered, "what has happened to us? I need you. "You *must* still love me!"

I thought then it would be easier if I just said I did not, that the years of fighting had taken their toll. But I did not have the courage. Instead, I reached down and tenderly helped my wife to her feet.

"I do love you, Kath," I said as affectionately as I could, "and I know you love me too. But that is precisely the reason we must split up. Don't you see? It is the only way we will not destroy each other."

She only gave me a puzzled look in return.

"Surely you'll admit you're not happy in this marriage, Kath," I went on. "And because I love you, I want you to be happy. I truly do." I smiled gently. "You'll see … this will be good for you."

Apparently no longer feeling needy or vulnerable, her face twisted in anger, and she harshly pushed me away. "You bastard!" she yelled. "Don't you dare pretend you're doing this for me!"

I stumbled back away but did not react in kind. Her outburst had not been unexpected. "I didn't think you'd believe me," I said softly. "But it is true. My concern for you is every bit as real as my concern for myself."

She stood tall then and asked smugly, "What about the girls, Mr. perfect? How can you just leave them this way?"

I had expected that question as well. It was what had haunted me the most. But I had a rational response prepared.

"I'm not leaving them, Kathy," I said. "We will just be living in different houses. In fact, I could be *more involved* in their lives than ever. And with you and I not clashing all the time, it will be much easier for them. And I am betting we'll be better parents apart than we ever were together."

"No, no, no!" she stomped. "You can't do this to them!"

"I'm not doing anything *to* them," I shot back, growing impatient. "In fact, I am doing this mostly *for* them. What they have now is not exactly the greatest, you know."

At that, Kathy lost her bluster and began to cry. "Please don't do this, Tom," she pleaded, holding her hands in prayer. "We've been together so long. We cannot just throw it all away over nothing. We can change, I know it, and it will be good for us again. Just like before. Remember Minnesota? How happy we were? We should never have left there, Tom. We can go back if you want. I love you so much, I will do anything for you, trust me. I need you, and so do the girls. We must stay together. We must." She held out her hands beseechingly, invitingly. "Can't we just make up like we always have? Can't we?"

My head was spinning, and I felt myself weakening, but I managed to set my resolve against this blatant tug at my heartstrings. "We've been through this so many times before, Kathy," I said with heavy eyes. "You know if we make up it won't last."

"Yes, it will!" She wailed desperately, talking amazingly fast. "It is different this time. I had no idea you were so unhappy. I know I said terrible things, and I know I lied to the girls. And … and … and I know I smothered you because I wanted you all to myself … but I am sorry, Tom. I am sorry. And I will never do any of that again. I can be different … and I will. You must believe me!"

"Oh, for chrissake, Kathy!" I yelled back, holding my head with both hands. "You will not be any different, and neither will I. Not for long anyway. In a month or two we will be right back in the same stupid situation, only with fresh wounds to deal with. Haven't we hurt each other enough? And the girls! My God! It is not fair for them to have to suffer through the bullshit that another attempt, and another failure, would certainly bring … I am sick of this. Aren't you? We are wasting our lives and destroying our children at the same time. Why do you want to keep doing this?"

"Because I love you, stupid, and Kristen and Amy love you too. And they need their daddy. Listen to me, Tom," she said breathlessly. "Even if you do not care about me, you owe it to your children! It is the obligation you always said you would never quit on. If you do not try again, you will never know what could have been. And we can make it this time, honey. I am sure of it. Please, Tom, do not leave us. We need you!"

She almost got me with that one, especially bringing obligation into it the way she did. I closed my eyes and fought back my own tears. I wanted so much to believe her. I wanted to be married. I wanted my children, and I wanted my wife. So, I questioned myself, *why am I doing this*?

She was right – we did owe it to our children to do whatever we could to keep the family together, and maybe one more try was all it would take. I could gather her into my arms, I thought, *and it would instantly be as if nothing bad had ever been between us. She would forgive, and I would forget. Everything would be good again – as she had said – if only for a while.*

But that was dangerous thinking, and I knew it. It was a line of thought that marginalized the harm staying together could bring, and my obligations included weighing the bad as well as the potential good. I could not afford to let myself be deluded again, and I could not let my emotions overcome my rationality. I shook off the fog in my head and blinked open my eyes.

I saw Kathy watching me intently, waiting for my reply. She was pacing a bit, but never taking her eyes off mine. She seemed stuck between wanting to hug me and wanting to slug me.

I did not know what to do – to cave into her certainly disastrous wishes, or to stick to my guns and follow through on what I had started. Like a department store mannequin, I stood in the middle of the floor, saying nothing, staring blankly.

After long moments of my paralysis and Kathy's silent pacing, each of us waiting for the other to make a move, she finally threw up her hands and broke the stalemate.

"What's it gonna be, boy?" she demanded impatiently. *"I can't wait all day!"*

The old familiar, bullying tone coming from my wife of seven and a half years snapped me out of my indecision and went a long way toward easing my mind. My shoulders relaxed as the weight of my uncertainty lifted.

Even while desperately wanting to show her love and consideration for me, Kathy's natural inclination to be bossy and noncompliant had easily risen to the surface. She just could not behave any other way, it seemed. I was grateful she had displayed those traits again sooner rather than later.

My nagging questions, thus, had been answered, and with new confidence I was ready to get back onto the evening's original path. I stood up straighter then, took a deep breath, and began explaining myself afresh.

*****

June 1975

About a mile from my former home, I rented a small second floor apartment. I did not have many belongings, but my dad helped me carry in a lumpy bed somebody had given me, most of my clothing, and my beloved golf clubs. After we finished with the small job, I grabbed two beers from the fridge and assumed a seat on the naked living room floor. It was then that we had our one and only conversation about divorce.

"You know, Tommy," the not-so-old guy said to me after taking a long swig of his Stroh's. "I think this is the right thing to do."

"What? Having a beer?" I said with a smirk.

"Not that, knucklehead. I mean your divorce. I do not see how you could do anything else."

"Do you think maybe I didn't try hard enough to stay married, Pop?" I asked sincerely.

80

"That is just it, son. You did try hard. I give you credit for that. Kathy's own father once told me he did not know how you were able to put up with her as long as you have. I am not saying I am happy with your divorce, mind you, but I think I'd be doing the same thing if I were in your shoes."

"No, you wouldn't, Dad," I said in return. "I know you better than that. You would tough it out forever. It does help me to hear you say what you said though. Thank you for that."

We sat silently for a while, leaning against the bare walls on opposite ends of the empty room. I spoke next with all I could think of to say. "I know this is hard on you and Mom. I am sorry, Dad."

He nodded his head, as if to say *Yeah, I know, son. It is okay, son. I understand, son.* But neither of us said anything for another minute or two, and then we were on to another subject.

My dad had said enough though, to relieve some of the guilt that had been piling up onto my not-so-strong shoulders. Marriages were permanent to my mom and dad. Divorce, they believed – particularly with children involved – was a complete abdication of responsibility. Besides, God does not allow it. I was grateful for him to find any kind words at all to say to me. It was more than I had expected.

*****

Once I had moved away from home, I do not remember Kathy ever trying to talk me out of the divorce again. Following the night of her dramatics on our living room floor, there were no more tears, no more begging, and no more consideration either. From that point on, everything from her was a demand, and little was reasonable.

"No, you can't have that table," she said with arms crossed and foot tapping in the usual fashion.

"But I need things, Kath. I need to live too, you know. And I am entitled to half the common property," I said, not so very sure that was true.

"That's not the way it works, dummy," she said. "I talked to a lawyer. The girls get what they need first, *then* you and I split up what's left 50/50."

"Okay," that's fair enough," I replied. "But surely I can have an end table."

"The girls need that table," she said without blinking.

"Okay," I asked politely. "Which table can I have?"

"You cannot have a table. We need them all."

"What furniture *can* I have, woman?" I asked then, already knowing the answer.

"You cannot have *any* furniture. The girls need it *all*," she said, not even trying to hide her delight. "And because they are in my sole custody, everything stays with me."

"But I need some things!" I said, raising my voice more than I wanted to.

The delighted look faded from her face and was replaced with a scowl. "That's not my problem, now, is it?"

"So, what *can* I have?" I asked loudly, my hands then firmly on my hips.

"You can have your clothes, which you have already taken, and your stinking golf clubs. I would say that's about all you can have."

"Oh, for chrissake, Kathy!" I yelled, pointing stiffly at the table, as if *it* were to blame. You do not *need* that table!"

Kristen and Amy had been standing anxiously by, watching the exchange with wide eyes, but not making a sound. I regarded them for a moment, recalling, of course, that the separation was supposed to end their witnessing such arguments. Gazing back at the end table, then again to their mother, I slowly lowered my arm, and, as usual, gave up the battle.

Forcing a softer expression, I took a deep breath and stood down to the height of the little ones. "M'ere you guys," I said, holding out inviting arms with a big smile. "Give your daddy a kiss. I will see you tomorrow."

*****

The details of the divorce were not difficult to work out. It was standard practice in Michigan, we were told, for the couple to be granted joint legal custody of the children. But the mother would always get physical custody, and the dad would get visitation. There was no talk between us of anything different. It seemed to me like the correct thing to do, anyway. All I asked for was to have lots of contact with the kids, and with all of us living in the same town, that was not foreseen as a problem.

I expected I would pay for the family house, and that Kathy and the girls would live there comfortably forever. I would have regular fatherly input into our children's lives, and everything would be fine. It seemed to me a solid plan.

*****

July 1975

"We're moving up north," Kathy said nonchalantly one afternoon.

"What do you mean moving?" I asked.

"We will live with my mom and dad for a while. You will have to sell the house and give me half the money, so we can get a place of our own."

83

"You already have a place of your own," I said, stunned. "You're standing in it!"

"This is not our home anymore," she came back with. "You made sure of that." A satisfied smirk spread across her face as she added, "You should have seen this coming; mister know everything."

The weight of the world shifted to my shoulders at that very moment. "It never occurred to me, Kathy," I said glumly. "You know I cannot follow you, and the girls will be too far away for me to have normal contact with them."

"That's *not my problem*," she said, stressing the words as if she were speaking to an imbecile, not the father of her children.

"But it *is* your problem!" I shouted. "You are supposed to encourage the children's relationship with me, not make it impossible. You cannot just forget about that."

"Oh, yes I can," she insisted, pointing a finger in my face. "You're the one who wanted a divorce … *not me*."

"I'm divorcing you, you idiot!" I screamed. *"Not Kristen and Amy!"*

"Calling me names won't change a thing," she said without passion. "We're leaving … get used to it."

~

Chapter 11   *Visitation*

August 1975

In short order, Kathy managed to pack up everything we owned from both the house and the garage into a U-Haul truck, withdraw all our money from the bank accounts, and leave town with the girls, the dog, and our one-year-old family car in tow. If nothing else, the woman was resourceful.

The house was still there, of course, along with the mortgage and the car payments in my name. She had said no goodbyes and made no arrangements for me and the girls to get together.

More than a week went by before I was able to reach Kathy on the telephone. Her parents lived in the small town of Hillman, about 20 miles of two-lane blacktop from the larger city of Alpena. It was in the far northern reaches of the Lower Peninsula of Michigan; four tedious hours' drive away from me.

"What do you want, Tom?" she deadpanned when she came to the phone.

"Well," I said, trying to sound friendly, "you're mighty hard to catch up with, girlie."

"What do you want, Tom?" she deadpanned again.

"Okay," I responded, still friendly. "If you don't want to speak with me, that's fine. So put Kristen on the phone, please."

"No," she stated flatly. "I won't do that."

"C'mon, Kath," I urged, losing patience. "This is not doing anyone any good. I have a right to talk to my daughter."

"Says who?"

"*Says me!*" I shouted into the mouthpiece. "*Says God! Says the fucking judge, that's who!*"

Click.

I pulled the receiver from my face and glared at it in disbelief, then quickly dialed the number again. Nobody answered, and after two minutes of ringing, I hung up, checked the number, and tried again. Nobody answered again, and I dialed again ... and again ... and again. After six or eight tries, I got the message, slammed the receiver down on the black handset, and cursed up a storm.

An hour later, having calmed down considerably, I sat at the makeshift kitchen table in my still mostly empty apartment, and slowly dialed the number again. Dialing slowly, however, did not change the outcome. I hung up softly, though, and noted the time, determined to call once an hour until I got through, no matter how long it took.

Even under normal circumstances, Kathy was not the type who felt compelled to answer a ringing telephone just because it was ringing. But I figured, if nothing else, her mother or father or one of the kids would eventually pick up. But they did not.

Around midnight, tired, angry, and frustrated, I finally admitted temporary defeat and went to bed. Somebody will answer the telephone tomorrow, I vowed, or I will call the fucking police.

As it turned out, I did not have to call the police. Kathy picked up the first time I phoned while I was on lunch break at work.

"What?" she asked without even saying hello, seeming to know it was me.

Having had time to think things over, I had a plan. "Don't hang up, Kathy," I said quickly. "I am coming to get the kids this weekend. I have a court order," I lied.

"No, you don't," she said just as quickly.

"Okay," I confessed. "I do not, but I will get one if I have to. You know the Friend of the Court wants me to have a visitation every other weekend, and they will not be happy when I tell them you are preventing it."

"I'm not preventing anything," she said calmly.

"Oh, then I can pick the girls up Saturday morning?"

"Nooooo!" she spit out, venom dripping from her voice. "My mother does not want you on her property!"

"Oh, bullshit," I shouted loud enough for her to hear me without the telephone. "If your mother said that, it's only because you influenced her."

Click.

My boss poked his head out of his office and raised an eyebrow at me. "Is something wrong, Tom?" he asked.

I shook my head. "No, Joe," I answered, red faced. "I'm sorry."

I did not try to call again from work, but instead waited till the evening when I was at my own table. The phone was picked up at that time on the first ring.

"Hello?" I heard my mother-in-law's hesitant voice.

"Hi, Mom," I responded pleasantly, not sure if she wanted me to call her mom anymore.

"Hello, Thomas" she came back with, not offering any small talk but not sounding mean either.

"I'm glad you answered the phone," I said right away. "I would like to have a talk with you if I may. Is this a suitable time?"

"Okay," she replied. "I guess so."

I had not been prepared for a conversation with that particular person, and I didn't know where to begin, but I did have something bugging me, so I just blurted it out.

"Do you really *not* want me on your property, Mom?"

"Well," she answered, "I did say that. It would just cause so much trouble, you know."

"Yeah," I conceded, "I can imagine how Kathy would behave … but I need a way to get the girls. I need …"

"Oh, I don't think Kathy's ever going to let you see the girls again," she interrupted. "You might as well give up on that idea."

"What the hell are you talking about?" I screamed into the mouthpiece.

"Don't raise your voice to me, young man!" she said without equivocation, "or I'll hang up this instant. Just like your ex-wife does."

"Sorry, Mom," I pleaded. "I am sorry. This is just so hard for me to take."

"Well, I don't suppose you want to hear this, Thomas, but you are the one who asked for a divorce, you know."

"That's true, Mom. I take 100% of the blame for that. But I thought it was the best thing to do for Kristen and Amy, and I am still their father, you know. I am not divorcing *them*."

"Well, that is the way Kathy sees it, you know. If you reject her, you are rejecting the girls too."

"But that is crazy! You know I am not rejecting the girls, Mom … don't you?"

"It doesn't matter what I think, Tommy," she said softly to me. "Kathy says you are an unfit father, and that's that."

"But you know that's not true!" I protested, raising my voice more than I wanted to. "She says stupid stuff like that when she is upset. The next minute she will say I am wonderful. You know she wants to stay married to me … so she cannot really think I am unfit, now, can she?"

"Well … no … I guess not," she agreed. "The way I see it though, is that she's using the girls to punish you for rejecting her." Her voice cracked a bit as if she had just then realized that point.

"That's not fair to the girls, is it, Mom?"

"Well … no … I guess not."

"You know it isn't!" I barked, "and she cannot get away with it. I have rights and so do the girls. If I tell the court she is doing this, they are going to be incredibly angry with her, and with you too for fostering this behavior."

"You think I'm fostering this behavior?" she questioned, her voice raising.

"Yes, I do," I said without hesitation. "But I know how you feel about your grandchildren, and I don't believe it's in your heart to act this way."

The kids' grandmother let out a deep sigh but said nothing.

"But I also know how impossible your daughter can be," I continued, less excited. "Nobody knows better than I. I understand the spot you are in, Mom, I really do ... but Kristen and Amy need your help, and I need access to them."

"What do you think I can do?" she implored. "Kathy is not going to listen to me, and I do not want to see fighting around here. What would the neighbors think?"

I leaned back in my chair, thinking that was a reasonable objection from her, and I said so. "If that is what you are worried about, Mom, heck, I can understand that. Your daughter and I can be plenty ridiculous at times. I do not blame you for not wanting the neighbors to see that, so how about if I wait in town somewhere, and Kathy brings the kids to me. Nobody will see us. But you will have to make Kathy do it, of course."

"Oh no!" she said quickly. "I'm not getting in the middle of this."

That was the last straw for me. I felt the veins in my forehead bulging and my eyes burning red. Whatever civility I had reserved for the mother of my ex-wife evaporated in that instant, and I let her have it.

"You are already in the middle of this, Mrs. Scapaticci," I said sternly. "You gave your daughter the means to steal the kids away from me and may have even encouraged it. Whatever bad comes to them, or to me, because of that, I hold you just as responsible as Kathleen. If you do not help me to get proper visitation with my children – and soon – I will show up at your front door with the police and a court order, and we will drag the kids out of your house, kicking and screaming, and strap them into the police car. Is that what you want your neighbors to see?"

"Oh, my God, Tommy, no!" she said with a heavy breath on the phone. "Please don't do that."

I resisted saying another word, sensing I may have finally gotten to her. Seconds of silence passed between us.

"Okay," she said at last. "I can see your point. I will see what I can do. Call me back tomorrow at about this same time."

*****

October 1975

Thus, I found myself with sleepy eyes at 5 am on a cold fall morning, headed north on empty I-75 in an old Pontiac Firebird I had bought just for that purpose. It had taken a few weeks of phone calls and letter writing between me, Grandma, and the Friend of the Court, but a *Visitation Agreement* had finally been hammered out. Throughout the process, Kathy had steadfastly refused to come to the telephone when I called, and likewise she did not allow either of the girls to speak with me all that time. I sure missed my two little darlings, but the wait was about to end.

"Since Grandma did not want any trouble on her property, Kathy was to pass the kids off to me in the parking lot of Glen's Market in obscure downtown Hillman. No contact was to be attempted before that moment – just be there Saturday morning at 10 am … and don't be late.

I had to arrange for time off from work, which really irritated my boss. Saturdays were big store days at Cadillac Fence, and I was needed there. Besides that, he was upset with me about the whole divorce thing. It was nothing religious with the old Jewish guy, just the usual taboos of the era, and his own strong belief in commitment to family. With sincere confusion, he had asked me a hundred times, "How could you let it come to this, Tom?"

I arrived at Glen's Market half an hour early, which I thought to be prudent; I did not dare be tardy. Kathy was an hour late, though.

90

It took her a moment to recognize me sitting in my new old car. She pulled forward into the empty parking space next to mine, so our drivers' windows were then face to face. She quickly opened her door into mine, got out of her car, retrieved the girls' overnight bag from her back seat, and shoved it through the open window into my face.

Kristen and Amy sat uneasily in their seats looking straight ahead. "Let's go girls!" Kathy demanded. "You *must* do this. Your father is going to call the police if you don't get moving. Hurry up!"

The girls slowly got themselves out of their mother's car, adjusted their hats and scarves, and walked around to where I was, stooped in front of my car with open arms and a big smile. They walked right past me without a look and crawled into the back seat of the Firebird.

Kathy laid out the rules. "Be back here at six tomorrow night, and don't do anything stupid with the girls." Abruptly then, without so much as a wave goodbye to her daughters, she left.

It was not perfect, but I was ecstatic to be around Kristen and Amy again - the first time in two months. I jumped into the driver's seat of the white convertible. "Hello yuz guys!" I said while cranking the big V8. "I am so happy to see you. I missed you soooo much."

They did not respond to me in any way, only casting glances at each other from the corners of their eyes. Kristen fiddled with her mittens and Amy squirmed in her seat. I did not bother to ask what was wrong.

I had not given one thought beforehand about where we would go or what we might do for two days. That really did not matter; there was always plenty to do in Northern Michigan. But I was caught off guard by the girls' lack of congeniality and was not at all sure how to crack the ice that had obviously formed.

"Aren't you glad to see me?" I asked.

Neither one responded, as if they had not even heard me.

I repeated myself, but with a louder voice the second time. "Aren't you glad to see me, girls?"

91

Still, they gave no response.

More than once in the past I had been given the cold shoulder like this by their mother, but never from Kristen and Amy. I thought it amazing, children so young could be taught such behavior.

"I know you can hear me," I said calmly. "Are you guys mad at me?"

No answer still, just blank looks.

"I hope not," I continued. "I got up here as fast as I could. It is a long way you know."

No response.

"How do you like my new car?" I asked with a big grin.

No answer.

"You wanna drive, Kristen?"

No answer.

"Okay," I spoke a little sternly then, looking over my shoulder at them for a moment. "I know this is not easy for you…. It is not easy for me either, but we really should try talking to each other, don't you think?"

Both girls just stared at their feet. A semi passed in the opposite direction on the two-lane blacktop, giving plenty of distraction.

"Don't you think?" I asked again with the same result.

I released a high-pitched sigh of resignation I thought they would find humorous. "Alright then," I said not unkindly, "if that's the way it is, then *I'll* do all the talking, but you two have to listen."

In the rearview mirror I saw them glancing at each other with questioning eyes. At least I knew they were paying attention.

"I love you two," I began, "with all my heart. I love you. No matter what happens between your mother and me, I will always be your father, you know; that will never change. And I will always be here for you and take care of you … always … and forever.

"And I know you love me too ... even if you do not want to say it right now. I understand you are upset. What, with all that has happened, who wouldn't be? I am upset, myself. But I am not upset with you. I want you to know that." I snapped my head back to them. "Did you think I was angry with you?" I asked. "Is that what's bothering you?"

They still did not answer, but the question did seem to arouse their interest. I was making progress.

"Okay," I said. "I am glad that is not it.... But what is it then, sweethearts? What is the matter?"

They stuck to their stubborn guns, having more of their mother in them than I had bargained for. Not a peep did the youngsters utter. I thought I should change the subject.

"So how do you like living up north?" I asked.

No answer.

"Have you started school yet?"

No answer.

"How's the dog?"

No answer.

"I really miss the dog. Does she ask about me?"

No answer. Not even a giggle at my dumb joke.

"Alrighty," I sighed again, "I give up. If you two want a *no-talkie* weekend, there is nothing I can do about it. But I do not know what we are gonna do with ourselves for the next two days. We could go horseback riding or fly an airplane, or something fun like that. But heck, I don't know what you want till you tell me."

I looked back over my shoulder again for a moment. "Whenever you are ready to talk to me, girls, just say so. In the meantime, it is a lovely day out, and I've got plenty of gas. I will just keep driving around, cuz I don't know what else to do."

Not saying another word, I cruised the highways aimlessly for the next 2 hours, hoping to nudge the girls into making some kind of move. The sun shone brightly on the stunning fall colors that blanketed the rolling hills. It was certainly the right time and place for a scenic drive, but it was taking a long, long time. I needed to find a restroom soon, and I suspected the kids needed a break as well. Determined not to be the next one to speak, however, I just kept driving.

The kids were certainly getting anxious; jostling and whispering, trying, it seemed, to make a plan of attack between themselves. I hoped they would figure it out soon.

Finally, Kristen sat up straight and took a deep breath. "We're hungry, Daddy," she said loud and clear.

"Ah hah!" I cheered, slapping the steering wheel, elated to hear her say my name. How I love to be called Daddy. "That's great!" I said, smiling over my shoulder. "I, myself, am *starving*. How 'bout you, Amy, you hungry too?"

"Yes, Daddy," little Amy shouted excitedly, bouncing on the seat. "Can we have a hot dog?"

"Does your mother let you have hot dogs?" I asked.

"Kristen hung her blonde head. "No," she replied sadly.

"Good!" I resounded. *"Then that's exactly what we're gonna have."*

*****

The rest of our time together that weekend was wonderful. We ate hot dogs and all kinds of other junk. We happened upon a Sweet Potato Carnival, which was a riot. We played in a beachside park and did lots of little girl shopping in the quaint resort towns.

That night in the motel we watched a rerun Disney show on TV, jumped on the beds, and laughed till we cried. The next morning, dressed in their new clothes, it was chocolate milk with pancakes and cherries and tons of hot syrup for breakfast. Not once did we speak of our troubles.

Six o'clock Sunday evening came around much sooner than any of us wanted. But all good things end, it seems.

We were playing *I Spy* in the parking lot of Glen's Market, the three of us still having fun, crammed into the two front bucket seats, when Kathy pulled in at 6:30. Instantly, everything changed, from noisy to quiet, from playful to serious, from me to mom.

The girls said nothing, neither smiled nor frowned, but climbed into the backseat and dutifully put on their hats and coats. Before I knew it, they were letting themselves out of my car.

"Hey you guys!" I called out. "Don't I get a kiss goodbye?"

But they were gone in a flash, efficiently loading themselves into the other backseat, not saying a word to their mother either, I noticed.

My ex-wife only cast me a dirty look, then sped away without even asking for the girls' overnight bag. I did nothing but wave meekly goodbye to red taillights.

*****

Five long hours later, in my barren bedroom in Madison Heights, I pulled covers tightly over my weary self. I had to get up too early the next morning to start the work week but did not fall quickly to sleep. The events of the last two days, and the faces of my children, played repeatedly in my mind.

My first *Court Ordered Visitation* had not been all that easy, but it was over, and it turned out mostly good, I thought. I got to be with the kids, and they got to be with me – that alone was worth all the trouble. But I did not like what took place in the last three minutes at Glen's Market and, unfortunately, that is what I remembered the most.

Then I began to question myself: once the girls had softened up, should I have pressed for a more serious conversation with them? Should I have tried harder to draw out their feelings? Should I have prepared them better for the moment our visit had to end? Why couldn't they at least say goodbye to me?

But I had no answers to any of my questions, and eventually I decided I was being silly feeling sad just because I did not get a final kiss from the girls. Surely the next time I saw Kristen and Amy, it would be better than the first, and the third time better than the second.

Warm under the covers then, remembering sweet little Amy's brightly lit-up face as she bounced on the car seat asking in great anticipation, *"Can we have a hot dog, Daddy?"* A smile eased across my face, and I drifted off to sleep.

~

Chapter 12   *West Branch*

Come rain or shine, every other weekend for the next several months, I made the trek up north to see my kids. We met each time at Glen's Market. Kathy was always late, of course, and always cranky. Every time, the girls were distant from me at first encounter, and every time, it was an effort to soften them up. But mellow they did, and, as predicted, each visit got progressively a little easier.

Things began to settle into a routine, and I hoped perhaps Kathy was beginning to mellow as well. Then I received a notice from the Oakland County Friend of the Court. A petition had been made for a modification to the Visitation Order and I had to be in their office the next Wednesday at 9 am.

I went as required, of course, but the issues brought up in that session caught me off guard. My ex-wife had asked that I not be allowed to take the girls to a motel during my weekend visits, and that the passing off the kids at Glen's Market be limited.

Joyce McKenzie, the Friend of the Court official, agreed with Kathy that it was unseemly for a man to have two young girls alone in a motel, and that the kids shouldn't have to be put through that transfer process any more than what was absolutely necessary. She therefore felt compelled, she said, to change my every-other-weekend two-day visits, from that point forward, to be Saturday only.

I argued vehemently against the idea, of course, but being ill prepared and without an attorney, I was at a huge disadvantage. Kathy was without an attorney as well, but she was clearly being helped in the matter by Mrs. McKenzie. I began to wonder then if the *Friend of the Court might not be more aptly named The Friend of the mother.*

"But this is terrible," I protested clumsily. "Overnight time is so important ... so is rising together in the morning, getting ready for the day's events ... I need *more* time with my kids to be a proper father, not less."

"Well, you should have thought of that before you asked for a divorce, Mr. VanBuren," the lady responded, casting a glance toward my ex-wife.

It seemed I'd heard that argument before. "Oh, c'mon now," I came back with. "At this point Mrs. McKenzie, we're supposed to be doing the best we can to provide support for the children, not pointing fingers in a failed marriage."

The official raised her eyebrows but did not seem to take offense from my comment. Instead, she backed off her chauvinistic attitude, perhaps sensing that I was competent and not going to be intimidated. "That's true enough," she agreed, "but I don't want the girls to be taken to motels anymore, and with your home being so far away, I really don't see another way to do this.... Do you?"

At least, I thought, *she was giving me a chance to offer a different solution to the problem. But what?* I closed my eyes and tried to think. After a long moment, I heard my own voice ask the question: "What about another home?" I opened my eyes then and looked with hope at the functionary.

"What do you mean?" asked Mrs. McKenzie.

Excited then, I continued. "I have a sister – a married sister – living in West Branch, not too far from Glen's Market. Could I take the kids there for the night?"

Mrs. McKenzie looked quickly at Kathy. "Do you know of this sister?"

My ex-wife, clad in a blue polka-dotted granny dress, pursed her lips, and nodded her head once.

"And do you approve?"

Kathy, taken aback by the change of focus, and clearly ticked off that this possible solution would thwart her plans to mess with me, looked rapidly around the room as if seeking a way out. Then, gathering some composure, she sat up straighter, smoothed out her dress, took a deep breath and sighed, "I guess so."

Mrs. McKenzie, obviously pleased, sat back in her chair and smiled. "Well then," she said rather loudly, "it looks as if we have a workable solution here."

*****

We all handled the new visitation method well enough; the only drawback being the extra driving time. It seems I had stretched the truth a bit when I told Mrs. McKenzie that my sister's home was not too far from Glen's Market. West Branch is a hundred miles south of Hillman.

So, after the four-hour trek up north to get the girls on Saturday mornings, it was another two-hour drive back to Mary Kay's house in West Branch. The very next day, it was six hours again of driving in the opposite sequence. All told, I was on the road 12 hours each weekend, eight of it alone. I didn't mind though, it was the only solution, except that I was quickly wearing out my old Firebird.

At least the new arrangements gave me and the girls something specific to do each time together – no more searching for carnivals and such. My sister's home, a small well-kept farmhouse with the town built up around it, was spacious enough to fit us in comfortably, and we were made to feel very welcome. Mary Kay, her husband Randy, and one-year-old towheaded Heather all could talk up a storm and seemed never to be in a bad mood. We cooked, ate, worked on projects, played games, and always had great conversation, usually late into the night.

I recall those West Branch visits as perhaps the best father/daughter time Kristen, Amy, and I ever had together in their early lives. It was certainly worth all the driving. I got to care for and fuss over my children – just me – without interference from their mother. And they got to run around all they wanted without ever losing my attention.

I heard my name called, "Daddy! Daddy! Daddy!" ten thousand times during each of those weekends ... and I melted at every rendition.

"Watch this, Daddy! Is it my turn, Daddy? C'mere, Daddy. I love you, Daddy."

"I love you too, girls."

*****

Besides wearing out my car, however, there was another downside – it affected my job at Cadillac Fence. "You know I like you, Tom," Joe had said helplessly to me many times over, "and of course I want you to see your kids, but how am I supposed to handle the store on the days you're not here?"

I had by then worked at that Plymouth Road location for more than five years. Joe had taken me under his wing, as if I had been his own son, and taught me the business from top to bottom. I hated to go, but I couldn't see another way out ... and neither could Joe.

*****

So it was that in the spring of 1976, I came to leave my job. I knew a lot about building fences, and I had a few hundred dollars saved up. *That ought to be enough*, I figured. I bought a 10-year-old black Ford pickup truck with red vinyl interior and smoking exhaust and filed papers in Oakland County to secure the name *Thomas Fence Company*.

~

Chapter 13   *Meet Nancy*

By the time Kathy and the girls moved up north (August, '75) it had been seven and a half years since I had left town with my pregnant bride for military duty in Minnesota. Now divorced, with the kids living far away, and no house to take care of anymore, I had pretty much nothing to do.

Hunched over the telephone on the living room floor of my empty apartment, I tried to make contact with my previous life. I managed to reach an old friend, Chuck Herman. We had worked together at Gemco Electric when we were both just out of high school. We arranged to meet for a beer after fielding some awkward questions from him, like, "Where the hell have you been for the last decade?"

I had never sat in a bar with Chuck before (we could not legally drink at 17, of course). It didn't take us long, though, to remember why we had hung around together for those two important years between high school and our future lives – we liked each other's company. Chuck had gotten married shortly before I did, to Gail, a pretty Mormon girl from the neighborhood.

We laughed recalling the times and the characters from our past life, but it was terribly sad for me to hear that Chuck and Gail were no longer married. They had no children together, so that at least made things easier for them. It took some hours and gallons of beer for me to tell my ridiculous story. I ended up crashing that night at Chuck's house, which was located next to a park in an old part of town not far away from my parents' home in Royal Oak.

*****

December 1975

As it turned out, Chuck had only one roommate and an empty bedroom. I broke the lease at the apartment and moved in with the two guys. My life quickly tried to shift into *bachelor mode.*

April 1976

Chuck didn't much like the idea of my starting a business, mostly because he was worried I would not earn enough money to pay him rent. The logistics of his corner house and the garage worked out well for me though, and I always managed to cover my expenses.

I worked eagerly each day to build my new business, and plenty of work came my way. Because I could set my own schedule, I simply cleared the weekends for my up-north visits with the kids. I also found enough time to chase around a bit, seeking female companionship. I had some success in that regard, but it did not come easy for me. Having gotten married so young, I had never really developed a single person's socializing skills.

June 12, 1976

I remember this date because it was exactly one week before my future wife's 20th birthday. Chuck's nephew, Lee Herman, affectionately known as Lee Boy, because he had just recently turned 21, asked me to go with him that night to a dance bar in Livonia. The bar was known for having a nice midweek crowd. "Sure," I said. "Let's go."

I had never been to that club on Grand River Ave near 7 Mile Road. I hadn't been to clubs at all and Lee hadn't even been allowed inside of bars but for a few days. Lee wasn't bad looking or good looking either, about the same as me, but we were both fit, witty, and friendly. I could dance well enough, but that was not really the mission. The mission was to meet girls and to get into conversation with them. We had half a chance with them that way. Lee couldn't dance for beans, but he would do what he had to do.

We found a table on the edge of the dance floor. The band was playing loudly, of course, and I soon found myself tapping my feet and wanting to dance. Lee was happy enough to sit around and watch.

"Look at those two," Lee said, nodding his head to his left. A few tables away sat two blondes who were somewhere around our own ages. Pretty girls drinking, alone, in a dance bar.

"Do you want to ask them to dance?" I asked.

"Hell no! They've already turned down six other guys."

"Oh bullshit. Why do you suppose they've come here if they don't wanna dance?"

"Well … they don't wanna dance with me. I'm sure of that."

"But you don't know that for sure, now do you, Lee Boy? If you don't ask, you never give them a chance to say yes."

"Well, go for it then, fella, if you want to," said Lee firmly. "I'm not stopping you."

"Yes, you are," I said, as if I were an expert at this. "The reason they turned down the other six guys was because they approached them one at a time."

"But you know I don't wanna dance, Tom."

"You brought me to a dance club to meet girls, dummy. How else do you plan on doing that?"

"Why don't you go and dance with one of them, mister know-it-all, and then bring them *both* back to our table for drinks?"

"Oh sure, why don't I just go and do that?"

'You're the suave one, buddy. Surely you can charm the pants off them."

"Look," I said sincerely to my young friend. "If we go over there together, maybe they'll say yes. You can do one dance, and then sit down with your girl, and I can keep on dancing. How easy is that?" Before he could respond, I added, "Which one do you want?"

"The one with the long hair," he quickly stated. "She looks like she's closer to my age, anyway. You can have the old bag."

"Okay, let's go," I said, pulling him up with me, and urging him along. They saw us coming and stopped talking to each other, waiting for our first words.

"Would you like to dance?" Lee said to the *younger one*.

"Yeah, let's go," answered the *old bag*.

She grabbed the shocked Lee by the hand and dragged him to the dance floor, leaving me standing there looking down at the young one. "Sit," she said before I could speak, gesturing to the empty chair next to her.

I sat. "Would you like a drink?" I asked.

"I'm okay," she answered without a smile.

The conversation went downhill from that point. I asked questions and got one or two-word answers. "Would you like to dance?"

"No thanks."

"Do you live around here?"

"Yes."

"Do you come here often?"

"First time."

"Me too."

She didn't talk much, but she sure looked good. She took a cigarette from me and touched my hand as I lit it for her. Long, full, very blonde hair covered part of her lightly tanned face. A few soft freckles sprinkled her nose. From what I could tell, her body was outstanding. There was enough to see through the three open buttons of her straining silk blouse to keep my eyes occupied for quite a while.

"Who's your friend?" I asked.

"My sister, Sharon."

Three words! I was making progress.

"She looks like she's having fun out there," I remarked.

"She likes to dance."

"So does Lee," I lied. "I'd rather just sit and talk though."

"Me too."

This in-depth, stimulating exchange went on for nearly an hour while Lee and Sharon danced their feet off. I ultimately learned from the quiet one that her name was Nancy Jean, and she was 19 years old. She had gotten into that place with a fake ID. Her 20th birthday was in a week. Sharon was 25 and married, but her husband didn't mind if she did this sort of thing without him. That's it ... in one hour. I didn't talk much about myself, mostly because she didn't ask. But I didn't mind. I was enjoying myself sitting with this hot woman-child, drinking beer, and watching Lee and Sharon dance. Damn, Lee was a lousy dancer.

When the band finally took a break, Lee and Sharon came back to the table. Lee wiped the sweat from his brow, while Sharon said to me, "Hello Popeye." I looked at her dumbly but didn't answer. "Your arms," she explained, pointing at me. "They're big ... like Popeye's."

"Oh, that," I said, a little embarrassed. "I've been digging a lot of post holes lately."

"Really?" Sharon said, as she took a seat. "What do you do?" The old bag didn't have any trouble with conversation, it seemed.

"I own a fence company," I answered.

"Bullshit," said Nancy Jean, briefly as always.

"He really does," insisted Lee, taking a heavy swig of his rum and Coke.

"It's just a little company," I added modestly.

"Bullshit," Nancy deadpanned again.

I didn't quite understand what she meant by her remarks, but I didn't care much. "It's really no big deal," I said with a little laugh.

105

"You *own* the company?" Nancy asked, as if that were not possible.

"Yes," I responded with glee. "Would you like to see my shovel?"

"*No, no*, we believe you," interrupted Sharon. "Don't we Nancy?"

"Sure," Nancy said.

At least the discourse was then easier to sustain with Lee and Sharon around. We talked and drank all through the next set. Lee refused to dance with Sharon again, and I didn't dare leave him alone with Nancy, so I turned Sharon down also. We stayed put, and we had fun. When it was time to leave, I asked Nancy Jean if I could give her a call sometime.

"Sure," she answered.

"Can I have your phone number?"

"522-0719"

"522-0719," I repeated.

"That's it."

"Okay ... goodbye."

"Goodbye."

If I could remember that number, maybe I could get a date with that chick. 522-0917. "Did you get Sharon's number, Lee Boy?" I asked on the drive home.

"No, she's married, remember?"

"Yeah, I remember 522-0717 Do you have a pen?"

"No, you'll have to do without."

"No problem 522-0919 I wonder if she gave me a fake number?"

"No doubt ... dumb shit."

106

I let a few days pass before I tried the number 522-0977. I didn't want to look too anxious. It was answered on the first ring. "Hello?" an older female voice said.

"Hello," may I speak to Nancy, please?"

"I'm sorry, there's no Nancy at this number."

"Oh, my fault, sorry," I said, as I hung up.

"Damn!" I said out loud. "She did give me a fake number!"

Maybe not, I thought. *Maybe I wrote it down wrong.* I tried 522-0179. "Harris Vacuum Service," a man answered.

Click.

"Boy, that sucks," I laughed at my own joke.

I tried another number -- no answer. Another -- no luck. I kept trying.

Finally, I dialed 522-0719.

"Hello?" a younger female voice answered.

"Hi ... this is Tom."

"Tom?"

"Yes, we met at Jamie's on the River last Wednesday."

Silence.

"Is this Nancy?"

"Yeah."

"Do you remember me?"

"Yeah."

"Is it okay that I called you?"

"Yeah."

"How's it going?"

"Okay."

"So … would you like to go for a motorcycle ride?"

"Sure."

"Tonight? As soon as I can get there?"

"Okay."

"What's your address?

She didn't give me her address. She instead gave me directions. "Okay," I said. "I'll see you in about an hour."

I didn't make it there in an hour though. Her directions were all but worthless. I found a payphone near the dance bar where we had met, and I called her for clarification on a few minor points; like left and right, and north and south. "Just go right at the Sands Bar," she said. "You can't miss it."

I took off again, still without an address, to search for the Sands Bar. After circling around two square miles for half an hour, I pulled into a service station at Five Mile and Beech Roads and asked a guy pumping gas. "Do you know where the Sands Bar is?"

"Sure, you can't miss it," he responded. "It's on 7 Mile Road between Middlebelt and Inkster."

"Thanks," I said gratefully as I rode away. "That's only four miles from here."

I finally spotted the Sands Bar. It was an old, faded farmhouse with a small neon sign over the side door. I couldn't miss it. I turned left onto the adjacent dirt road (the street did not go to the right). I struggled to read the scribbled directions in my hand while steering in the dark around the potholes and bumps. "Go two blocks to the corner house." Which corner? I wondered when I had gone two blocks. Lucky for me only two of the corner houses had lights on. I chose one of the lit-up houses for no reason and parked my bike in the drive. Feeling like a real dope, and not altogether safe, I walked up to the front porch carrying the extra helmet in my hands like it was a bouquet of flowers.

Nancy Jean answered the door promptly, as if she had been expecting me. She stepped gracefully onto the front porch, looking like Venus in blue jeans. She wore a little leather riding jacket which barely contained her assets. The moonlight sparkled on her golden tresses. I lost my breath. If I had been irritated about her lousy directions, I forgot all about it.

No hellos were exchanged between us. She took obvious notice of my interested eyes, and then gave me her first ever frail smile. Her expression that moment made words between us forever unnecessary. I only smiled in return and handed her the bouquet of flowers.

My Honda 750 did not have a passenger backrest, which I was grateful for at that moment. Venus would have to hold tightly onto me. As it turned out, a motorcycle ride was the perfect date for us – we didn't have to talk.

The radiant night was warm and quiet. I felt a comfort around my waist that had been missing for what seemed like forever. We began our journey together, wordlessly, down many winding roads until then unknown to either of us.

~

Chapter 14   *Dennis*

July 1976

I was smitten. I struggled only briefly with the idea that maybe it was too soon for me to bind myself to any one person. I wanted friendship and companionship, yes, and I had a normal sex drive, but by that time I had only been out of my last commitment for about a year. *I should be more careful, perhaps*, I thought. But careful I was not.

After our first motorcycle ride, Nancy Jean and I had a few non-contact, getting to know each other on different types of dates, like having coffee at Clancy's Grill on 7 Mile Road near Middlebelt. We always sat in one of the booths by the windows overlooking the parking lot. It was usually in the evening when we both were finished with our long day's work. I still didn't know what Nancy's long day at work was; I was soon about to learn a few things though.

On our third date at Clancy's, I watched in amazement as Nancy blazingly scanned through the selection cards on the jukebox terminal and picked out a few songs she wanted to hear. As I deposited quarters, I commented, trying to sound funny, "I marvel at the speed with which you dispatched a normally arduous task."

"You use too many big words, Tom," she responded.

The waitress brought us the usual coffee and French fries, and our conversation began. This time Nancy spoke more than usual. I learned that despite having just turned 20 years old, she had already been married once and divorced. That was surprising enough to me, and then she casually mentioned that she had a 3-year-old son at home. "Holy shit!" I blurted out before I could check myself.

Her eyes grew large, and she pushed her coffee away. "That means you don't want to see me no more."

"No, it doesn't," I objected with a slight smile, not yet knowing that she was serious.

"When you say it like that, that's what you mean," she said earnestly.

"You think *holy shit* means I don't want to see you again?"

"Yes, that's what it means."

"No, it doesn't," I insisted.

"Yes, it does," she insisted in return. "Because I have a child."

"But I have two children myself; why would I think that?"

"I don't know why … but you do."

"But I'm telling you now, that's not what it means."

"What you say first counts the most," she said with certainty.

Her logic escaped me. "Can't what I've had time to contemplate carry at least as much weight as what I say when caught by surprise?" *Surely, she would understand this*, I thought.

"You use too many big words, Tom," she said without blinking.

"I'm sorry, Nance, and I'm sorry I said what I said. I didn't mean to offend you. I am very sorry." I slowly eased her coffee back to her. "It's just that you're so young to already have a 3-year-old. It surprised me. That's all. Please forgive me."

After further explanation from me, and three more cups of coffee, she did forgive me. Then she invited me for dinner the next Saturday evening at her home to meet her son, Dennis, and the rest of the Rashauer family. Her mother had asked her to extend the invitation to me. *Pretty nice of her mother*, I thought. "Don't expect my family to be normal though," she added as a warning.

It was the first time I had set foot inside the rundown white bungalow on the corner of Floral and Exford streets. Some unfamiliar cars were parked on the dirt road and in the driveway by the big Elm tree. I knew that Nancy had a bunch of older and younger siblings, but I didn't know what to expect that evening.

Venus answered the door and took my breath away, as usual. The inside was filled with people of all sizes and ages, barely enough room for me to step into it. I met everyone and had a beer in my hand

111

in about three seconds. There was only one little blond-headed kid with teeth too big for his face. I knew right away who he was.

For the next six hours, Dennis dominated the activity. Even later in the evening when most of the adults were drunk, Dennis was in the middle of everything. He paid no attention to me.

Nancy's mother was busy mashing potatoes, steam billowing from her mixing bowl. Older sister, Phyllis, was making gravy in a large blue roasting pan on top of the gas stove. Dennis was pestering both women, incessantly. "I wanna eat. I wanna eat."

Brother-in-law, Harold, and Nancy's dad were inspecting the kitchen ceiling which was threatening to fall onto the night's feast any minute. Herald lifted little Dennis up to put his hands through the holes in the plaster to see what was on the other side. Phyllis chased them all out of the room. Dennis begged again to be fed.

Later, we all somehow fit around the table, which filled the entire dining room. The toddler was seated in the middle on a booster chair, out of the reach of his mother. Grandma started the serving with Dennis, of course. "Be sure to eat all your carrots, Dennis," she said sweetly.

"Here Dennis," said Sandy, Nancy's younger sister, who was seated next to the boy. "I'll cut your meat up for ya … there you go. Now start eating, please."

Dennis sat still in his seat, quiet for the first time since I had known him. "Here's another beer, Tom," mother said to me as she took away my half-full can. "Let's get going, Dennis. I thought you were starving," she said as Grandma.

"Leave him alone, Ma," said Phyllis. "He'll eat when he's ready. Sandy, try to feed him," she demanded.

"Try these sweet tatoes, Dennis. I know you like em, with all that butter on em," coaxed Sandy, holding the full spoon up to his closed lips.

"C'mon Dennis," begged Grandma. "You've not eaten all day. You must be starv'n. My goodness."

"Dennis!" barked Uncle Harold, sternly wagging his finger at the stubborn little fellow. "If you don't eat ever' last bit of food on your plate, you don't get no apple pie."

"Oh, shut up, Harold!" scolded his wife, Phyllis. "Dennis, if you don't start eating right now, I'm gonna smack your face."

"You will not!" Grandma shouted. "My goodness!"

"Leave the poor boy alone," pleaded Grandpa. "Can't you see he's not hungry? Ain't that right, Dennis?"

Dennis sat silently, as did his mother and I, as this discourse continued for the entire meal. The boy never left his seat, and he never took a single bite of food, including his apple pie.

The meal ended, and all the females, except for Nancy, pitched in to clear the table and do the dishes. The rest of us retired to the living room for more beer and conversation. Dennis took up residence in Grandpa's oversized easy chair, and Grandpa deposited his oversized self onto one half of the sofa.

Dennis looked angelic, regally sitting with his arms spread over the leather wings of the chair, like Abraham Lincoln on his monument. A tall lamp from behind cast a warm glow onto his tiny presence. His bare legs extended straight out in front of him through his short pants. His little white sneakers barely reached the end of the seat.

I seemed to be the only one in the room who was now concerned about the boy eating something today. If this sort of thing went on all the time, surely the angel would wither away, I surmised. Come to think of it, he *was* rather skinny.

The conversation in the living room got progressively louder and more animated, with many trips to the beer cooler and many excursions to the toilet. The girls, apparently finished with their chores in the kitchen, appeared one at a time, each carrying a fresh brew for themselves. Except for Grandma. She carried, instead, a gigantic silver bowl of hot buttered popcorn, and she ceremoniously marched up to Abraham Lincoln and placed the steamy prize onto the little guy's lap. The mound of fluffy white treasure rose to his chin. The prince, expecting this reward, smiled slightly at his subject and nodded his towhead once, completely forgetting to say thank you.

"See!" I told you he would eat when he was hungry!" Grandpa shouted, laughing. "Ain't that right Dennis?"

"Yea!" a cheer came from the crowd.

Long live the king, I thought, glancing over at my smiling girlfriend.

Around 10 pm, Sharon, the sister I had met at the bar with Lee boy, and her husband, Tim, were arguing fiercely over who was the best ever first baseman for the Detroit Tigers, when a sandy-haired fellow about my own age pushed through the front door with a case of longneck Budweiser.

"Ha, ha!" he said, obviously happy about something. "I just ran over Stinkley's cat. Ha, ha!"

"Did you do it on purpose, Carl?" Mother asked, aghast. "My goodness."

"Well, I didn't drive up on their lawn, if that's what ya mean, Ma. But ole' lady Stinkley's mad as hell, and she's calling the cops."

"If that bitch calls the cops," Phyllis said angrily, "I'll kick her skinny ass all over Livonia."

"Yeah!" Father bellowed, almost rolling off the sofa.

"Norm Cash was the cutest first baseman on the Tigers, ever," said Sharon.

"We're not talkin' 'bout cute here, Sharon!" Tim shot back.

The cops never showed up that night, but I was told they were a common sight around them thar hills, breaking up fights between the Rashauers and the Stinkleys.

I was taking all of this in, watching Nancy watch me. She looked to be anxious about my reactions to her family. Perhaps embarrassed, she whispered in my ear, "You wanna go for a drive, Tom?"

114

"Nothing doing," I said teasingly. "I wouldn't miss this for the world. Besides, you shouldn't be leaving your son alone here, should you?"

Around midnight, Carl went out to the party store for more beer, and he reported back: "The cat has been scraped up from the road, dammit."

The gang, including Dennis, was now sitting around the dining room table again, munching on leftovers. The old man was telling a story when he stopped abruptly in the middle of a sentence and scrunched up his big round face in a terrible way. I tensed up, not knowing what was happening, and the room went silent. I thought he needed help, but nobody moved. Suddenly, giant tears poured out from his squinting eyes, and his huge fists began to thump the table. "I love you guys," he struggled to get out of his mouth.

That's it. That's all he said.

Phyllis went to him and patted his back. "We know, Dad," she said. "We love you too."

The room slowly came back to life and Dennis stole Grandpa's apple pie when he wasn't looking.

*****

It took me a few days to recover from my first party with the Clampetts – I mean the Rashauers. Ellie Mae – I mean Nancy Jean – was heavy on my mind. So was little Dennis. I really liked this girl, but what was I getting myself into? I already had two kids in a troubled situation; did I need to get involved in another high-maintenance affair? Along with Nancy, would come the clan, and, of course, there was Dennis.

But I still wanted to be around this stunning and seemingly lost female. I had passion for her, yes, but the road that I appeared to be headed down was not so clear anymore. Maybe she was correct when she analyzed my holy shit remark? *No, that's not it,* I thought. I just wanted to see her again, that's all … and again … and again.

The problem, of course, was Dennis. I cannot say that I at once fell in love with the little fellow, and that I wanted to take him into my care and make him my own. But I owed him something, didn't I? Yes, I owed him respect, just because he existed. After all, he had first dibs on his mother; I did not.

I resolved, then, that I could not mess around with this boy's mother unless I had noble intentions. I felt no such obligation towards Nancy's mother or father, or brothers or sisters, or to Nancy herself for that matter. But I felt an inescapable obligation to this little human being, who I hardly knew.

With all this in mind, then, I phoned Nancy Jean and arranged what I hoped would be another chance to be around her, to touch her, without the need for words – a motorcycle ride.

I took the sunny weekday afternoon off from work and meandered my way down Floral Street, carefully avoiding the potholes and ruts. I pulled into the empty driveway in front of their one-car garage. The pigtailed cutie came dancing out the front door before the wheels of the Honda had even stopped turning. "Let's go!" she said.

"Where's Dennis?" I inquired.

"Oh, he's down the street playing with his friends," she said, pulling on her helmet.

"Alone?"

"No, with his friends, I told you."

"I mean, are there adults with him?"

"Yes, there are other mothers in the neighborhood, ya know. Let's get going before he comes back."

"Is your mother here for him?"

"No, she's at work. But Sandy and Gary are here. Don't worry 'bout it."

116

"I tried not to worry 'bout it."

~

Chapter 15　　*Everything Changes*

September 1976

　　For a few weeks following my introduction to Dennis – my future adopted son – I saw Nancy Jean every day, except for when I traveled up north on the weekends to see Kristen and Amy. The *court ordered visitation* was going well enough. Usually, we steered south to my sister's place in West Branch. One weekend, though, with permission, we spent our time together about 20 miles from the girls' home, alongside the waters of Lake Huron, in the historic town of Alpena.

　　We explored down a tremendous wooden dock extending like a fortress into the cold, merciless ocean of freshwater. Enormous breakers smashed against the huge boulders below, as we stood safely above. Countless seagulls filled the sky with endless chatter. Ships and boats of all sizes dotted the horizon.

　　The girls, although they were just eight and five, had lived in that area for only about a year and knew a great deal about the town, the history, and the waters. They delighted in teaching me all they knew, and I delighted in learning.

　　"Daddy, Lake Huron is the second largest of the five Great Lakes," said the 8-year-old, like a schoolteacher instructing her students.

　　"Nuh-uh," said the younger Amy in return. "Lake Michigan is, isn't it, Daddy?"

　　"Well, all I'm sure of is that Lake Superior is number one. Do you remember going there when we lived in Minnesota, Kristen?"

　　"No," she answered, trying hard to recall. "I must a been too little, Daddy."

　　"Look!" shouted Amy, excitedly jumping up and down on the dock and pointing out to sea. "There's Uncle Ronnie's boat!" My brother-in-law, Ron, had been the first of the Scapaticcis to move to northern Michigan four years earlier.

"No, it isn't!" exclaimed Kristen. "Uncle Ronnie's boat has a flying bridge."

"What's a flying bridge, Princess?" I asked, not knowing.

"I know, I know, Daddy," chimed in Amy. We waited patiently for her description, but instead, putting her finger into her mouth, she only giggled.

"It's a place way up high where you steer from," Kristen took over. She stretched her arms in amazement as high as she could reach.

Later, the three of us sat on swings in a lakeside park. Our time together was nearing an end. I decided then to share with my children the joy I was feeling in my life at that time.

"I have something to tell you guys," I said with a smile.

"What, Daddy? What?" They both responded at once.

"Well … I hope you're happy for me," I said, delaying the moment to build the excitement. Then I burst out, *"I have a girlfriend!"*

"But we thought *we* were your girlfriends, Daddy," they reacted with pouting lips. "You said! You said!"

"Oh, you are," I corrected myself quickly. "But I meant, a *lady* friend. A very nice lady friend."

Amy said nothing, but looked a little puzzled, putting a finger into her mouth again.

"Really?" Kristen said happily. "What's she look like, Dad?"

"Well," I began. "She has blonde hair and big blue eyes, just like you guys. She's very pretty, very nice, and we have lots of fun together. She likes kids too, and she can't wait to meet the two of you. So, what do you think? Is it okay with you?"

Smiling comfortably, Kristen neatly folded her hands in front of herself. With a knowing look on her face, she answered sophisticatedly, "Yes, Father."

I then looked at little Amy for her response. She squealed in delight, scurried onto my lap, and held tightly onto me and said: "Swing me as high as you can, Daddy!"

I was soon heading south on US 23, the usual drive home, the usual things on my mind. This time though, I was feeling more content. I had just completed a satisfying day with the two most important people on Earth. I disclosed to my children that I had a new girlfriend, and they wished me well. Kristen and Amy had been carefree, playful, and loving with me. What more could a man ask for?

*****

Following the spilling of the beans to the kids about my having a girlfriend, Nancy and I had a special evening together. We went out for a nice dinner to someplace other than Clancy's, and then returned to my bedroom in the bachelor house for some private time together. We had been dating by then for a couple of months, but we had not yet consummated our relationship. It seemed as if that was going to be the big night.

Soon we were under the covers. Oh my God, what a thrill, lying face to face with Venus without her blue jeans. But I found I could not go on. She waited patiently for my next move, but I could not make it. She asked if I was okay, but I did not answer. Instead, I brushed the hair from her face and, for a long while, beheld the awesomeness of the moment. Then, for the very first time, I spoke softly the words I needed to say: *"I love you."*

Her eyes grew wide like they often did when she was surprised. Then her expression softened, and a gentle smile crossed her lips, but she did not reply. She did not return the words "I love you too." But I didn't mind because I was then free to continue.

The next day, I recalled our first night together in the bedroom. I concluded that I must have felt my children had given me license to pursue a relationship with Nancy, by their gracious acceptance of another person into our lives. But why was I not able to go on with the act, until I had uttered the words, *I love you?* Perhaps it was my way of honoring my self-imposed obligation to Dennis. I had resolved, after all, that I would not mess around with his mother, unless my intentions were noble.

Ten days later, still on a high from my new love, and anxious to see Kristen and Amy again, I phoned my ex-wife to arrange my next visit.

"Your visits with the girls cannot continue," Kathy said coldly.

"What are you talking about, Kathleen?" I responded with like coldness.

"This is too hard on them. It's harmful for them to be around you. So, it's going to end."

I fumed, "Even if that ridiculous statement were true, snotface, there's nothing you can do about it! We have Orders from the Court."

"The Court will not force me to put the girls into harm's way," she continued with her planned speech. "I've already spoken with them about this."

I thought about that statement for a moment before I angrily spoke, "and I suppose they gave you permission to withhold the kids from my *court ordered visitation?*"

"Yes."

"On what grounds?"

"On the grounds that I don't have to put my children into a position I deem to be harmful for them."

I could not believe my ears. I screamed incredulously at her, "You think you can just arbitrarily do your own deeming like that?"

"Yes, I can. They said I could."

"I don't believe it."

"Too bad for you."

"I'm coming Saturday morning to get the kids at Glen's Market."

"We won't be there."

I hesitated for a moment, then challenged, "I'll go then to your parents' home."

"The police will be waiting for you. I've already spoken with them too."

The witch spoke in such an icy way that I believed her, but I continued anyway. "Then I'll be on the school grounds on Monday at 3:30 to pick them up."

"Boy Tom," she said, still calmly. "You're really asking for it now. I'll get you for kidnapping."

"Okay ... I won't do that. But why are you doing this to me?" I asked, about to cry.

"I'm not doing anything to you, you bastard!" she spat out like a rabid bat. "You did this to yourself."

"I'll fight you on this, Kathy," I said, my voice cracking. "Do you think I'm going to just drop out of sight?"

"That would be delightful," she said with contempt. "Why don't you just stay home and play house with your new little friend."

"Oh," I said slowly, "so that's it."

"Go to hell, Tom." Click.

*****

Sitting across the table from my *new little friend* in our favorite booth by the window at Clancy's Grill, I didn't know where to start my story. "Well, I'm not going up north this weekend," I simply said.

"How come?" Nancy Jean inquired between French fries.

"The bitch won't let me."

"Your ex-wife?"

"Yeah, her," I answered, slumping in my seat, resting my head in my hand.

Suddenly looking puzzled, in mid-bite she put down her fork, cocked her head, looked me in the eye and asked, "How can she stop you?"

"She won't bring the kids to meet me, that's how," I said tersely. "And I don't dare go to their house. And I don't know what to do next." Exasperated by the situation, I shut my eyes and rubbed my temples.

If You Leave Me Now by *Chicago*, was playing on the jukebox as Nancy searched the charts for her next choice. I thought I had lost her attention when she turned and asked me, "Won't the Friend of the Court make her follow the rules?"

I thought about that for a moment, wondering how much she knew about the Friend of the Court. "I don't know if they will or not, honey," I answered. "She says she has their blessing, and I don't doubt she does."

"Let's play *Lou Rawls*, B17, next," she said to me.

"I don't even know how to approach the Friend of the Court without hiring a lawyer," I continued, "and I don't know how smart that would be anyway. That might lead to even more trouble. What do you think, Nance? What should I do?"

"Heck, I don't know, Tom," she squirmed self-consciously in her seat. "A man don't stand a chance with the Friend of the Court though ... I know that much."

"What about the needs of the kids though?" I asked. "Doesn't the court care about that?"

"That don't matter," she responded knowingly. "The mother always wins, whether she's right in what she's doin' or not."

"That's just great," I said, folding my arms and turning my head to look at nothing through the window.

She reached across the table and gently placed a hand on my arm to draw me back. She gave me a sympathetic smile and said, "She'll prob'ly change her mind in a while, don't you think?"

*****

I began making phone calls up north every couple of days. Grandma would not talk to me. I asked for the girls – nothing doing. I begged and threatened Kathy – no help. Finally, the snotface forbade me from calling that number again under the threat of police protection from harassment. I called a friend of a friend of a friend to find a lawyer to whom I could ask some questions. Ultimately, I reached a seasoned family attorney in Pontiac, who had experience with the Oakland County Friend of the Court. I arranged to go to his office the next day for a free consultation.

I arrived at the offices of Clarence C. Wyatt, attorney at law, late on a Tuesday afternoon. It seemed to be his last appointment for the day, and his secretary escorted me directly in to see him. His office was only of average size but was richly appointed and comfortable. The large man walked around his desk to greet me with a firm handshake from a giant paw. He sported a bushy gray mustache on his smiling leather face.

"Nice to meet you, Mr. VanBuren. Please, please, have a seat," he said loudly.

I felt like I had just met Teddy Roosevelt. "My pleasure, sir. Thank you."

"So," the president began, "tell me your story, son, but try to give me the Reader's Digest version."

After explaining to this warming man my eight years of BS in 10 minutes, he gave me his free advice.

"This is going to cost you, son," he counseled in a grandfatherly way. "And it will likely take a long time, if you want to challenge *the Friend of the Court*, that is."

Ignoring his mentioning the cost, I responded, "I don't want it to take a long time, sir, and I don't care if we involve the Friend of The Court or not. But what else can we do?" I asked with a touch of desperation in my voice.

"My advice," he began, "is to first try to get your ex-wife to come to her senses. If you've told me everything, and I believe you have, then she doesn't have a legal leg to stand on. But she can probably drag things on forever if she has a mind to."

I shifted myself around in my seat to gain some comfort, but I remained intently focused on his every word.

"I can write an official-looking letter explaining a few things to her," he continued. "She can't just deny you your visits on a whim. She must have cause. There are serious consequences to violating an *Order of the Court*. You have parental rights, also. The children need both parents. Those sorts of things." He sat back in his large chair and folded his arms, signaling to me that it was my turn to talk.

"She has heard those things before, Mr. Wyatt, but coming from you, instead of me, it may make a difference. And this will be less costly than filing a lawsuit?"

"Yes, yes," he acknowledged, moving forward in his chair again. "A couple of letters from me won't cost you much, and maybe she'll respond properly on her own. How does that sound to you?"

"It sounds like a sensible approach to me, Mr. Wyatt. Although I don't expect she'll respond properly, as you put it. But let's give it a try and see how it goes."

"Okay, okay," my new family attorney said, nodding his head in agreement.

"One more thing," I continued, changing the subject. "I am thinking of moving out of state, for business purposes, to North Carolina, specifically. I need to know how that will affect my standing with the courts."

Thinking for a moment first, Mr. Wyatt furrowed his brow, then asked, "How would you make your visits from North Carolina?"

"I can fly from Raleigh to Alpena and rent a car quicker than I can drive from Detroit," I answered. "As long as I can afford it, it may actually be easier for me."

"I see, I see," responded Mr. Wyatt. "Well, there's nothing in the law that says one has to reside in Michigan." Wagging a finger at me, he continued, "But don't ever miss a visit. That would look bad for sure. And, you still must make your child support payments. Remember, support and visitation are separate issues."

So it was with that that Mr. Wyatt and I made the deal and set into motion what turned out to be a six-month letter writing campaign. I was content that this was at least a good way to start the battle. Now I was free to begin thinking about other things, like how I was going to earn money in the immediate future.

~

Chapter 16　　*North Carolina*

October 1976

It was getting cold. Michigan has a way of doing that in October. I was already seeing a drop in my fence business, and soon, I figured, my income would be down to zero. I relied mostly on residential customers who were now moving indoors for the winter. I had to find something else to do during the cold months – like plow snow or sell Christmas trees – or I had to move my enterprise, and my life, to somewhere warm.

Moving south had multiple advantages. There was nice weather, of course, to enjoy all year round, and an increase in business. A bonus was that I could end the terrible drive from Detroit to Alpena twice a month to see the kids. If I had an excuse to fly, I reasoned, it would be nicer for me. My cousin Larry had moved to North Carolina a couple of years earlier. He and his family were thriving there, and they thought that getting out of the cold and the snow was reason enough to make the move.

Another appealing thought for me was to get Nancy, and myself for that matter, away from her domineering family. But Nancy Jean had not yet even returned the *I love you* words to me, so I didn't know if she would go with me or not. I had to ask her. *Would I leave town without her?* I wondered. *I didn't have that answer.*

Parked that night in her driveway, next to the big Elm tree, we sat in my pickup truck. It was the way we ended most of our dates, with a little bit of talk and a little bit of smooching. Her mother would soon be turning on the porch light, as if we were high schoolers. If I was going to find out that night what I wanted to know, I had to move quickly.

"You know, honey, I've been telling you I love you for some time now," I said. She was cuddling on my chest, so I could not see her face. She gave no response. "I'm not asking you to say it in return or anything. I just want to know if I'm barking up the wrong tree or not."

She suddenly sat up straight, inspecting me with a little smile. The moon cast a soft glow onto one half of her young face. "You're not," she said.

Not sure what to make of her response, I asked, "I'm not what?"

"Barking up a tree," she answered.

"Yes, I am," I insisted. "But I want to know if I'm barking up the *right* tree."

Baffled by my speech, she questioned. "What are you talking about, Tom?"

I grinned at her, understanding now that once again I was using words in a way with which she was not familiar. I was determined, however, to expand her lexicon.

I sat up taller in my seat and cranked open the driver's window to let in some of the unusually warm night air. Pulling her closer to me, I stole a couple of soft kisses. "Nancy, sweetheart," I then inquired, "are you my girlfriend?"

She did not verbally reply, perhaps thinking that her passion was answer enough. The porch light would soon spoil the moment. I had to get back into the conversation quickly. Taking both her hands into mine, I looked her closely in the eyes. "Honey," I began, "I've been talking to you about moving my business down South."

She nodded exaggeratedly in understanding. "Yes," she affirmed, but puzzlement dominated her expression.

Now that I had her complete attention, without further ado, as if on bended knee, I then popped the question. "If I choose to leave these parts, in search of gold and fame, my tender morsel, will you follow me?"

"Oh!" she reacted, as her face lit up. "I won't let you go without me. If that's what you mean."

"That's *exactly* what I mean, honey," I said, greatly relieved. "I love you."

Then, with the grandest smile I had yet received from her, she replied, "I love you too ... honey."

*****

The decision to migrate south had not yet been made when I received an invitation to attend a family wedding reception in the nearby city of Clawson. All my siblings were there, including my younger sister Mary Kay from West Branch and her husband Randy. This was not the first time I had taken Nancy to a family function, but it was the first time we behaved as a couple around others.

Mary Kay was almost exactly Nancy's age, and Randy was only a year or two older. They were always great company, especially at functions like this. In between socializing, drinking beer, and dancing with two hundred different people, the four of us managed to sit around a table and carry on a disconnected conversation. It was the first time Nancy and I had discussed with anyone the idea of us moving to North Carolina.

"What a great idea!" Mary Kay said. "I would love to do something like that. Just to get out of the damn cold if nothing else."

Randy was showing off his new lime green platform shoes to Aunt Mary Carol. The shoes made him 6 foot 4 instead of 6 foot 0. "I wonder if they do siding and roofing all year round down there?" he questioned as he pranced around the table.

"Oh, sure they do," answered Aunt Mary, even though she had never in her life been out of the state of Michigan.

I tried on Randy's silly shoes. I was then 5 foot 11, instead of 5 foot 7. Randy was still taller than me in his stocking feet, but we made a fine couple doing the hokey pokey together. When we returned to the table I suggested, "Why don't you guys come South with us?"

"Are you kidding?" asked Mary Kay. "We can't just pick up and leave town like you two."

129

"Why not?" I countered. "What's holding you back?"

My talkative sister, with her dark hair and dark eyes, sat in contrast next to my quiet, yellow-headed girlfriend. "Would you want us to come with you?" Mary Kay questioned Nancy seriously.

Nancy then strung together the longest statement any of us had ever heard her speak. "Well, we haven't yet decided if we want to do this or not, but if we do, it would be way better to go with friends than to go alone ... I know that much for sure."

The three of us froze and stared in the middle of eating our wedding cake. Not sure if I should make a comment about Nancy's newfound voice, I only pitched in, *"Hell yeah!"*

Randy was then clearly considering the proposition. "I've got no work going on right now," he said, soberly. "And we're on a month-to-month lease at the farmhouse. Would you and I join our businesses together, Tommy?"

"I suppose," I answered, gaining excitement about the idea. "We could do home improvements *and* fencing; whatever came our way first. That would make it easier to get started. Wouldn't it?"

Before long we had the entire VanBuren family involved in the conversation, including our cousin Larry. Larry then invited the four of us to his home in Raleigh to check things out. "Now that's a great idea!" Mary Kay said.

"Let's drink to that!" Randy added.

By the time they had shut down the bar and shut off the lights that night, we had all but made up our minds. We agreed then to meet at 11 the next morning for breakfast at Denny's to iron out the details. By 2 pm that Sunday afternoon, stuffed with pancakes, bacon, and gallons of coffee, we had a consensus. Before the snow began to fall in miserable Michigan, we would all be living in sunny North Carolina.

So it was that we soon found ourselves optimistically traveling down the Ohio Turnpike in a two-vehicle caravan of heavy-duty Ford pickup trucks towing U-Haul trailers. Two adults and a child sat in each cab, with furniture, clothing, tools, and motorcycles packed tightly behind each. Six happy souls in search of warm weather, adventure, and a good life – together.

*****

We moved collectively into a large brick home in an upscale Raleigh neighborhood. The neighborhood was more fashionable than any of us had ever lived in before. "You sure get a lot for your money in North Carolina," Mary Kay said. The rent in the area was so low, in fact, that Mary, Randy, and little Heather soon took a nearby apartment for themselves. Nancy, Dennis, and I remained in the house. Surely, at these rates, we could afford two homes for two families.

Nancy and Mary Kay got busy right away setting up the two households. Randy and I promptly spent much of our working capital on furniture, dishes, and such. It was a fun time for all of us, including Dennis and Heather. The mothers genuinely liked each other, Randy and I were splendid partners, and the kids got along famously together.

When it came time to get to work, with whatever cash we had left, Randy and I secured the name *Palace Construction Company*. We had business cards printed with our fancy new home addresses and phone numbers and placed ads in newspapers looking for customers. We also visited the local building supply houses seeking subcontracting opportunities and discounts on materials.

Some nice residential work came our way from the newspaper ads – a few backyard fences and ceiling replacements. We also bid for and won some commercial projects. We just didn't earn much money on any of the jobs. Overall, profit margins were much lower in the Carolinas than what we were used to in Michigan.

One memorable job we landed was to install a tall fence around three sides of a McDonald's restaurant. The problem was that the project was in Morehead City, four hours away from us on the Atlantic coast. We had a wonderful time. Along with the fence posts and cement, we also packed up the girls and the kids. It was challenging work for Randy and me, but the six of us got to spend plenty of time playing around on the empty winter beaches. Returning home after a week of work and play, we were promptly paid for our efforts. When we added up the motel and food bills, however, we discovered we had lost money on the deal.

We would have to find more profitable projects, we figured, if we expected to pay the bills. But we were charging as much for our work as possible in that part of the country. It turned out the marketplace and cost of living were much different than what we had known in Michigan. We never earned half what it was costing us to live.

Things might have turned out differently if the six of us had stayed living together in one house, or if we had had more working capital to start with, but probably not. It was just not possible, with the money we were earning, to live the life we had hoped for. As we ran low on cash, we began to sell things. First our motorcycles, then one of the trucks, then some of our tools. *What next?* we wondered.

*****

With little money left, and down to one truck with a few tools, our prospects for a Merry Christmas that year were not all that good. But we were by no means giving up.

One quiet evening, Nancy and I were telling each other stories of home. I recalled that on the day we had left Michigan, as we were saying our final goodbyes, that I had seen tears in my father's eyes.

"You never mentioned that to me," she said.

"Yeah, I know," I replied. "It's no big deal, really. I'm sure he was just sad to see us go."

Dinner was through, and the dishes had been put away. Nancy was folding clothes on the bed next to me. Dennis was playing quietly in the kitchen.

"Why don't you give him a call?" she suggested.

Bob Seger was moaning on the radio in the background, *Wish I didn't know now, what I didn't know then.*

"Now that's a good idea!" I said, jumping up from the bed. "Why didn't I think of that?" I grabbed the phone and dialed good ole Michigan.

Little sister Connie answered on the second ring. "Hello."

"Helloooooo Connie pie," I replied slowly.

"Tommy!" she screamed. "Where're you at?"

"I am here. Where're you at?"

"I'm right here, too," she laughed.

The four youngest kids still lived at home then. Anne Marie was 18, then came Teresa, then Connie, and Paul was the baby at 13. I spoke with Theresa next (I interrupted her studies at the kitchen table, of course).

Mom was at Saint Dennis Church for Tuesday Night Novena, while Dad read the newspaper with the TV on at super low volume. Dad came to the phone next.

"Hello Tommaso," he said lightheartedly. "Why are you calling so soon? You only just left town two months ago."

"Hello Pop-o," I responded. "I'm just calling to see if you want to play golf on Sunday."

"There's 2 feet of snow out here, knucklehead."

"Well, there's 2 inches of brown grass out here, and I can't get Randy or Larry to play with me. I need a partner."

After 10 minutes of kibitzing about nothing, I got into some serious conversation with my dad about how well we were all doing in our new homes.

"We live in a fine house, Dad ... the weather is great ... we have all kinds of work ... Mary Kay, Randy, and Heather are all happy

… Nancy and Dennis are right here with me … we're all doing fine … don't worry about us."

Suddenly, Nancy broke the peacefulness of the moment by letting out a booming whoop of delight. She had found a crumpled up $20 bill in her pants pocket. "Look what I found!" she cheered, as if she had just won the Irish Sweepstakes. She danced around the room waving her newfound treasure in the air. "Ha ha!" she cried. "I'm going grocery shopping first thing in the morning."

"What's going on, Tommy?" my dad questioned.

"Oh, nothing, Pop," I answered. "Nancy just found a wad of cash in her pocket. I told you, didn't I? *Life's good in the Carolinas!*"

~

Chapter 17   *Marry Nancy*

December 1976

After dinner one evening at their apartment, Mary Kay took me aside for a private conversation. "We're packing up Tommy," my sister said, tears welling in her eyes. "We need to go home."

To hear those words did not surprise me. I had been expecting it. But not that night. And I couldn't bear to see my little sister cry. "You don't like it here, Mar'?" I asked somewhat unfairly.

"That's not it, Tom," she answered, wringing her hands. "You know we like it here. It's just that we're out of money, and if we leave before January, we can save a month's rent."

Mary Kay sat down on the edge of her bed and nervously folded her hands onto her lap. I stood, leaning against the dresser, hands in the pockets of my Bermuda shorts. "Does Randy want to leave too?" I asked.

Her lip quivered as she thought about an answer. "Yes, yes he does, Tom, but he's afraid to tell you." She looked me in the eyes, blinking back tears. "He doesn't want to let you down."

Randy had been a great partner for me, I thought, *but it was utterly like him to send Mary Kay about this.* I paced around the room for a few seconds to formulate a good response. "Randy is *not* letting me down, Mary Kay," I insisted. "Our business is not earning enough money to pay its own way. I don't see another answer myself. Doing what is best for your family … I don't consider letting me down."

"But what about you guys, Tommy?" Mary Kay questioned, totally concerned for me. "What will you do?"

I answered quickly, without thinking. "We'd stick it out, MK, if we could. But if you're leaving … I suppose we'd have to leave too."

My little sister's face took on a combined look of horror and sorrow. The tears flowed ever harder. I knew I had just said the wrong thing.

"I'm sorry, Mar'!" I pleaded. "I didn't mean it that way." I sat on the bed, putting an arm around her shoulder. "I don't blame you or Randy one bit for anything, really. None of us have any obligation to stay or to leave. Besides, nudging us to get out while we still can is probably good advice. Nancy and I have had this discussion, you know."

"Are you sure, Tommy?" she responded, sniffling. "If you think …"

"I'm sure Mar'," I interrupted with a smile. "Besides, soooo many people are counting on me anymore, it doesn't seem right for me to be trying to build a business this way any longer."

She took hold of both my hands, looked at me with some hope in her pretty face, and asked again: "Are you sure, Tommy?"

"Yes, Mary Kay," I answered firmly, squeezing her hands. "I'm sure, and I'm betting Nancy will love you for this. Now where's that husband of yours? I want to kill him!"

That night in bed, Nancy and I didn't get much sleep. "What are we going to do in Michigan, honey?" my girlfriend asked me.

Propping my head up on an elbow, I studied her draped figure in the glow of the table lamp and answered, "Well, I'm going to get a job, and you're going to get pregnant."

Her eyes widened in the usual way, which always made me smile. Then she asked with her voice rising, "You want me to get pregnant?"

"No, sweetheart," I responded. "I just want to work on getting you pregnant. Would you like that?"

Abruptly sitting up in bed and clutching the sheet tightly around her body, she answered, "Not if we're not married."

I sat up myself and tugged at the sheets a bit. "Then let's get married."

"When?"

"Tomorrow," I said anxiously.

"What's your hurry?"

"I want to get to work on getting you pregnant, that's my hurry."

"But I thought you wanted to get to work on a new job," she teased.

"First things first, my dear."

"I always wanted a *big* wedding, ya know."

"I don't know if I can afford *big*," I said. "But I can probably do *medium*."

"Can I have a fancy white dress? And a church? And bridesmaids and flowers?" she asked breathlessly, the covers rising and falling with her voice.

I watched intently, and, as her excitement rose, of course, so did mine.

We stopped talking.

*****

So it was that we decided to get married, leave North Carolina, and find a new job – not necessarily in that order.

My new fiancé made some collect phone calls the next day and quickly arrived at a suitable wedding date for us – January 8th. Her three sisters found a church and planned for a reception at the VFW Hall in the dumpiest part of Livonia. Invitations were put in the mail. All we had left to do was get home as soon as we could and buy a fancy white dress.

We didn't own my pickup truck any longer, so we had a hitch installed on our new/old, 1969 Cougar XR7 convertible and loaded up a U-Haul trailer. Nancy, Dennis, and I left our house in North Carolina empty and clean and set out just a few days after our former business partners, Mary Kay, Randy, and Heather. All of us were happy and hopeful, looking forward – again – to new beginnings.

It was a tough two-day haul across snow-covered mountain roads and lonely highways. We entertained ourselves along the way listening to The Eagles on 8 tracks, while Dennis ate, slept, and played in the backseat. We arrived at my parents' place in Royal Oak early on a Friday evening, ragged, but in one piece. We had been gone for less than three months, but it seemed to us a long, long time.

As we pulled up next to the house, 13-year-old, mop-headed Paul flew out the side door to greet us. He seemed more interested though in the slush-covered black Cougar we had just arrived in than in his big brother. Before I had finished stomping the snow off my feet in the foyer, my dad had me firmly in his embrace. "I'm glad you're back, Tommy," he said.

I answered his embrace and said quietly in his ear, "Me too, Pop-o."

It wasn't long before mom had dinner set out for us on the large yellow kitchen table. Meat and potatoes, of course, and devil's food cake slathered with butter cream frosting for dessert.

I assumed my usual chair against the wall on the long side of the table. Nancy, Dennis, Mom and Dad, Anne Marie, Connie, and Paul filled in the rest of the seats. We stuffed ourselves with good food and good conversation. "You don't need dessert with a meal like this," my dad announced as he sampled the icing with his finger. We all just grinned as we ate our cake.

Afterwards, still basking in the glory of reunion, I wondered how I could have ever voluntarily left that family of mine, which I loved so much. But that didn't matter then – we were home.

Considering my mom and dad's strong Catholic ideals, Nancy and I knew that, until we were married, we could not stay overnight together in the family house. Therefore, that night we continued our migration a block and a half away to my sister Donna's place. Donna, Mike, and 3-year-old Scotty took care of the three of us for some days, while we searched for a place of our own.

Two days before the wedding, my dad, Mike, and Paul helped us move into a little two bedroom, red-painted, block house that we rented in northern Royal Oak. It was a major step down from the stately brick palace in the tony North Carolina neighborhood we had recently left behind, but we didn't mind. We were finally settled in, and we were together.

*****

The evening ceremony, on a warm but snowy Friday night, was near perfection. All manner of family and friends swelled the quaint, warmly glowing neighborhood church. Nancy was dazzling in her flowing white gown. I was as handsome as I could manage in my crisp, dark blue tuxedo. The preacher waited calmly in front of the altar, Bible in his hands, surrounded by a garden of yellow flowers. Brother-in-law, Mike, and big sister, Sharon, stood proudly with the bride and groom. Dennis, in his own little, crisp, dark blue tuxedo, carefully carried two rings on a pillow up to his mother and me. Music and flashes of light filled the air.

"I love you, Nancy Jean."

"I love you, Thomas Walter."

There would be no honeymoon, but we didn't mind. There were jobs to be found and life to be lived.

*****

January 1977

A few days after the wedding – for $5 per hour – I began work as a draftsman at *Sure Weld Engineering*. It was one of a zillion growing engineering companies bursting at the seams in southeast Michigan at that time. Unbeknownst to me, the skills I had gained from two years of mechanical drawing in high school, and seven years on the drawing board at *Gemco Electric* and *Cadillac Fence*, had made me nicely marketable in that area.

It seemed to me that $5 per hour was rather good pay, but two weeks after starting work at *Sure Weld*, I was surprised by a $7 per hour offer from *Modern Engineering*. I, of course, quickly changed jobs. Another month brought another job offer of $9.50 per hour to move to the *Automated Pneumatic Systems* company in Farmington Hills. It felt as if we were soon to be rich!

Along with the latest job move, I moved my new family into a much nicer, three-bedroom brick ranch in the well-known State Street area of my bride's hometown of Livonia. Our standard of living was on the rise. Dennis was calling me daddy by then, his biological father was nowhere in sight, and it quickly became my intention to make the happy little fellow my own. My stepson was then 4 years old. I had not yet even known his mother for a full year when I filed papers in the Wayne County Courts for his formal adoption.

~

Chapter 18   *Kathy in Court I*

March 1977

Throughout the move to and return from North Carolina, my marriage to Nancy, several job changes, and the adoption of Dennis, I had kept in telephone contact with my family-affairs attorney concerning my daughters. Mr. Wyatt had been trying to gain me equitable visitation with Kristen and Amy, without involving the Friend of the Court. His efforts, however, had gone for naught. It had then been six months since my last visit with the girls in the park alongside the waters of Lake Huron.

From a pay phone at *Automated Pneumatic Systems,* during my scheduled work time, I spoke with my attorney again. "I can't take this any longer, Mr. Wyatt," I said. "I knew we would never sway that stubborn snot. In the meantime, I am forgetting what my daughters look like. We must move to Plan B, don't you think? … I can pay attorney fees now."

I could hear Mr. Wyatt breathing on the other end of the phone. He had been resisting my argument for a great while. He really did not want to give up on his court-less approach, but I heard him heave a sigh as he finally relented.

"Okay, okay, I agree, Tom," he said firmly. "We'll ask for a hearing for her to show cause as to why she is denying your visitation."

"Okay, great," I answered with relief.

"It's not as simple as it sounds, Tom," Mr. Wyatt warned me. "As you know, I really did want to avoid approaching the Friend of the Court. They can be incredibly difficult for a father. But you are correct: appealing to your ex with reason is a dead end. I'll get moving on this right away."

*****

Mr. Wyatt was spot-on – it was not simple. After getting the case put onto the court docket, Kathy had to be served a subpoena ordering her to appear in court at the proper time and place. She would then be questioned under oath. Only then, after hearing the details right from the witch's mouth, the judge may or may not fix things in my favor.

The first hurdle, however, was to get my ex-wife served. After cases were assigned a court date, the papers had to be created and then served within a certain timeframe, or we had to start over again from square one. The process took weeks and weeks under normal circumstances. Throw in 200 miles distance and a hick town like Hillman, and we were just as likely to never get it done. And Kathy had to be handed the papers directly by a process server. This meant someone from the Hillman area had to be hired who was authorized to do such things, and they had to get the job done in a timely fashion.

Kathy would not come to the door on our first two attempts at serving her, and we ran out of time. We then had to secure another court date. In the second go around, we caught up with her on the first try, as she entered her workplace one morning. Kathleen VanBuren was successfully served, and the date was set in stone, for July 14, 1977, 9 am, in the court of the Honorable Judge Malcolm J. McLean.

*****

The day of the hearing was blistering hot, the traffic was overwhelming, and the courthouse was extremely busy. The awesomeness of the building and the activity of the attorneys, the police, and the judges made my case seem small and unimportant at that moment. As my attorney led me down the halls, however, greeting others along the way, I was pleased to see that he was familiar with the building and the people. We sat in the back of Judge McLean's courtroom – *a rather large room*, I thought – and listened to two other cases before we heard my name called.

"VanBuren vs. VanBuren."

My attorney, in his blue suit and red tie, presented himself to the court. No opposing attorney responded, however. After some questioning from the judge with no forthcoming answers, he noted that the defendant, Kathleen VanBuren, was not present in the courtroom. He then asked my attorney to brief him as to why we were in court that day. Mr. Wyatt, in a professional manner, stated the case in somewhat complete form, and then we waited for the judge to speak.

Shuffling papers on the bench, the judge put on, and took off, and put on again his reading glasses, before saying loud and clear, "Counselor, in light of the fact that we can't have a *Show Cause* hearing today, what do you propose we do?"

"Your Honor," my attorney asked matter-of-factly, "I move that my client be granted full physical custody of the two minor children."

Removing his glasses again, the judge replied, "This is not a custody hearing, Counselor."

"I ask then, Your Honor, for the court to enforce the terms of the existing *Visitation Order.*"

"And how do you propose we do that?" Judge McLean asked.

I stood next to my attorney. We shared a single podium. I thought I knew where Mr. Wyatt would take the conversation. Instead, he said, "I ask that the courts supply an order requiring the defendant, mother, to release the children to my client for his scheduled weekend visits."

"Okay, I can do that," the judge said quickly. "Is that what you want, Mr. VanBuren?"

"*No,* Your Honor!" I responded loudly to my attorney's surprise. Throwing two palms to the sky, I asked, "How would I enforce such an order?"

The judge reacted a bit sarcastically. "Do you believe, Mr. VanBuren, that an order from this court, demanding the release of the children to your care, would not be enforceable?"

"Yes, Your Honor, it would *not* be enforceable by me." I stood with both my hands on the podium, leaning a little towards the judge. "Not if it were written the same as the existing *Visitation Order,* to include only the hours from 10 am Saturday to 6 pm Sunday. She would simply not be available at that time. She has a court order in her hands, right now, to attend this very hearing, doesn't she? And she's defied that order … hasn't she?"

The judge seemed to be taken aback by my impertinence. "At this point, Mr. VanBuren, we don't know if she is in contempt, or if she has a good reason for not being here."

"That's just it, Your Honor," I said quickly, happy the judge brought the word *reason* into the discourse. "She will always create her own *good reason* to justify the way she wants to behave. There is no way she will *ever* gracefully follow *any* order that you may issue."

The judge put his glasses back on and seemed to read something in front of himself. He then looked at me over the top of his spectacles and asked sincerely. "Then what would you have me do, Mr. VanBuren?"

"Why don't you hold her in contempt of court, Your Honor?" Mr. Wyatt spoke out on my behalf, and I nodded in agreement.

The judge stared scornfully at my attorney for long seconds and then bellowed out, "I am *not* going to arrest a mother of two, Counselor, and haul her away from the care of her dependent children – for days on end – just so I can determine if she purposely skipped out on a Friend of the Court hearing or not."

When the judge ran out of breath, Mr. Wyatt and I exchanged glances with each other. I inhaled then and began to answer the original question, which I thought had been directed at me anyway. But Mr. Wyatt correctly took over again. "Can you supply a more usable court order, Your Honor? One that has less time restrictions. Can you allow my client to collect the kids during, let's say, a 24-hour period, and then return them to their mother 48 hours later? He believes he could manage that."

The judge thought about this for a long moment. He looked as if he might accommodate our wishes, but instead he responded,

"Now you're asking me to alter the Visitation Order, which I can't do at this time."

"*Why not?*" I blurted out, frustrated. My attorney gently nudged me in the ribs, reminding me of courtroom decorum. "Please forgive me, Your Honor," I continued. "But is it not possible to alter the Visitation Order?"

"To do that, Mr. Van Buren," the judge said, "without a proper hearing, you would have to show an emergency. Is there an emergency here?"

"Only that I have not seen my girls now for almost a year, Your Honor. For no good reason, I might add, and against this Court's dictates. Surely, there must be some harm being brought to the children by their being improperly withheld from a parent."

The judge leaned back in his chair and responded with a slight smile, "You might be able to demonstrate as much, Mr. VanBuren. But if you did that, and in light of the fact that we don't have the mother here today, and that I have no way of ascertaining your own fitness as a custodian, if I thought the children were in danger, I would then have to remand them – at least temporarily – to the custody of the State of Michigan." He then tilted forward in his chair, raised up a bit on his forearms, and peered down at me. "Is that what you want, Mr. VanBuren?"

"No sir, of course not," was all I could find to say. My attorney looked at me, perplexed. I looked at the judge. The judge looked at me, and then to Mr. Wyatt, but nobody spoke. I closed my eyes and bit my lip then abruptly exclaimed, "There must be something that can be done. The answer can't just be to do nothing!"

"Yes, there is," the judge then began. "I suggest we pick out another court date – right now – for three months from now, and then you serve your ex-wife again, Mr. VanBuren, to come here and show cause. *Then* I can do something effective."

"She won't come," I said calmly, shaking my head.

The judge responded with equal calmness, "If she fails to show a second time, I will then consider more stringent measures."

"What about child support, Your Honor?" my attorney chimed in.

"What about it, Counselor?" the judge said sternly. "You know support and visitation are separate issues."

"Yes sir, yes sir, of course, Your Honor," my attorney responded, picking up some papers from the podium. Raising a finger in the air, he then added, "But perhaps the Friend of the Court could hold my client's payments in escrow, until the mother shows up in this court to claim the money. She would then have more *good reason* to show up."

"Hmmmm," the judge said, considering the question. He looked again as if he might accommodate our wishes. "Yes, okay," he said slowly, pointing a finger at us. "But when she shows up in this court, I will *first* give her all the escrow money. *Then* we'll begin the hearing." He looked carefully at me again. "Would you be satisfied with that approach, Mr. VanBuren?"

What else might I accomplish here? I asked myself. *Probably nothing.* Fidgeting with a button on the front of my gray wool suit, I searched for an alternative solution, but found nothing. Dejected and unable to hide my disappointment, I could only sigh, "Yes, sir."

~

Chapter 19   *Nancy and Ma*

July 1977

I was so upset. There would be at least three more months without seeing my daughters. I missed them immensely. So much happens so quickly in the lives of children; precious time that can never be recovered. I was missing it all.

I was happy though with the tactic of trying to starve Kathy into cooperation. *It would be a real hardship,* I thought, *for her to go without the support money.* She would be forced to put her financial needs ahead of her own vengeful character.

Trying to take my mind off the issues with Kristen and Amy, I poured extra attention into my new life. Repairs were needed around the house, games needed playing in the yard, and time was needed between a man and his new wife. A pleasant and welcomed normalcy crept into our lives.

Nancy had missed a period and had been feeling sick in the mornings. We hoped she was pregnant, but we were waiting for the definitive test results from the doctor's office before celebrating.

One day, while I was at work, my mother stopped by our home unannounced to drop off a bag of hand-me-down boys clothing that my nephew, Scott, had outgrown. Nancy later related the story to me.

"I think this will fit Dennis just fine, Nancy," my mother had said, holding up a striped t-shirt, "and everything is in very fine shape."

My wife, happy to receive the clothing, made a pot of coffee for the two of them. They sat down at the secondhand kitchen table and began their first-ever girl-to-girl chat. Both were a little nervous, I'm sure.

Mildred VanBuren was an extremely gracious lady to everyone whom she had ever met. She never had an angry word for a single person in her entire life. Nevertheless, try as she might to

147

hide it, her strong Catholic beliefs about marriage and divorce always showed through. Nancy naturally felt some disapproval from her new mother-in-law.

Ma naturally loved her son, and by extension her son's choice of a partner in life. She struggled, though, to find some common ground with her new daughter-in-law. For her part, Nancy was not sure if she was even liked by my mother, let alone loved.

"Look what Mimi brought you, Dennis," Nancy said, as the 4-year-old came zooming through the room, arms outstretched, making airplane noises.

He stopped long enough to check out what was in the bag. He did not care that much about the clothing, but he thoughtfully said, "Thank you, Mimi," before continuing his airplane flight outside to play.

"Dennis is always such a polite little guy, Nancy," my mother said while folding a pair of blue jeans on the table. "You've taught him so well."

I'm sure Nancy replied with only a smile. She then poured each of them a cup of coffee and apologized for not having a cookie or something in the house to eat.

Taking a sip, my mother replied, "I don't need a cookie, Nancy. Don't worry about that."

The telephone rang. Nancy quickly picked it up from her seat by the window. "Hello … yes … yes … oh my God! ... yes … yes … okay, goodbye." Replacing the phone firmly onto the cradle, she looked at my mother all wide eyes and smiles, and announced with glee … *"I'm pregnant!"*

Ma, astonished, clasped her hands together and proclaimed, "Oh my, Nancy! I'm so happy!"

My wife, suddenly remembering who she was sitting across the table from, changed her expression from joy to puzzlement. "Really?" she asked.

With a puzzled look of her own, Ma sat up a little straighter in her chair, then began to understand Nancy's question. She replied, "Of course I'm happy, Nancy. Why would you think otherwise?"

"I don't know," Nancy said. "I thought … I thought …" she stuttered, tears beginning to show. "I thought you didn't approve of our marriage … *or of me!*"

My mother, then with tears of her own, placed her hands calmly over her daughter-in-law's. "I'm so sorry, Nancy," she said. "I didn't mean for you to think that way of me. I can see why you would though."

Nancy wiped her eyes with one hand while allowing my mother to continue holding the other.

Ma, probably thinking she knew what was on the young lady's mind, offered further, "The whole idea of divorce is just so hard for me to accept. Not just yours or Tommy's … but anyone's." Shaking her head slowly, she lowered her eyes. "So many things nowadays clash with Catholic teaching." Looking up at Nancy then, she quickly added, "But that's just me. I don't expect anyone else to think the way I do." She then took her hand from Nancy's, sat back in her chair, and asked, "May I please have another cup of coffee?"

Getting up to fetch the coffee pot from the stove, "Sure," Nancy said, feeling some relief.

While my wife poured the coffee, my mother continued, "I don't see how young people like you two can be expected to behave any differently than you are. But I also can't say that divorce and then marriage outside of the church is okay." Surrounding her freshly heated cup with her slender fingers, finding a way to humble herself, my mother then asked, "Can you accept that of me, Nancy?"

Sniffling as she sat back down, Nancy Jean nodded in agreement. "Yes … yes, I can," she said. "I'm sorry, I misunderstood."

Now smiling, my mother dug a Kleenex out of her coat pocket and handed it to her daughter-in-law. "I don't judge you, Nancy," she continued. "That's another Catholic teaching, you know. I struggle with some things that go on, of course, but only God can judge. I do my best to love and accept everyone though. Certainly, I cherish the wife of my son, whatever the circumstances." The tears began to flow then from my mother's own warm face, as she choked out a few more words. "And I am certainly thrilled at the thought that God is blessing me with another dear grandchild."

Nancy later told me she was feeling emotions which were entirely new to her. No one had ever spoken to her of God before. No one – particularly one whom she hardly knew – had ever shown unquestionable love this way. Finding courage, she did not previously hold, my young wife got up from her chair, rounded the table, and wrapped her arms lovingly around her mother-in-law from behind. Mixing their tears, she then whispered to her new friend, "I'm happy to have you … Ma … thank you."

~

Chapter 20   *Kathy in Court II*

When the time came for our second attempt at a Friend of the Court hearing, our hired hand in Alpena managed easily enough to serve papers to my ex-wife. We had then, with the same Honorable Judge Malcolm J. McLean, another date set in stone. This time it was Thursday, November 3, 1977.

We stood in the same courtroom as the last time, and Mr. Wyatt was sporting his same blue suit with red tide. I wondered if anyone would notice I had on my same gray outfit. Unfortunately, the first 10 minutes of that hearing also went the same as the last time. Kathleen VanBuren, again, was a no show.

"Okay, Mr. VanBuren," the judge began. "I release to you the funds currently in your Friend of the Court escrow account, and, until further notice from this court, no further support payments are required from you."

When my attorney offered no response to the proclamation, the judge adjusted his reading glasses and peered over them directly at me. "Now then," he said, "just what are we going to do about your visitation?"

Mr. Wyatt spoke up then. "Your Honor, under the circumstances, I would like, once again, to suggest that my client be given physical custody of the two minor children. It should be clear to the court by now that the defendant does not have the best interest of the children in mind."

"Let's not go there," Judge McLean said harshly, irritated by the diversion. He leaned forward and glared at my attorney. "At this point, we have no evidence the mother is unfit. It would take more than just a visitation dispute to warrant a change in custody. If that is what you seek, you'll have to pursue it in a different venue than this. Do you understand me, Counselor?"

My discomforted attorney responded meekly, "Yes sir, yes sir, Your Honor, I understand. Ummm … ahhh …"

"Mr. VanBuren," the judge interrupted, "Short of a change of custody or a rewrite of the Visitation Order, what can I do for you?"

I was a little embarrassed for Mr. Wyatt and didn't want to upstage him in that setting. Nevertheless, I responded directly to the question. "Your Honor, can you make an order requiring my ex-wife to turn the kids over to me at a certain time and location?"

"Yes," the justice replied, paging through a notebook on his desk. "I can do that." He made a notation, then stated: "At 10 am, three weeks from Saturday, November 26th, at the Hillman address. Is that okay?"

Thrilled with the thought of seeing the girls in only three weeks, I replied buoyantly, "Yes sir, that would be great! Can I get the police to help me?"

"Yes, certainly," the judge answered. "We'll guide you on how to accomplish that."

"Remember, Your Honor," I said stupidly. "Hillman is 200 miles away."

The judge smirked a bit. "This court has jurisdiction anywhere in the State of Michigan, Mr. VanBuren."

"Can I have a longer time with the kids than just one night?" I asked next.

"Judge McClain sat up and adjusted his glasses again, which I learned to take as a bad sign. "Let's not try to change the Visitation Order at this time, okay?"

"Yes sir," I responded promptly while my attorney stood by watching. "What if they're not home when I get there?"

"I think they'll be there," the judge said with confidence. "We'll send out notice to defendant Kathleen VanBuren that she is required to be at that address, at that time and day, and to peacefully release the children to your care or she'll be held in contempt of court by me."

"That ought to do it," I agreed. "And I can use this new order again in another two weeks?"

"No sir!" the judge barked. "This is a one-shot deal. Following that you fall back on the existing order."

I pursed my lips and stood silently staring at the judge. He seemed to be reading my mind, when he then asked, "Do you believe, Mr. VanBuren, that after all the effort we're going through here, and the loss of her child support money, and the threats from me, your ex-wife would be bold enough to defy the Visitation Order once again?"

I took a deep breath. "Yes sir," I answered. "Of course she will."

The judge sighed and lowered his head, seemingly in disgust at the situation. Brushing the gray hair from his forehead he looked up at me again but did not speak. I took the judge's silence as an invitation for me to explain a few things, and I gave it my best.

"My ex-wife is very mad at me," I began. "It was bad enough after I divorced her ... but then I got remarried ... and she's been impossible ever since. She's determined to punish me in any way she can, Your Honor. And she uses our children to that end. She coaches them to hate me, and to be afraid of me.

"The last time I saw or spoke to Kristen and Amy was a year and two months ago, when, during a visit with them, I made the mistake of talking about my new girlfriend. The kids were happy for me ... but their mother apparently was not. The girls and I have always been close, Your Honor. I'm their daddy ... we ..."

My throat constricted at that thought, choking off my words, but after a moment I was able to continue. "We love and need each other. I sure need them. I'm sick without them.

"Normally they would want to be with me too, but their mother has had all this time to poison their minds. The next time I show up on their doorstep they're *not* going to be eager to see me, and if it takes the police to load them into my car, it'll scare the daylights out of them. They are only 6 and 9, Your Honor.

"They'll cry for hours as I drive around trying to figure out what to do next. It'll be all I can do to calm them down and get them talking again before I have to return them to their mother at 6 pm the very next day."

The judge squirmed in his seat a bit, but still did not speak. I wondered then if I might be harming my own case by painting such a glum picture. But I had no choice but to continue.

"That sounds dreadful, Your Honor, I know. But it would get better the next time, and the next. We have been through this before. It *does* get better. But we need the means to have consistent, regular time together. Not just one shot at it.

"What you propose, sir, with a *Special Order* and the police help, I think will work and I'm grateful for that. But my ex-wife is very stubborn and very revengeful. She will never cooperate beyond that one visit. What do we do then?" I asked.

The judge made no attempt to answer my question, so I carried on.

"Following the first visit, Your Honor, if all I have when I knock on their door is the old Visitation Order," I said, waving an imaginary paper in the air, "they just simply won't be home. Or if they are, they won't come out. And if I holler and scream and make a fuss … *I'll* be the one arrested, not the mother."

Although I felt I had said woefully too little, no other words or points to be made came to my mind. Generally, I could rant endlessly on the subject, but at that important moment I had frozen up. I glanced at my attorney for some help but received none.

After a long moment, when it was more than obvious that my side had run out of steam, the judge mercifully took over. "I see," he said, messing with his glasses again. "Unfortunately, Mr. VanBuren, I cannot offer you relief, *now*, for something that only *might* happen in the future. If what you just described to me takes place, I'm sorry … especially for the kids … but come back to me if it does, we'll be able then to take different steps." He looked at my attorney. "Mr. Wyatt, do you have anything to add at this time?"

"No, Your Honor, that is all."

"I can only suggest then, Mr. VanBuren," Judge McLean concluded, "that you do your best with what the court has given you today ... good luck to you." He banged his gavel, and then shuffling papers announced, *"Next case."*

*****

I had not won the complete battle in court that day, I knew, but at least in three weeks I'd be spending two days with my children. I was sure excited about that, and I tried to feel positive about the future.

*****

"I can't believe you're going to go through with this, you bastard!"

The voice I despised so much caused my knees to buckle a bit as I stood at the payphone in front of the open room of drawing boards where I worked, but I recovered quickly. "I told you I wasn't going to just disappear, didn't I?"

"Well, the girls don't want to go with you. What do you think of that?"

"Of course, they don't, Kath, after what you've told them."

"I haven't told them anything. They just don't want to go with you."

"They'll get over it," I said tersely. "Don't worry about it."

"Don't tell me not to worry about it!" she screamed. "Especially when it comes to *my* daughters."

"They're my daughters too, Kathleen," I responded calmly.

She then spat out venom that struck directly in my heart. "They don't even call you *Dad* anymore!"

"Bullshit!" I hollered, reeling.

"It's true, they don't," she insisted in a superior tone, "and I didn't have anything to do with it. They call you *Tom*. What do you think of that?"

"I don't believe it."

"Do you want to talk to Kristen?"

"Of course, I do."

"Just a minute."

I waited for a long time, feeling the stares of my co-workers at my back. Finally, my 9-year-old daughter, who I hadn't spoken with since she was 8, came to the phone.

"Hello … Tom," the small voice said.

The blow staggered me, and it took a moment to reply, "This is your dad, Kristen."

"Hello," the small voice said again.

"Can you not say *Dad*, honey?"

No answer.

"I love you, Princess. I miss you so much."

No answer, just some sniffling.

"I'm coming to get you on Saturday, honey."

"Please don't!" she cried out.

"Yes, sweetheart. I'm coming. It'll be okay, I promise. Remember how much fun we used to have? You liked it before, didn't you?"

She began to cry. "No … Tom … I hated it!" she managed to get out between sobs, then hung up.

With the phone in hand, I stood in stunned silence for a long moment staring blankly at the block wall. Tears began to fill my eyes. Suddenly I remembered where I was and searched self-consciously around the room at the many gawking faces. I wanted to run. Quickly hanging up the phone, I staggered down the aisle toward the engineering room door. I broke through the small lobby without my coat and stumbled into the snow-covered parking lot. Fumbling for my keys, fighting the wind, the snow, and the hurt, I sought a way out. Eventually, I found my way to the relative privacy of my home, where I could cry alone.

*****

The next morning, I phoned my boss and apologized for walking out of work the way I had. After he forgave me, I asked for the day off to take care of some personal business. "Sure," he said. I then phoned my attorney.

"I can't do it, Mr. Wyatt," I began. I then told him about the phone call between my ex-wife and me, and then my seemingly ex-daughter.

"Okay, okay. I can see your point, Tom," he sympathized. "So, what do you want to do next?"

"I sure don't know what to do next. I just know I can't be part of bringing such pain to my children."

"But it's not your fault, Thomas," he insisted.

"Yes, it is!" I insisted in return. "If I can prevent something and I don't, then it's my fault."

"We went through so much effort and money to get to this point, Tom," the attorney in him complained. "It seems like such a shame to waste it."

"It does seem that way, Mr. Wyatt, I admit, but I can't stand to hear my kids cry anymore, and to be afraid of me. Even if it *is* unfair, they don't want to be with me, and they won't come willingly, and I don't want to use the police to force them into it and, if nothing else, I can't take the rejection."

"But what else can we do?"

157

"All I know is I'll never find a way into my children's lives, Mr. Wyatt – *never* – without the goodwill of their mother. Short of giving me custody, nothing the Friend of the Court can ever do will help – *nothing* – without the mother's willingness."

"You're not going to give up, are you?" he asked with surprise.

"No, of course not," I stated adamantly. "But I'm not going to force things onto the kids this way. It hurts too much."

I could hear him thinking and pictured in my mind his furrowed brow. Then I heard him say, "You know we still have the support issue going on. You're not sending any money, are you?"

"No."

"How long do you suppose she can hold out without it?"

"Well, I suppose she'll hurt pretty soon," I answered. "But it'll hurt the kids too. I don't want that."

"Of course, you don't, Tom, but it may force her into appealing to the Friend of the Court. Don't you think so?"

"I don't know, maybe."

"If she can't get her money turned back on until visitation is back to normal, she will be forced to cooperate, don't you see?" Mr. Wyatt was getting a little excited then. "She'll be calling *you* before you know it, to make amends, I bet. She'll be *full* of goodwill then."

"If you say so," I finally admitted, but without enthusiasm.

"I'll contact the Friend of the Court right away," he added, exuding confidence, "to see if I can push the issue. I'll let everyone know not to expect you this weekend, too. Then I'll tell them why."

"Okay, Mr. Wyatt," was all I could muster.

"Keep your head up, Thomas. We'll get this thing fixed … one way or another."

~

Chapter 21   *Motherly Advice*

February 1978

While my younger siblings were at school, Mom and I sat together at the yellow kitchen table in Royal Oak and talked all afternoon. In desperate need of some expert advice and some loving counseling, I had taken yet more time off work to seek it.

It had been three months since I had canceled the police-escorted visit with my daughters, and no progress whatsoever had been made toward normalizing that situation. What I needed mostly from my mother, though, was not practical, legal, or even moral advice, but how to deal with my seething anger and bitterness.

"I hate that woman," I said with a vengeance.

"No, you don't Tommy," she calmly suggested. "You hate her behavior, of course, but you don't hate her."

"I don't know, Ma. It sure *feels* like *hate* to me." I took a gulp of my coffee. "Yes, I hate her. I hate her!"

"I'm not so sure you do, Thomas," she reasoned, sitting up straighter in her chair. "I don't think you have it in you to actually hate someone." Feeling a chill then, she fastened the top two buttons of her well-worn cotton sweater.

"Don't I have reason to hate her though?"

"I suppose you have *reason* to," she said, level-headedly, "but you don't *have* to, you know, and it is not good if you do."

"She's keeping your grandchildren from you too, you know. What have *you* ever done to deserve that? And what about what she is doing to Kristen and Amy, for Pete's sake? Don't you hate her for that?"

"Heavens no!" she responded. "You know I don't hate anyone. Hate is a very destructive emotion, and I won't let anyone's conduct affect me that way, and neither should you."

"That's not so easy for me, Mother," I rebutted quietly.

"Yes, it is," she assured me, placing a warm hand over mine. "You've never been a hateful person, Tommy. Don't let Kathy cause you to become one now, or then *she* wins. Don't you see? Just be yourself. It's easier to love than to hate anyway."

"Not when you're talking about my ex-wife it isn't. But it's not just Kathy, Mom. I'm getting screwed as a parent every step I take, just because I'm male. How did our society get to the point where the father has no importance?"

My mother looked surprised. "That's a strange thing coming from you," she said. "Does your father have no importance in your life?"

"Of course he does, but is that only because you let him? You could have stolen us from him if you had wanted to."

"I can't even imagine such a thing."

"I know you can't, Mom, but what if you had gone mentally ill and packed us into the station wagon and took off for Timbuktu? What would have happened?"

She laughed. "They'd have put me in a nut house!"

"Exactly! That's how it used to be. They wouldn't have just let you do anything you wanted to, just because you're the mother. Nowadays, they say, you *go girl*, here's some money; don't let that *evil* man take advantage of you."

"Oh, you're crazy!"

"No, I'm not. Remember that Christian idea about the man being the head of the household? *Ha!* What a joke that is! If a woman has total say in the raising of the children – and in 1978 America they do – then the man is rendered completely useless, not needed. That's what I am, useless, except maybe as a sperm donor and a money giver." My shoulders dropped. "My own children don't even want me, Ma. Do you know how much that hurts?"

She took a moment to respond, brows drawn down, lines of trouble in her face, considering the question. "Yes, Tommy, I think I can imagine how you feel. But you're making a mistake if you expect Kristen and Amy to be able to overcome their mother's evil ways better than even you can."

"There!" I snapped, pointing a finger at my mother and grinning. "You think Kathy is evil too."

"No, I don't," she came back quickly. "I said her *behavior* was evil. I didn't say *she* was."

"What's the difference, Mother?"

"You know the difference, Tommy. Don't pretend you don't. But we were talking about your daughters. They're only 6 and 9. They love you very much, you know they do. But they're far too young to be able to openly defy their mother and tell you so.

"And they certainly need you. They have to learn restraint, patience, and love from someone. And that someone is you. But you're no good to them, angry and bitter. Even if you're not around them a lot, they learn from your example, and you're a huge influence on their lives. They know and they understand more than you may think."

I blinked back tears as my mother reached across and took my hand again. "You're not lost to your children, as you may be thinking, Tommy," she said warmly. "Not by a long shot."

I sat for a while digesting my mother's words as she watched me. Inhaling deeply then, I was about to offer my next discussion point when suddenly the side door burst open and in blew a flurry of cold snow and fresh air. It was my little brother Pauly, 16 years younger than me, wearing no hat and carrying no books.

"Hey, Tommy!" he said too loudly, running over for a quick hug.

Still feeling defeated and sullen, I struggled to change my demeanor to something less dismal. "Hey man, how's it going?" I responded lightheartedly. "Don't you have any homework?"

"Yeah, I have homework, but I have two study halls now, so it's no sweat."

161

"Boy," I complained, "school sure is a breeze nowadays."

"Don't worry, big brother, it's not so easy," the little hard-bodied guy insisted as he poured himself a tall glass of milk.

"So, man," I said, sinking back in my chair, "in a couple of weeks Nancy is having a baby shower that you and I are not invited to. Why don't you come over to my house with Dad that night?" I leaned toward Paul and added impishly in a loud whisper, "and we can have some beer."

"Ahhhhhh!" Mom gasped in surprise. "You better not give him any beer!" she admonished, shaking a finger at me.

"I'm just kidding, Ma."

"No, he's not!" Paul retorted with a big grin on his face and milk for a mustache.

We all laughed.

Feeling lighter then, having had some comic relief, I wanted to stay longer, but it was getting late. "I better get going now," I said. "Nancy will be expecting me home soon."

After my little brother said goodbye and left the room, Mom had a few parting words for me. "I'm so excited about the new baby coming – both you and Mary Kay! Wow! We're so blessed. Do you think Nancy will let me help her when the time comes?"

"Oh yes," I answered, putting on my coat. "She's counting on you. She told me so."

"She's counting on *you* more than anyone, Tommy," my mother said seriously in return.

I only smiled, buttoning my coat, and letting her continue.

"I hope you can get your mind off your worries about Kristen and Amy and focus back on Nancy and the new baby. You've done all the right things for your daughters, son. There doesn't seem to be anything else to do now in that regard except to wait, really. Quit second guessing yourself. Quit fretting. Put it into God's hands." She folded her own hands then. "I pray that you will."

162

I lifted my hands up in mock surrender, grinned broadly, and spoke. "If that's what you're praying for, Mother, then I don't have a chance. I have no choice but to stop worrying and whatever else you just said."

"No, you really don't have a choice, Thomas," she said, turning my collar up behind my neck. "You got yourself remarried. You have a lovely wife. You have a new son, and a new baby on the way. They need *all* of you," she continued, then holding my lapels with both of her diminutive hands. "Not just part of you."

~

Chapter 22   *Baby Shower*

March 17, 1978

For the next few weeks, I took my mother's advice; I put my troubles where they belonged – behind me. No more bitterness. No more complaining. Nancy and I had lots to do.

We turned the third bedroom of our little brick house into a nursery. We attended birthing classes twice a week, and the two of us picked out baby names for hours in front of the fireplace. I built a wooden baby cradle from plans we found in *Better Homes and Gardens*, and Nancy dressed it smartly in yellow and white muslin. Ma was correct – it was easier to love.

Nancy's three sisters, Phyllis, Sharon, and Sandy, planned a baby shower. It was to be held at Sharon's house – a nice three-bedroom brick ranch in the newer section of Livonia. Sharon's husband, Tim Heath, a paramedic for the city fire department, was fortunate to be scheduled for work that night, so he didn't have to worry about being displaced during the girls-only event.

Most of my seven sisters attended. Dad dropped off Mom, 15-year-old Connie, and 17-year-old Theresa at the party. He then drove his red station wagon the two-mile distance to my house to spend the evening with me and Dennis.

The night was moonless and unusually warm. Dad, wearing a short sleeve shirt and cotton slacks, entered my abode through the side door. Rising the two steps from the landing to the kitchen, he greeted me with his normal good cheer. "Hello, Tommaso."

Before I could even respond, my 5-year-old son flew noisily into the room and wrapped his arms tightly around his grandfather's legs. Stepping on top of my dad's new blue canvas sneakers, Dennis looked up with his smiling chocolate-covered face and said, "Hi Pipi! Are you staying long?"

"Hi there Dennis," Pipi replied, mussing the boy's hair, not even trying to regain the use of his own feet. "I'm here for a while. What are you up to?"

"Oh nuttin. Wanna play Nintendo?"

"What's Nintendo?" Pippi asked.

"You don't know what Nintendo is?" Dennis said incredulously, jumping off the poor man's feet.

"Later Dennis," I interjected. "Give the guy a break. And go wash your face, wouldja? Come on in, Pop-o. Take a load off."

The three of us men moved to the living room. Dad and I each relaxed in easy chairs next to the end tables. Each end table just happened to feature an ice-cold longneck Stroh's. "Oh man, that sure looks good!" Dad said, rubbing his hands together.

Dennis plopped himself down on the blue shag carpeting, right between the two grown-ups. He crossed his bare legs, folded his hands in his lap, and waited for the conversation to begin. He had not washed his face yet.

"Where's Pauly, Dad?" I asked. "I thought he was coming with you?"

"Oh, he was supposed to, but he went to his first ever Bishop Foley dance instead. The bonehead forgot all about it though, until we were about to leave the house. We had to drop him off at the high school on the way here." Looking a little concerned then, he added, "Somebody else will have to give him a ride home, I guess."

"I'm sure he'll be alright, Dad," I consoled him. "I bet he can dance like a wild Indian, ey?"

"Yeah, he sure can. But I don't know if he will or not. He can be shy, too, you know."

"Man, I used to love my high school dances," I reminisced, draining the bottom of my first beer. "What a wonderful time in a kid's life. Sometimes I wish I were young again."

"You are young, kiddo," Dad responded.

"I'm young too, Daddy," Dennis chimed in.

"Yes, you are son," I assured him. "But you're old enough to wash your own face. Why haven't you done that yet?"

"Oh jeez, Daddy," the lad complained as he raised himself up from the floor in one quick motion, and then bounded off to the washroom.

Noticing that my beer bottle was empty, I hastened to the fridge for a fresh one, asking along the way, "Did you just drop off the ladies, Pop-o, or did you go in?"

"I went in for a while," he answered.

I stood leaning against the wall in the archway listening to my dad. I had one ear on the conversation and the other on Dennis splashing in the bathroom.

My dad continued. "I saw Nancy and her mother. Man, she's big!" Then he added with a smirk, "Nancy, that is. When is she due, anyway?"

"Not for another month," I chuckled. "Mary Kay's due about the same time, you know."

"Are you sure?" he asked, scratching his head. "She doesn't look as far along to me."

"I could be wrong about that, I suppose. Who knows? Who else was at the party?"

"Well, I met Nancy's three sisters again, but I've forgotten their names. We got there late, you know, because of Paul. Your other sisters were already there, Janice, Donna, Mary Kay, maybe Linda and Ann Marie too. I remember *their* names for some reason. They tried to feed me, but I skedaddled out of there pretty fast."

At the mention of food, I took a step towards the kitchen. "Are you hungry Dad?" I asked. "I've got some Gino's pizza rolls for us."

"Yeah, I'll have some," Dad answered, polishing off his first beer. "But it doesn't have to be now. Whenever you're ready."

"Why not now?" shouted Dennis as he pranced back into the room with only the left side of his face washed.

Dad and I each did a double take at Dennis, then we looked at each other and broke out laughing.

"Whaaaat?" asked Dennis. "Can't we have pizza rolls now?"

"As soon as you wash the other half of your face, goofball," I quipped.

The telephone rang. It was Nancy, calling from the shower. "Your mom passed out," she said in a panic. "She's on the floor."

"What?"

"She just dropped to the floor, Tom. I don't know why. They're working on her now."

"Who's working on her?"

"Your sisters. We called an ambulance."

"Oh my God! We'll be right there!"

"Hurry!"

I hung up the phone in the kitchen and rushed the few steps to where Dad and Dennis had been waiting and listening. I stood, speechless for a moment, stunned, staring at my dad sitting on the edge of his chair. "Something's happened to Ma," I finally spoke. "I don't know what, but it sounds bad. We've got to go there right now."

The table lamp shone harshly on my dad's pale, drawn face. His eyes were dark and frightened. He seemed to want to speak, but nothing came out.

I reached down and took my son by the arm. "Let's take your car, Dad," I directed. "You're blocking me in."

While we raced to the scene, there were no words spoken between my dad and me. We had nothing to ask or to answer. Dennis was quiet in the backseat, also. I thought that when we got there, we would find my mother recovered, smiling, telling us not to worry about her. I didn't know what my dad was thinking. I was afraid to even look at him.

167

As we turned onto Sharon's street, we saw ahead the flashing lights of the ambulance. My heart sank. My dad gasped. A sea of people parted as we drove up. Everything was in slow motion and silent. I saw Theresa and Connie standing on the curb, terrified, clutching at each other, crying, sobbing. Their mouths were moving, but I heard nothing. Tim Heath soundlessly closed the back doors of the emergency vehicle and glanced over his shoulder, squinting in the glare of our headlights. He turned then and ran sluggishly to his driver's seat. I watched the ambulance snail away.

I stepped out of that surreal dimension and stood helplessly on the pavement. Here, the noise and the chaos seemed amplified. Phyllis and Sandy were helping Aunt Shirley back towards the house. Curious neighbors flooded the street. My sisters were hurrying someplace, no place. Everyone was panicking, except my dad. He sat deathly still in the other world of the car, looking ashen, not stirring from his seat, not asking questions, or even speaking at all.

"They're taking her to Garden City, Tom!" my wife shouted at me from the front lawn, pointing frantically down the street. "Follow them!"

The spell broke, I jumped back into the station wagon, back into reality, and took off.

"Where are we going, Daddy?" I heard the little voice from behind me say.

"Oh my God! I have Dennis!" I slammed on the brakes, pulled the boy out of the back seat, and carried him quickly to his mother who was still watching from the front lawn. She seized him from my arms and held him fast. "Go!" she cried.

We could see the flashing lights, then blocks away small and fading.

*****

168

We gathered together in the family waiting room of the Garden City Hospital; 20 or 30 of us crammed into a space built for 10 or 12; 20 or 30 of us crying, huddled into small groups, exchanging facts, comparing notes, not knowing, not believing.

A silhouette appeared framed in the doorway of the dimly lit room backed by the harsh lights of the corridor.

"Who's that?" Aunt Shirley asked, sniffling.

Everyone's eyes turned to Aunt Shirley for a moment, and then followed her gaze to the shape in the doorway. The figure entered the room and slowly closed the door. He turned to face his anxious audience, but then stood silently, somberly, hands folded in his front. He appeared to be more like a shy young priest than an emergency room physician about to do his job – a job that he hated.

My sister, Janice, spoke first. "Doctor, tell us how she is."

He swallowed hard but did not answer.

Gut-wrenching moans spilled from around the room. The doctor, seeing that he was being misunderstood, then quickly and considerately spoke, "She's still alive."

None of us knew whether to cheer or to cry. "What do you mean *still* alive?" Ann Marie demanded. "What does that mean?"

"She's had a massive stroke," he said deliberately. "A blood vessel in her brain has burst. She has suffered severe damage."

"Severe *brain* damage?" Donna asked.

"Yes," he answered, hesitantly. "Severe brain damage."

Fourteen-year-old Pauly, the youngest of my mother's nine children, gently pushed his way through the crowd. His lip quivering and his voice an octave higher than usual, he said to the doctor, "But, she'll live … right?"

"I don't know, son," he answered faintly. "I just don't know. But if she does live," he directed now to the first rest of us, "there will be nothing left. She will be …" He just couldn't get it out of his mouth. He closed his eyes, and at last said the word. "*Nothing.*"

"Noooooo!" screamed Linda, clenching her fists in anger. "How can you say it like that!"

Uncle Russell slid down the wall to the floor in disbelief. Aunt Bea and Donna helped him to his chair, consoling him. My poor dad did not speak; he only sat helplessly with Theresa on his lap and his other daughters surrounding him.

I did not fully understand what was taking place, but my sister Janice did. Being a registered nurse, she discerned well what the doctor was telling us, and she knew she had to speak for the family.

She stood up from my father's side and stepped purposefully to the young physician and, looking him eye to eye, said, "You must do everything you can to keep her alive, Doctor ... *Everything.*"

The doctor moved back a bit and put a hand to his chin, before he stammered, "Even though ... even after what I've just told you?"

"Yes, Doctor," she insisted. "Even after what you've just told us; we want her alive, no matter what. You must do everything ... you must!"

The world went totally silent. The doctor regarded my sister carefully. She stood defiantly in front of him, struggling to keep her composure, tears streaking from her stoic face. He softly sighed and, almost imperceptibly, nodded in agreement. Without another spoken word, he turned and withdrew from the room.

We stood alone in frozen anguish, dissolving hope, godforsaken, desperately frightened, 20 or 30 souls, in utter agony.

*****

Two days later

I watched my dad as he saw the fleeting scenery from the passenger seat through the side window. The sky was bright yellow, and the air was extra clear. Buds were showing on the spring trees. Cars, trucks, buses, and people were about as usual. *People* – what were they doing? Didn't they know?

Dad had chores that morning – a casket to be chosen, a plot to be purchased, arrangements to be made. So many arrangements – and it had to be him – at a time when he could hardly think. None of us could think, really, not much more than automatic functions like breathing and blinking. For the next few days, the next few months, the next few years, I did my best to help my dad. But really, it was the other way around.

Dad came out of his funk in a day or two. He began to speak, sparingly at first. His words were so much needed by his children. "All we can do is go on," he said. Then he showed us how.

He picked out a pewter casket with tiny purple and pink flowers, then met with the priests and the nuns of St. Dennis Parish. He spoke with hundreds of friends and family members, all of whom wanted to know about Mom, wanted to talk about her, and wanted to cry with him. Dad cared for his children by letting his children care for him.

There were three days of visiting at the funeral home. It was a tremendous outpouring of love. So many people, so upset. It seemed that Ma had quite an effect on everyone she had ever touched – neighbors from 30 years before, neighbors from yesterday, school kids and their parents, in-laws, and forgotten friends. And absolutely every soul from our entire, large, extended family. *Everyone,* it seemed, loved our mother.

My sister Donna gave a very emotional eulogy at St. Dennis Church. I marveled at her ability to do so. I, for one, could not yet have strung together three words without breaking down. Donna was always better than any of us at finding the right words and using them.

My very pregnant wife - and my very pregnant sister Mary Kay - were stunning reminders of the tragic loss of the future years of precious and unconditional love that would have come from Ma. Sitting together in the church, they grieved together – one who knew her very well, and one who hardly knew her at all. Each carried with them a piece of the Mildred VanBuren legacy. Each carried with her a life that Mimi would never know – each a life that would never know their Mimi.

171

Mildred Marie VanBuren

February 6, 1920 – March 17, 1978

Mom	58	Nancy	21
Dad	59	Kristen	9
Janice	34	Amy	6
Linda	31	Dennis	5
Thomas	30		
Donna	28		
Mary Kay	21		
Ann Marie	18		
Theresa	17		
Connie	15		
Paul	14		

~

Chapter 23   *Jamie*

April 20, 1978   Tom 30, Nancy 21, Dennis 5

I followed the nurses towards the bright lights. My hands were well scrubbed, and I was dressed in light blue hospital garb – complete with hairnet and footies. I was excited – perhaps like never before – but also nervous. This spotless room, filled with machines, wires, and tubes, was smaller than I had expected. A single patient's bed, placed in the center, was surrounded by an array of technology. The air was cool and antiseptic as doctors and nurses bustled in and out.

I stopped two steps short of the head of the bed and stood with my fingers spread in front of my face as if I were waiting for the nurse to install my latex gloves, but I already had gloves on. My wife was lying on her back, with the head of the bed raised a bit. Her knees were in the air making a tent out of the sheets, keeping her lower half from my view. She strained to look over her shoulder at me and tried to greet me with a smile. She screamed instead.

Awake then from my momentary fog, I rushed the final steps to her side and took one of her moist trembling hands into my own. "Push! push!" I heard the doctor demand.

"Oh my God! Am I late?" I said to no one in particular. Nancy screamed again and she squeezed my hand ever harder.

An otherwise busy nurse brought a stool over for me. "Have a seat here, Dad," she said in an obvious hurry. "Look into that mirror and you can see everything, okay?" Before I could respond she hurried away.

I looked up into the mirror into a staggeringly beautiful spectacle and was instantly struck motionless with wonder. I forgot everything entirely of what was going on around me, what was needed of me, and why I was even there.

*****

It had only been 34 days since Mom had passed away, but a lot had taken place in that time. I spent the first eight of those days at the family house in Royal Oak with my dad and the rest of his kids. We might have stayed there forever, grieving together, but slowly, cautiously, we emerged back into the routines of our individual lives.

For me that meant getting back to my job, getting back to my wife and son, and getting ready for the new baby. Together, Nancy and I finished decorating the nursery and building the cradle. We went to our last few birthing classes, and we completed our boy or girl name pics – Thomas for a boy, but not a junior, and Jamie for a girl – Jamie Jean.

One day, about two weeks after the funeral, I came home from work in my usual subdued mood. I pulled the black Cougar into the garage, got out, and talked for a moment to Dennis's chicken in its cage. With my jacket over my shoulder, I walked slowly to the side door, trying not to notice the grass needed cutting. I took the two steps up from the landing into the kitchen just as Nancy was hanging up the telephone. She was clearly excited about something.

A swollen belly was peeking between the top of the too small maternity pants and the partially unbuttoned white cotton blouse that she wore. Her hair was wild yellow, just blown dry after a shampoo. Her cheeks were freshly rosy red from a steamy bath, and her smile was radiant. She smelled of Ivory soap and dusting powder.

"Hi honey," I said as she wrapped her arms around my neck. "Why the smiley face?"

"Guess why?" she asked impishly.

"I give up … why?"

"Because the doctor's office called, that's why. Guess what they said?"

"I give up … what?"

"Noooooo … you have to guess."

174

"They told you April is a free delivery month?"

"Noooooo, that's not it," she said in a singsong voice. "Guess again."

"You're going to have twins?"

"No, knot head! You know I'm not going to have twins." She stomped her feet in mock frustration. "What have you been *asking* for lately?"

"Well," I said, rubbing my chin. "I've been asking for a beer for about an hour now, but I didn't think anyone was listening."

She looked away from me for a moment as if she didn't even care about my beer. She gave a little shutter, her eyes widened, and her eyebrows rose. "Whooooa! she said in amazement. She looked back at me again, pushed her belly into mine and pulled me tight to her. "Do you feel that?" she said urgently. "The baby's kickin, do you feel it?"

I felt one, two, three, four little thumps into my own belly. "Yes, I feel it!" I said excitedly. Five, six, seven. "Holy cow! It feels like that little fella really wants to get out. Are you having pains?"

"No, she's just been kicking a lot lately."

"*He's* been kicking," I suggested. "A girl couldn't be that strong, could she?"

"Well, I think it's a girl and so does the nurse."

"Is that what the office called to tell you? How'd they know that?"

"No, bozo, they don't know if it's a boy or a girl, she was just guessing about that. But they called to say you can be in the delivery room with me if you want to." She stepped back from me a bit so she could get a better look at my face; she always wanted to judge my feelings by my first reaction.

I had a smile on my face as big as a slice of watermelon.

"Oh good!" she said, clasping her hands together, "you're happy."

"Yes, yes, of course I'm happy." I pulled her back into my arms, embracing tightly. "When can we go?"

"It won't be long, Tom, I don't think, but you've got to get some training." She gently pried away from me a bit, trying to keep me focused on the subject matter. "Doctor Graybaum's never done this before, ya know."

"He's never delivered a baby before?"

"No, stupid, he's never allowed a dad in the delivery room before. He wants to make sure you know what to do."

"What's for me to be doing?" I said teasingly. "You'll be doing all the work." I rubbed my belly into her once more. "Now, let me feel my son again."

*****

I received my training alright but sitting there on the stool looking into the mirror, I had forgotten it all. There was little for me to do anyway, except to gape in amazement. I saw flesh that I had never seen before, and a swelling sphere of golden curls. Was it the top of the head? It was growing, pushing, straining to escape. Relaxation then, and quietness. It moved away. There was a sudden gush of fluid that splashed across the bed and dripped onto the floor. Once more then, the intense pressure and the stretching came, and once more it eased slowly back. With the next push the crown grew to an impossible size and a head popped out with a flood of fluid and blood.

I clenched my teeth, but went on watching, holding tight to my wife's quivering hand. She dug her fingernails deep into my skin and made an enormous grunt of effort. The doctor put his fingers in and turned the shoulders slightly to help. There was a slurping sound and a long, wet figure slithered out onto the soggy bed. I had never seen anything so beyond belief astonishing in my entire life. I was staggered. I cried.

She was beautiful. Not the purple, scrunched up, and bruised form I had expected, but a perfectly beautiful *she*. She was not crying, but making rousing sounds, taking short explosions of breath, and punching the air with tiny fists. Her black, unfocused eyes were filled with unexpected self-assurance. It was clear she was happy to be alive and that she knew she could do anything in the world she wished to do – *anything*.

I swear I heard her say, *"I am here."*

~

Chapter 24   *Angela*

Three days after I watched our daughter enter this world with her eyes open and her fists pumping, we took the little cherub home and rocked her to sleep in her newly completed white and yellow cradle. Dennis was thrilled with his new little sister, and he was anxious to help in any way he could. Nancy recovered easily enough from the delivery, and she expected no trouble caring for two kids instead of one.

I went to work the following day (late as usual) and passed out three boxes of *It's a Girl!* cigars to the guys in the Engineering Department. It seemed, in those days, that just about everyone smoked. After lunch we all lit up at the same time, filling the air in our windowless surroundings with billowing clouds of white puffy toxicity.

Angela Malansky, a refined 50-year-old Armenian immigrant, sat wheezing and coughing at the drawing board directly behind me. "I am happy to you, Mr. Tom," she said, waving the smoke away from her face. "But if you have any more babies, I'm going to have to find a new place to be working."

Angela reminded me of my mother, and we talked to each other every day about our families. Her experiences in life were much different than mine, of course, but we shared many of the same values. She, being much older than I, also had wisdom. If she took a special interest in me, I suppose it was only because I happened to sit near her at work. Nevertheless, I respected Angela and valued her opinions, and she knew it.

As I took a heavy drag of my cigar, a piece of Pink Pearl eraser bounced off the back of my head. I looked back at Angela, and she said, "You were late for work again today, Mr. Tom, and you really should quit smoking, you know."

I ignored the late for work remark, and responded, "Oh, I would like to quit smoking, Angela. I have been trying to quit for the last 10 years. It's not possible."

"You don't smoke around your new baby, do you?"

"Well ... do you think I shouldn't? What does it hurt?"

"It hurts *plllllllenty*," she said, stretching out the word. "I can tell you that. But you know that already. Does your wife smoke too?"

"Yes, actually ... she does."

Angela sat up straighter in her chair and blurted out loudly so that others took notice. *"In the house?* You and her both smoke inside your house? With the new baby there?"

Embarrassed by her accusations, I did not respond, but instead turned slowly around and pretended to go back to work. I did not cherish Angela's chastisements.

Shaking her head in disbelief, she whispered to my back, "I am surprised at you, Mr. Tom."

I sat quietly at my drawing board the rest of the afternoon, thinking about what Angela had said. Although I no longer enjoyed it, I finished smoking my cigar. I then switched to smoking cigarettes in my customary fashion – one after another. During my drive home I smoked two more cigarettes.

When I arrived home, my wife was sitting peacefully at the end of our blue velour sofa with the baby in her arms. A newly lit cigarette smoldered in a large glass ashtray which sat underneath a table lamp. Next to the ashtray sat a fresh, warm bottle of infant formula.

"Hello, my dears," I said as I bent to gently kiss the faces of my two special angels.

"Hi Tom," Nancy Jean said with a smile.

"Bleh meh," Jamie Jean said, also with a sweet smile.

"Can I feed her for you, Nance?" I offered.

"That's alright. I'm okay," she answered.

"But I would like to, and then you can smoke your cigarette."

179

"I can feed her *and* smoke my cigarette," she said with pride. "I don't mind."

I sat down heavily on the sofa next to the two of them and removed the shoes slowly from my feet. "We should probably keep smoke out of her face, don't you think?"

Shifting the baby in her arms, she said curtly, "I'm not blowing smoke in her face, Tom. Don't worry about it."

"I'm not worrying about it, Nance. Well ... maybe I am. We talked about it a lot at work today. Don't you think smoking can harm the kids?"

"I'm not going to allow them to smoke till they're at least 6 years old, Tom," she said with a smirk. "So, don't worry so much."

"Some people think that breathing in someone else's smoke is just as bad as smoking yourself. And why wouldn't it be, Nance, if they're breathing it in?"

Nancy propped the bottle into position on the blanket that was keeping Jamie warm while cuddled in her left arm. With her now free right hand, she reached over and picked up her cigarette from the ashtray and took a deep drag. She then exhaled away from the baby's face.

"See?" she said with a big smile, "no problem."

I looked at my wife's silly grin and chuckled. *I would have done the same thing just yesterday,* I thought, *but not anymore.* I took the pack of Marlboros out of my shirt pocket, looked at it longingly for a moment, and came to a final decision. Tossing the pack onto the coffee table I announced, "I've just decided, I'm going to quit smoking."

Nancy rolled her eyes and said, "You've said that before, pal."

"Yeah, I know, honey, but this time I have more incentive. It would be easier, you know, if we both quit. Why don't we quit together?"

"I really don't wanna quit."

I heard about this place where you get hypnotized, and it's really supposed to make it easy, and it's only 40 bucks."

"For 40 bucks I can buy 10 cartons of cigarettes," she said. "And besides, I like to smoke. But you should do it if you wanna, Tom. Go for it."

"Okay," I said, somewhat dejected. "I think I will. But I sure wish you'd come with me."

*****

A few days later, I and four other guys from work went to the William Hoak Hypnotherapy Center for their guaranteed to quit smoking in a one-night clinic. It was an interesting and entertaining night out with the guys, but I doubted that many people actually quit smoking because of it.

The following morning, I arrived late for work without a pack of Marlboros in my shirt pocket. I was in a hurry and suffering, and I was looking for someone to bum a cigarette from. By then I had gone almost 11 hours without a smoke, and that was about long enough. I knew I was going to give in sooner or later, so it might as well be sooner.

As I was removing my jacket and looking around the room for a friend with a cigarette, I noticed on my table, a foil-wrapped chocolate mint sitting on top of a hand-lettered note. The note said:

Dear Mr. Tom,

Thank you for not smoking.

I am enormously proud of you.

Angela

I turned around and smiled meekly at the nice lady. She was sitting erect on her stool with her hands folded neatly in front of herself. She wore on her face a broad prideful smile, like a mother whose son had just graduated from medical school.

181

Damn! I thought. *What am I going to do now? I really wanted a cigarette! How dare she do this to me. How does she know if I went to that stupid stop-smoking thing or not?* I reached up and checked my forehead for a gold star. Nothing there!

I was stuck, and I was weak, but I had no choice. There was only one thing I could do. I studied Angela for a long moment, then took a deep breath and said, "You're welcome, Angela. Thanks for the mint."

I popped the mint into my mouth, folded the foil wrapper into a neat square, and placed it in my shirt pocket where my cigarettes used to be. I carried that piece of foil with me for the next three months, fingering it from time to time, whenever the urge to smoke would get intense, which was often.

Quitting smoking was an extremely challenging task, but I always had Angela and Jamie on my mind, so I did not give in. Little by little it got easier and easier, and eventually I broke through the barrier – I became a non-smoker.

*****

Angela was *happy to me* for having quit smoking, and *happy to me* for having a new baby, but she was not yet satisfied. The woman was such a nag. One day, during our morning coffee break, as I was enjoying a sausage biscuit slathered in mustard, she attacked me again.

"What is wrong with you, Mr. Tom?" she demanded.

"Nothing is wrong, Angela. Why do you ask?"

"I ask," she said deliberately, "because you come to work every day late."

"Not every day," I insisted, wiping mustard from my face. "Besides, I'm never more than half an hour late."

"You cannot get promoted that way, Mr. Tom, and you might get fired."

182

"You think?"

"Yes, I think," she said sternly. "So, answer me, please. What is wrong with you?"

I had an idea what she was asking me, and why, but I didn't really want to talk about it. "Nothing is wrong with me, Angela. I just have a tough time waking up in the morning. The baby keeps me up at night, you know."

Angela raised her hands to her chest and exaggerated her best injured mother expression. "You are lying to me ... no?"

I shrugged my shoulders, shook my head no, then shook my head yes but I did not answer. I turned around and went back to work.

Angela dropped the subject and went back to work herself, but she had gotten her point across well enough. I *did* have a problem with getting to work on time. If I didn't fix that situation soon, I certainly would get fired. My boss, Mr. Fairman, had already told me so. I wondered then if he had been talking about me to Angela. I turned around in my seat and asked her.

She looked up from her work but did not put her pencil down. "Heavens no!" she said. "You think you are so important to Mr. Fairman?"

"No, I guess not," I said, breaking eye contact with her.

She leaned forward, trying to find my eyes again. "You are ready now, maybe to tell me what is wrong with you, Mr. Tom?"

I threw up my hands in surrender. "I stayed up too late, Angela. That's all there is to it."

Angela wobbled her head and frowned. "If that is what is ruining your life, then it is easy to fix, no?"

"How so?" I asked stupidly.

She leaned forward and whispered as if telling me a secret. "Go to bed on time!"

I lowered my eyes and spoke softly. "That may not be so easy to do."

She tilted her head and raised her eyebrows a bit. "Maybe there is a little more to the story, eh? Possibly you are drinking too much, also, no?"

"I suppose, a little. But that's really not the problem Angela, honest."

*****

I *was* drinking too much – obviously more than I should have. It had started two years earlier when I first started hanging around Nancy and her heavy-duty beer-drinking family. Before we had met I seldom had more than a beer or two at a time, but that quickly changed. Almost from our first date, I was a heavy drinker. The change in me happened so fast, in fact, that Nancy never really knew me to be any other way.

It was our routine to visit someone in her family, or for them to visit us, three or four times a week. Sometimes the gatherings were planned – a cookout or to play cards, for example. Mostly, though, they were impromptu events. Either way, we always had plenty to drink. The fact that we had two little kids didn't seem to slow us down.

I was better at quitting a party than my wife, but not by much. If I suggested leaving at 10 or 11, so that I could get up for work the next morning, the answer would invariably be: "Go ahead if you want, Tom. I'll catch up with you later." No matter that Dennis and Jamie were already asleep somewhere, and that we only had one car. My wife always wanted to stay, so we would stay, and we would drink, and we would have fun. Then I would suffer mightily the next day, while she slept it off.

Angela was correct – this situation had the potential to ruin my life. But it was easy to fix, no?

~

Chapter 25　　*Party Time*

August 1978　　　　　Tom 30, Nancy 21, Dennis 5, Jamie 4 months

　　　One sweltering Tuesday evening after a particularly long day at work, I sat patiently at the kitchen table with Dennis and Jamie, waiting for dinner to be served. A cold Stroh's was the only item on the speckled Formica surface. A stiff breeze from the 5,000 BTU window air conditioner blew directly onto my face. My young wife, a cigarette dangling from her painted lips, stood in front of the cooktop. She diligently stirred – exactly right – the ingredients of the original Hamburger Helper recipe.

　　　She placed the sizzling cast iron skillet, filled with its enticing contents, directly onto the middle of the table. Taking a seat herself, she said, "Tim Heath is having a birthday party Sunday night."

　　　"Oh," I responded as I reluctantly got up from the cool air of my seat to fetch plates and silverware for everyone. "Too bad it's on a Sunday."

　　　"Why's that?"

　　　"Cuz I have to work on Monday."

　　　"Don't worry about that," she said. The party's at 6 o'clock. Will you make a pot of beans for it? And will you grab the big jar of applesauce out of the fridge?"

　　　"I'll make beans for Sunday," I said as I scooped some applesauce for Dennis, "but I probably won't go to the party. I have to get up for work on Monday, remember?"

　　　"Don't be so stupid," she replied. "The party starts at 6 o'clock, remember?"

　　　"But you know it'll go till 2 in the morning."

　　　"You can leave anytime you wanna, Tom. Nobody's stopping ya."

"Really?" I said with good cheer. "You won't mind if I leave early?"

"Course not. Why would I mind? As long as you take the kids with you. I can get somebody to give me a lift home later."

"Okay," I said, "but if I've got to take the kids with me, it'll be around 9 o'clock, so I can get to bed by 10."

"No problem, Tom"

*****

Sunday morning, we slept in till around 10, then spent the rest of the day doing nothing. I did manage, though, to make a pot of *Tommy-Beans* for the party. Around 4 o'clock we took showers and bathed the kids. By the time we got everybody and everything loaded into the car it was half past 6. We drove the 10 minutes needed to get to the Heath estate.

We were the first ones there. The backyard was filled with balloons and Tiki Torches, but no people, and no fire in the grill.

Two of the Heath boys broke out of the back door to greet us, followed closely by Tim and Sharon carrying a cooler full of ice and beer. "Bout time you guys got here," Tim said, thrusting a beer into my hand.

I gladly took the beer. "Are we late?"

As Tim was about to answer, a throng of partiers burst through the chain link gate. Grandma and Grandpa, moms and dads, brothers and sisters, and kids and dogs appeared. In tow were babies and playpens, toys, food and of course, beer. The party had begun.

Four beers into the party, Tim decided it was time to light the fire. The kids were begging for food. Carl helped Harold carry in a hundred-pound bag of charcoal briquettes that Harold had brought as a birthday gift. Tim put on his chef's hat and a big grin.

"Look at that!" Nancy's father shouted. He stood next to the picnic table staring into a big bucket that Nancy's mother had brought to the party. "There ain't no tuna fish in your pasta salad, Mother!"

"My goodness," Mother said, embarrassingly covering her mouth. "I forgot to put the tuna fish in! I can't believe I did that. I bet it's still draining in the kitchen sink." She got up from her lawn chair and began looking around for her purse. "I'm gonna hafta go home and get it."

"No, you're not Ma," Carl insisted, holding up a hand to stop her. "We don't need no stinkin' tuna fish."

"Yes, we do Grandma!" Dennis chimed in, bouncing up and down. "I'll go with ya. Let's go! Let's go!"

Meanwhile, a crowd was gathering around the charcoal grill.

"Stack the briquettes up in a pyramid first, Tim," Harold directed. "Then soak 'em with lighter fluid. Then, just before you throw on a match, top it off with a little gasoline. That'll get 'em going real good." Others nodded their heads in agreement.

"Well, yeah!" Tim responded while pouring a scoop of briquettes into the grill. "But I'm a fireman, member? We hafta do things safely 'round here."

"Safe, bullshit!" Carl barked, taking a swig of his beer. "We don't got all day, ya know."

Mother stood nearby wringing her hands, and said sheepishly, "Father don't like his pasta salad without tuna fish."

"Look here," Harold said, waving a can of lighter fluid. "It's gonna take Tim an hour to light this friggin' fire, and I'm going to the party store for some more *Cool Aids* anyhow … "

"Dennis! You kids get that dog outta that tree!" somebody yelled.

"Like I was telling ya," Harold continued, "I'll run by the house and get your tuna fish, Ma."

Relieved, Mother said, "Thank you, Harold. Thank you. Thank you."

187

It did take an hour for Tim to get the fire going *real good,* but at least he didn't blow the place up. Harold eventually saved the day by returning with more beer and Mother's tuna fish. By 9:30 the pasta salad was all fixed up, and the hot dogs were ready to go on the grill.

I spoke softly to my wife sitting next to me at the picnic table. "I better get going now, honey, it's getting late."

She answered with surprise, "Dennis has to eat first, Tom."

I pursed my lips, trying to find a solution to the dilemma. "Why don't I leave him here with you, and I'll take the baby home with me."

"No way!" she insisted. "Besides, it's rude of you to leave before we sing happy birthday."

"At this rate, my dear," I whispered cynically into her ear, "we won't be singing happy birthday till midnight."

I was wrong about that though. It was hardly past 11:45 when Sharon brought out the flaming cake and we roused the neighborhood with a thundering song to the birthday boy.

By then the river of beer had been flowing for more than five hours, Dennis was still running wild with the dog and the other boys, the Tiki Torches were blazing brightly in the warm breeze, and Jamie was sound asleep in her padded travel crib. All this underneath the smooth blanket of a black velvet sky.

"Let's go home, honey," I said wearily to my wife. "It's really late."

She snapped her head quickly to her sister Sharon sitting next to her at the picnic table and made a silly face. They both broke out in deafening laughter. No way was Nancy ready to quit the party.

"Let's sing a little Lesley Gore to him, Nancy," Sharon shouted, "1, 2, 3, 4." They swayed arm in arm on the bench and belted out, off tune:

"Don't tell me what to do.

Don't tell me what to say.

And please, when I go out with you,

Don't put me on display.

Cuz, you don't own me.

Don't try to change me in any way.

You don't own me.

Don't tie me down

Cuz, I'd never stay.

Ha Ha Ha Ha."

"That's really nice you guys," I said. "Can we go home now?"

"You can go if you want to, Tom," Nancy said defiantly. "Go for it."

I didn't want to *go for it,* as she put it. I hated it when she talked to me like that. We were both drunk, and I could feel the anger building inside of me. "I need some help with the kids, dammit, and you've had enough to drink."

"Oh, shut up Tom."

"I'm not shutting up!" I shouted, *"and we're leaving right now!"* I grabbed her by the arm a little too forcefully and pulled.

"Let go of me, asshole!" she screamed.

Big brother, Carl, jumped out of his lawn chair to come to the rescue of his little sister. As he lunged towards me, he stepped onto the pole of a Tiki Torch, and slammed its flaming contents onto the head of Tim Heath.

Tim howled in terror. I let go of Nancy's arm. Sharon threw a tablecloth over her burning husband.

The party was over.

*****

189

I arrived at work the next day during the lunch hour. Angela was eating a ham sandwich at her table.

"Well," she said, "I'm glad to see you could make it to work today, Mr. Tom."

"Boy Angela, I'm glad too. You wouldn't believe what I've just been through." I then told her the entire sorry story.

Angela never took another bite of her sandwich. "As it turned out," I continued, "Tim was not burned too badly. But man, it could have been awful. Jamie's crib was not 6 feet away! *Just think about that!* We didn't get home from the hospital and didn't sleep till 4 o'clock this morning."

"I warned you something like this could happen, no?"

"Yes, Angela," I said, morosely. "You warned me. Now I've got to talk to Mr. Fairman and hope he doesn't fire me."

*****

Mr. Fairman did not fire me, but only after I convinced him that I'd never be late again, that I was turning over a new leaf, and that I would give my job the respect it deserved.

I *was* never late again, either, and I began to thrive. Mostly because – as Angela had suggested – I went to bed on time, and because I quit partying with my wife.

To my new way of life, I tried and tried and tried to bring my wife along with me. "You're changing, Tom," she would often say, "and that's a good thing. I like that in you, but I'm still the same girl you married – don't expect me to change too."

~

190

Chapter 26   *Concord*

In those days there were about 300 people working at Automated Pneumatic Systems in Farmington Hills, where I was jobbed-in as a mechanical draftsman. It was an acceptable position for me, but I, like most of the other 30 or so *jobbies,* hoped to be hired directly into APS someday. Being a contractor, after all, was not as good as being a direct employee.

All of the management and sales people at APS wore ties to work. Some wore suit coats as well. The rest of us had dress codes varying from business casual to clean jeans and safety shoes. Except for the three department heads and the chief engineer, none of the 50 guys in the engineering room at APS wore ties to work.

My friend and mentor, Angela, figured that while I was improving my attitude about my job, I would have a better chance for advancement if only I would upgrade my dress a bit.

"About all I can do, Angela, is to put on a tie," I said, pinching my Adam's apple.

She leaned forward across her drawing board and said, "That is maybe a clever idea, then, no?"

"I'm not so sure," I reasoned. "Nobody else wears a tie in here except the bosses."

She raised her eyebrows. "You want to be higher-up, do you not, Mr. Tom?"

"Right now," I said, putting my chin in my hand, "I'd just like to be a designer, like Jim, Al, Gary, and Bruce. I'm already as good as they are. Don't you think? And *they* don't wear ties."

"They have all worked here for many years," Angela said, shaking her pencil at me. "Do you want to wait so long? Or do you like to be noticed now?"

"Do you think wearing a tie will get me promoted?" I scoffed.

"Not just promoted," Angela said with certainty. "But much more, Mr. Tom."

I stop scoffing. "You're serious, *no?*"

"Wearing a tie will not change your abilities one bit," she continued. "But it can change the way people think of you. That is necessary for you. Unless you are satisfied with being a detailer all your life."

I did not want to be a detailer all my life, of course, and putting on a tie seemed like an easy enough thing to do, so I agreed to give the idea some thought. A week later, Nancy and I went to Hudson's and picked out a few business-looking shirts and ties. The hard part was still to come, though, which was showing up at work in that stuff, feeling totally overdressed and foolish.

Angela had recommended that I read a book written by John T. Malloy, *Dress for Success*. In the book the author directed me to wear only white, off-white, or light blue long-sleeve shirts, with conservative red, burgundy, blue, or gray ties.

Mr. Malloy would have been proud of me as I arrived for work (on time) Monday morning, decked out in my fresh new business attire, but I felt like a total idiot. For days I took heavy duty ridicule from my cohorts. But I stuck it out, and, eventually, I became comfortable in my new duds. And the teasing subsided.

*****

September 1978

No one of importance ever made a comment to me about the way I was dressed. Maybe the quick rise that I made in stature, and the tie thing, were just a coincidence. Maybe not.

Not a month after I put on a tie, I received a call into Mr. Fairman's office. Mr. Fairman was a kind old fellow, but as a typical engineer, he was very thorough and tolerated *no* mistakes. Therefore, he was naturally intimidating to his underlings. Upon exiting his office, it was standard practice to flash your armpits to your coworkers to demonstrate whether you just got chewed out or not. There was no chewing out this time, however, and he quickly got to the point.

"Do you think, Thomas, that you can handle writing the logic for the transfer line on the Windsor Engine job?"

"Yes, sir, I can," I answered without hesitation.

With no further explanation he spread out engineering drawings onto his too small desk and began to show me what he wanted. He puffed away at his ever-present pipe and directed me for 30 minutes. There was no talk of promotion or a raise, but I didn't mind. I walked out of Mr. Fairman's office with dry armpits and a smile on my face. A design project had been placed in my care, and I had a chance to show my worth.

*****

December 1978

When I received my next call to Mr. Fairman's office, there were no thank yous for doing a decent job on the Windsor Engine project, but that was not expected. I knew he was satisfied with my work, because he immediately gave me my next assignment, and it was a beauty.

"Are you ready to head up a project, young man?" he asked without cracking a smile.

My eyes widened a bit, but I tried to contain my excitement. "Yes, sir, I am," I responded without emotion.

"We have here an interesting project for Eldon Axle," he began. "It involves a Modicon 484 Programmable Controller. It's a new product that you'll have to learn."

Holy cow! I thought. *This is my big chance.* "Will I go to Modicon school?" I asked.

"No!" Mr. Fairman said. "We don't have time for that. I have here the instruction manuals you'll need ..."

Forty minutes later, emerging from the Fairman Sweatbox, I stepped outside of his door and looked around the engineering room. I caught the eye of Angela, who had been watching for my exit. Then I smiled smugly, adjusted my tie, and strutted boastfully back to my area – the Modicon manuals proudly in my possession.

Once again there had been no mention of promotion or more pay, but I didn't mind. I had been given the lead in an important project, and I was a happy camper.

*****

January 1979

The Eldon Axle project was coming along just fine when my two-year anniversary at APS arrived. Engineers were earning about $12 per hour then, but I was still at my $9.50 wage. This was reason enough to ask for a meeting with Mr. Fairman.

"I can probably get you hired directly here, Tom, if that's what you want," he said. "But I can't get you paid $12. That's how much seasoned engineers get."

I squirmed a bit in my seat, stuck as I was between the window at my back and Mr. Fairman's desk. I asked him, "How much can you get me then?"

Mr. Fairman sat back in his chair and tried to light his pipe as he thought through my question. "Ten dollars, tops," he said with a puff. "It wouldn't be fair to the others to pay you any more than that."

"But I'm doing the same work as the so-called *seasoned engineers*," I insisted. "Maybe even *better* than them. Do you agree with that?"

He re-lit his pipe and took a few puffs before answering. "Maybe," he said as he wobbled his head a bit. Then he wagged his pipe at me and smirked, "Except for Bruce. You don't think you're as good as Bruce, do you?"

Okay," I said. "I'll give you that one. Maybe I'm only your *second-best* designer. But isn't that enough to warrant *$12*?

"Perhaps it should be, Tom, but the pay scales are set for us at the home office in New York. They're based more on education and seniority than anything else."

I understood what Mr. Fairman was telling me. Regardless of the work I was doing, I did not qualify for the position I wanted. I had no college degree and I had only two years' experience. I began to question if I should even try to be hired by APS.

"What if I remain a contractor?" I asked. I waited for a response through a few more puffs.

"I could probably get you $10.50," Mr. Faiman finally said. "If you remain a contractor, that is."

A dollar would have been a huge raise for me, but I resisted. I pretended to think it over for a minute, then I asked the question I had planned from the beginning. "Could I contract myself here, Mr. Fairman?"

"Whoa! I don't think so," he said, sitting back deeply into his chair. "At any rate, you'd have to talk with my boss Mr. Pritchley about that."

Chief Engineer Chuck Pritchley was about a decade younger than Mr. Fairman. Even though his office was next to the department I worked in, other than an occasional *hello* or *good morning*, I'd never spoken to the man. By the time of our meeting, though, he had obviously spoken to Mr. Fairman about me.

"Come in. Come in, Thomas," he said. "Have a seat. I know what you're looking for, and we really can't do it."

I shook his strong hand and tried to hold his gaze for a moment, but he quickly retreated to his chair behind his desk. He crossed his legs and put his hands behind his head. "Go ahead, have a seat," he said, nodding to the appropriate guest chair.

"I know we have a couple of guys who have contracted themselves here at APS," he began. "But it's really a pain in the ass and we really shouldn't do that again. You can't just do it as an individual, you know. In your own name, that is. It's a federal government thing, because of withholding taxes and such. The rules to be an independent contractor are so tough anymore. It's best to just *not* do it. Besides, if I were to let you do it, then others would want to as well. And that's not the way APS wants to do things, you know. We'd like to have you as a direct employee, though, Tom. Wouldn't that work out best for all of us?" He took his hands down from behind his head, uncrossed his legs, leaned forward on his desk, and waited for my reply.

I let a few awkward silent seconds pass between us before I spoke. I absently wiped my lips, looked away for a moment, then looked back at him. Then I said unemotionally, "I'll save you money."

Upon hearing this, Mr. Pritchley sat back in his chair again, re-crossed his legs, and put his hands back behind his head. "How much?" he asked.

"Two bucks," I said instantly. "I'll work for two dollars *less* than you're paying Progressive Engineering for me right now. And I'll form a company so you can pay the company instead of me."

He thought about what I said for about three seconds, nodded his head *yes*, and said, "Okay. Write me a proposal and I'll get you a purchase order."

At that I jumped up from my seat, thrust my hand into his, and said, "Yes, sir, Mr. Pritchley. Thank you very much."

Skipping merrily back to my work area, I leaned over Angela's drawing board, and answered her inquiring eyes. "I think I did pretty well," I said with an enormous grin. "But, do you know what a *purchase order* is?"

*****

The day I had my big meeting with Mr. Pritchley also happened to be a racquetball night. Every Wednesday after work a league of 15 of us went to the Farmington Racquet Club for an hour of vicious competition. Afterwards we would always go together to a local bar for food and beer. After playing that night, however, I made plans to meet my wife and kids for a family dinner at Fonte De Amore, our favorite Italian restaurant.

"Oh man, these calamari are great!" I said as I dug into the appetizer. "Wait'll I tell you what happened at work today." I talked and ate, and talked, and ate.

"Boy Tom," my wife said. "You're actin' like you never ate before."

"Well," I said with a chunk of ossobuco on my fork, "we don't exactly eat like this every day, you know. Maybe we should start cooking like this at home?"

Nancy responded, forlornly, "You know I can't cook like this."

"Neither can I," I said with my mouth full. "But we can learn, can't we?"

"You can try if you want, Tom," my wife answered sincerely. "But I sure don't know when you'd find the time."

"How about if I buy the ingredients and you cook it for us?"

"No way."

"It can't be that hard, honey, if my ex-wife could do it," I foolishly added.

She folded her arms and shot daggers at me with her eyes. "I hate it when you compare me to her," she growled. "Maybe you should have stayed married to her if that's what you want."

"Oh man. I'm sorry I said anything, honey. It's just that I'd like to eat better at home. Wouldn't you?"

"I don't think that's it at all," she said with a sneer. "You just want to change me, that's all."

I put my fork down and absently moved Dennis's chocolate milk away from the edge of the table. "Why does wanting us to *grow* together always have to mean I want to *change* you? Don't you like to accomplish new things?"

"It's obvious, Tom, I'm not good enough for you anymore. You always want to change me. First you want me to quit smoking. Then you want me to quit drinking. Now you want me to cook like your ex-wife." She grabbed her wine glass a little too forcefully, spilling a bit as she did, and emptied it in one quaff. "I like my life just the way it is," she spat out, refolding her arms, and looking away. "I don't want to change what I am."

Knowing the conversation was going in the wrong direction, I had to get off the subject. "Forget I said anything, sweetheart," I said with a smile. "I love you just the way you are. I wouldn't change one hair on your pretty little head." I reached across the table for her hand. "Now … what would you like for dessert, dear?"

She turned back to me, unfolded her arms, and smiled in return. Taking my offered hand, she then replied, "Jamie and I will split a cannoli, thank you."

*****

For sure Nancy had no desire to learn how to cook, but she took a keen interest in my new business idea. Not that she wanted to work at anything, but since I was going to form another company, then she very much wanted to be my partner.

"So," she said with enthusiasm the next morning as she watched me dress for work. "You're going to be a business owner again. That's exciting!"

"It's not exactly like that, honey," I said, putting on my tie. "It's just a way for APS to *pay* me instead of making me an employee."

Ignoring what I had just explained to her, she bounced on the bed like a little kid. She asked me with a big smile, "Are you going to make me your partner, mister?"

"You *are* my partner, sweetheart," I said, bending over for my goodbye kiss. "We're married, remember?"

She grabbed my tie and pulled me onto the bed beside her. After planting a long juicy kiss onto my lips, she pressed her body to mine, and whispered softly into my ear. "Then I'll own half the company, right?"

I glanced through her perfumed hair to the bedroom clock. Dennis and Jamie were still sleeping, and I didn't have to leave for work for another 10 minutes.

"Well," I said as I began to loosen my tie. "A husband and wife ought to have equal status on certain things, I suppose. But we only have nine minutes left, so can we talk about this later?"

*****

During the next few days, with the help of an attorney, Nancy and I registered a business partnership in the County of Wayne, in the State of Michigan, that we called *Concord Design*. The word *Concord* means "harmony," and it was also a supersonic airplane, and I liked the way it sounded. I then created a proposal from our newly formed venture to Mr. Pritchley at APS, offering the engineering services of Thomas VanBuren at the bargain rate of $12 per hour.

Two weeks later, on February 12, 1979, I received my first-ever purchase order for Concord Design. More correctly I should say, Nancy and I received *our* first purchase order.

~

Chapter 27   *Opportunity*

April 1979

Concord Design was originally started simply as a way for APS to avoid hiring me directly. Very soon, however, other opportunities opened. APS was looking to bring in some temporary engineering people to help get them through a busy period. I knew the procedure, that's how I came to work there two years earlier. So I asked Mr. Fairman if he would consider contracting some detailers for his department through my company.

"Who are these people?" Mr. Fairman asked as he looked up from a pile of papers.

Standing in front of his desk as if holding my hat in my hands, I answered, "Friends of mine, sir."

"Have a seat, Thomas," he said as he sat back in his chair. "Tell me what you have in mind."

"They know how to draw, Mr. Fairman," I began as I sat down on the edge of the chair. "But they've never worked in our field before. I'd train them, though, at my home, with everything they'd need to know to be productive here on their very first day. And I can get them to you for $10."

Mr. Fairman knew a good deal when he heard one. He never hesitated. "When can you have them ready?" he asked.

"When do you need them, sir? And how many?"

"I need four pencils here as soon as I can get them for about six months. I don't see why I can't use your people as well as anyone else's. They need to know Allen Bradley controllers, though."

"I can teach them that easily enough," I said, trying to conceal my excitement. "Then I offered the nearly impossible: "I can have two detailers here on Monday, and two more a week from Monday."

My boss reached absently for his pipe and lighter, but he never took his eyes off mine. "Okay, fine," he said after a few moments. "Get me a written proposal with their names and billing rates, and I'll get you a written purchase order."

"Really?" I asked stupidly.

"Yes, really," he said with a raised eyebrow. "But don't wait for the written purchase order to get going. Consider this a *verbal order* for four detailers at 10 bucks per hour to start no later than a week from Monday. Get them here as soon as you can, though. One or two at a time is okay."

"Yes, sir. Yes, sir," I said, as I hastily shook his hand. I tried to leave, but he didn't loosen his grip.

"And make damn sure," he said while holding my gaze, "that they can draw a good line, and that they know what the hell they're looking at."

Hastening out of his office I wondered why it had been so easy. *I'd never employed anyone before, but it couldn't be that difficult,* I figured.

On my way home that evening I stopped *at* Robert Stein Accounting Service on Farmington Road and asked for some emergency consultation. Two hours later – and $150 lighter – I walked out with enough information and supplies to *get going* as Mr. Fairman had suggested.

By that weekend I had managed to hire and train two young friends of my wife's family. Monday morning – wearing white shirts and ties – Gary Rontain and Barry McDonald began working at APS as the first two employees of Concord Design.

The next two hires were a little more difficult, as I didn't know anyone else looking for work. I placed a help wanted ad in the *Livonia Observer* similar to the one I had answered two years prior. After fielding phone calls for three days, I interviewed four experienced draftsmen in the APS parking lot after work, and I hired the best two. The following Monday – fulfilling the purchase order – Ross Tomitter and Rod Grandon began working as Concord Design employees' number three and four.

July 1979

Meanwhile, Chuck Pritchley, the man who had allowed me to set up Concord Design in the first place, had left APS for a similar position at crosstown rival, Spalding Automation. I had heard that Spalding was terribly busy and were looking for outside engineering sources. It seemed to me an appropriate time for me to give Mr. Pritchley a call.

I offered Concord Design as a moonlighting crew for any engineering overflow that Spaulding might have. Mr. Pritchley only had one concern. "How much can you handle, Thomas, just working part time?"

"Well," I responded, "there are five of us now, and I can get Al Everett and Jim Abbeville too. So that's at least 70 hours per week."

"I see, I see," he said. "Well, I do have a ton of work here, and you guys would be perfect for it. So, yeah, I'll give you a couple of stations. When can you come and see me?"

*****

August 1979

The money started to flow – not vast amounts, mind you, but enough for Nancy and me to buy the little house we had been renting. Then, of course, came a new Pontiac Grand Prix for myself, and a white Camaro with t-tops for my sexy partner.

Chuck Pritchley was more than pleased with the two stations Concord Design had done for Spaulding. The evening I delivered the approval drawings to him, he was alone in the building. He broke out a couple of cold beers from the little fridge behind his desk.

"Would you be interested in a larger project, Tom?" he asked.

"Yes, of course I would, Chuck," I answered. "But how large?"

He took a swig and a deep breath, then said, "You know we got the St. Lawrence 3.6 Engine Line. Well, I'd like to give the *whole damn thing* to you."

I almost lost a mouthful of beer! *He couldn't possibly have meant what I thought I'd just heard. The entire line?* I didn't even try to hide my surprise. I sat in stunned silence with my eyes wide, staring at the man behind his big oak desk, with his legs crossed and his hands behind his head.

"What's the matter, Thomas?" he asked with a grin. "Cat got your tongue?"

"Uhhh, uhhhh," I stammered. "How many years do you have to get this project done, Chuck?"

"Oh, it's about the same as usual, I suppose – six or eight months."

I began to gain back some of my composure. I said, half to my beer and half to no one, "We could never do it part-time then, could we?"

"No," he said emphatically, regaining my attention. "Part-time would not cut it. But I figured maybe it's time for you to expand a bit."

Still dumbfounded, "I see," was all I could produce.

"You would need your own shop, for sure," he said. "You'd probably have to take one of the heavies with you too, like Al or Jim. That might piss off APS. But they'd get over it, I suppose. What do you think?"

I didn't respond for a moment, but the gears were turning in my head. Shuffling in my seat and running fingers through my hair, I then said, "I think you're right Chuck. They wouldn't miss me all that much. After all, they could have hired me had they wanted to – but they didn't. If I take Jim or Al, though," I said, shaking my head. "That'd be different. I'm doing well with the six guys I have working there now. I'd hate to mess that up."

"That's not going to last forever, Tom," Chuck responded. "As soon as there's a slowdown at APS, your guys will be the first to go.

203

Eventually you'll be needing something else for them to do. If you have any long-term thoughts for Concord Design, you'll need more than just *one* customer."

*****

I didn't just jump into that new opportunity with blazing guns. I gave the idea some heavy thought. There wasn't much time to make up my mind, though. Chuck wanted an answer in a week, or he'd have to look elsewhere. I knew I had to talk with my partner about it.

"I don't care what you do, Tom," my wife said with a smile during our drive home from Thursday evening breakfast at Denny's. *"Go for it!"*

Turning on to Ann Arbor Trail I steered around a family of Mallard ducks waddling down the street. "But I might be walking away from a secure position for nothing but a pipe dream."

"What's a pipe dream?" Nancy asked unfeigned.

Giving her a funny look, I said, "You know what I mean, blondie. What if it doesn't work out well? We could spend all our money getting set up to do this one job and then what if I can't find any more work? What would you think of me then, if I went broke in a year?"

"You're not going broke, silly. You gotta make my Camaro payments, remember?"

Yes, I did *remember* the Camaro payments, and lots of other payments too, but there were other things on my mind. *Was it wise for me to risk what we already had going on, for only the possibility of gain? Would I be biting off more than I could chew? Would an opportunity like this ever come again?* It was useless to ask my wife these questions, I knew, so the next Sunday afternoon, I went to see my dad.

"Boy, Tom," my dad said as we all sat around the big yellow kitchen table. "You know better than I do whether you can make a go

204

of this or not. I don't even understand how you learned this stuff in the first place," he said, shaking his head. "But if they're willing to give you this big order, then you *must* know what you're doing!"

"Yes, Pop-o, I know what I'm doing, technically, but that's not enough. I still have to get the work done somehow – and on time. And I'd have to put out a lot of money beforehand and hope that the project comes in under budget. All sorts of terrible things can happen, you know. I could easily lose money, particularly on the first project. And I really can't afford to take any losses. I'd be bankrupt and out of work at 32 years old. How would that be doing right by my family?"

Dad sat quietly, along with Pauly and Dennis, listening to my long-winded dissertation. Jamie sat, not so quietly, impatiently waiting for her dinner. I dished out food for all of us from the buckets of Kentucky Fried Chicken I had brought for the occasion. The food was at least better than the Hamburger Helper we would have suffered through had we stayed home with Mommy.

"On the other hand," I carried on, "this could be a springboard to something really good. I can imagine myself at the head of a large engineering firm someday. I don't have a college degree, so it's not likely anyone will ever pay me much to work for them. My best chance for success – perhaps my only chance – is through business, *my* business.

"I can't expect opportunities like this to come along every day either," I continued, chomping on a big juicy thigh. "Anyone can buy a building and put up a sign, you know. But how often does one get the chance to open up a shop on the first day with a $100,000 order in his hip pocket?"

"It seems to me, Tomaso," my dad said, scooping out more mash potatoes, "that you're young enough and smart enough to overcome a setback if things don't work out perfectly. But man, I'd never have had the nerve to try something like this myself, I can tell you that. Not with a houseful of kids."

*****

That was it then. I had my dad's blessing, it seemed; even though he never would have done it himself. I had my wife's blessing too – as long as I made her car payments. My own ambition was none too small, but I knew that no matter what, I could deliver a good product. The worst that could happen then is that I'd lose a little money and be out of a job.

My overriding reason, though, for choosing the path I took was that I couldn't stand the thought of someday having to look back and wonder what might have been – if only. In the end, all I could see was an opportunity that should not be squandered.

The next day I gave my two weeks' notice at APS. They made no effort to get me to stay. I then accepted the purchase order from Spaulding Automation.

Lives changed.

~

Chapter 28   *Partners*

October 1979

Somehow, two years slipped by since I had last seen my daughters Kristen and Amy. We had sat in the park by the shores of Lake Huron when I told them about my new girlfriend. So very much had taken place since then:

- o   A migration to North Carolina and back.
- o   Nancy and I got married.
- o   I adopted Dennis.
- o   Twice, I went in front of Judge McLean about my ex-wife.
- o   I made the decision *not* to go through with police-escorted visitation.
- o   My mother passed away.
- o   Jamie was born.
- o   I quit my job and started Concord Design.

For the last year and a month, Mr. Wyatt consistently predicted Kathy would cave in any day now, due to the money squeeze we continued to apply. But that hadn't happened yet.

Through it all I carried with me a heavy grudge and a terrible ache for the loss of my two older children. But my mother had directed me to put what I couldn't help into God's capable hands, and give my best to my new life – so that's what I tried to do.

*****

Before my two weeks' notice at APS had even expired, I had taken a one-year lease on some nice office space on Grand River Avenue in downtown Farmington. Then came the purchase of drawing boards, desks, tables and chairs, filing cabinets, office machines, telephones and, of course, the staffing of people.

Inside of a month we looked like a genuine engineering firm, and we were busy, busy, busy. The only thing we lacked to make the organizing complete was a blueprint machine of our own, but I was out of money.

"I guess I'm going to have to sell your Camaro, honey," I teased my wife one evening at the dinner table.

"Bullshit you are!" she countered, not really seeing the humor in my comment.

Scooping out the potato-and-cheese-flavored Hamburger Helper, I thought I'd push her button a bit more, just for the fun of it. "We've got to have a blueprint machine, you know, *partner*. And I don't see where you really need a car. We can buy another one for you in a year or two, though."

"Ha, you're a funny boy, Tom."

"Yeah, Daddy," Dennis parroted, "you're a funny boy."

"Oh, so you think I'm funny, do you?" I said to Dennis with a wink. "Well, this is between your mother and me, pal. So, you just butt out of it. And get your sleeve out of your applesauce, will ya?"

"So, where *are* you gonna get the money from, Tom?" my wife demanded. Before I could respond, she added, "You shoulda thought of this beforehand, ya know."

Getting defensive, I quickly came back with, "I *did* think of this beforehand. I always knew raising money to get started would be difficult. What did *you* expect?"

Her face contorted as she slammed her fork down and wailed, *"I never expected to have my car taken from me!* That's for sure!"

"Don't get your underwear in a wad, dearie," I said with a smile. "I'm just kidding about the car."

At the mention of underwear, Dennis began chuckling. His mother shot him a look, however, that cut him off mid-giggle.

"No, I don't think you're kidding at all. I know you, Tom," she said quite adamantly, jabbing a finger into her own chest. "It's a good thing I own half the company, or you'd have *everything* screwed up."

Her words cut deep. She had never taken issue with anything I'd done in business before. And when did she start thinking I was incompetent? I blinked in disbelief. "Is that really what you think of me?"

She never answered my question. Instead, she stared through me for a full 20 seconds, expressionless, something of greater importance on her mind. Then she spoke softly with little emotion.

"I'm pregnant."

*****

The next few weeks Nancy hardly spoke with me at all. She was clearly unhappy about the pregnancy, but she wouldn't say why. Naturally, we both had questions, but the more I pushed her for discussion on the matter, the more she pushed me away.

Personally, I was thrilled with the idea, and I told her so. "I'm so ready for another baby, honey," I beamed. "I couldn't be happier."

My with-child wife, a cigarette in hand and beer on the table, sat on the end of the blue velour sofa pretending to read a book. "I told you I don't want to talk about it, Tom," she replied coldly without looking up from her reading. "Now go away."

"Okay, Nance," I said pacing in front of a drift of smoke. "I don't want to upset you. I won't try to get you to talk. But I have a few things to say, and I'd like you to at least listen. It won't take long. Is that alright?"

She cast her eyes to me for one second, which I took as a signal of her approval. Carefully I took a seat beside her.

"Whatever your apprehensions are, honey," I began. "I'll try to understand, whenever you want to tell me. In the meantime, I want you to know how I feel."

I smiled broadly. "I think you and I are the luckiest people on Earth. We have each other, and we're gonna have another baby!"

209

Getting no reaction, I continued. "Dennis is 6 years old now and Jamie's 18 months. It's the perfect time for our next baby. *Absolutely* perfect.

"I know it's easy for me to say, cuz I go to work every day and leave you with the feeding and the diapers. But this is what we said we wanted when we got married, and I'm *so* excited!"

Nancy, still staring blankly at her book, gave no hint of a response. The cigarette smoldered beside her. I couldn't help but ask a question.

"Won't you tell me how you feel, sweetheart?"

At that she turned slowly to face me. "I knew you wouldn't do what you said, you never do. I told you I'm *not* going to talk about this, Tom. I'm just not, get it through your fat head ... now please go away!"

*****

Having been cut out of my wife's thoughts and deprived of her company, I poured myself single-mindedly into my work. But even with me and the whole staff working 10 hours, 7 days a week, we began to fall behind schedule. We needed another designer on the job, but there wasn't enough money in the project to pay for one. It seemed that either we were going to be late delivering (which would hurt Concord's chances for future work), or we were going to lose money on the project. Neither possibility was good.

Nancy had little sympathy for me when I tried to discuss the situation with her. It only served to distress her all the more. "You shoulda thought of this beforehand, blockhead," she told me.

*****

November 15, 1979

Six weeks after we had opened our doors, Concord Design still needed a blueprint machine. But, more importantly, we needed to get our designing done faster. I telephoned an old friend and co-worker from APS, Jim Abbeville, and asked him to meet me for lunch at Ginopolis's.

Jim was a few years older than I: a tall, lanky, quiet guy with a handsome face and quick smile. He had been in engineering for two decades, as opposed to my two years. I really needed his talents. After an hour of hamburgers, beer, and reminiscing, I finally got to the point of the meeting.

"I need some help, Jim, ole buddy. We're falling behind on the Saint Lawrence project. Would you be interested in some moonlighting work?"

Sitting up straighter on the bench seat, he answered, "Maybe," then ordered two more beers with just a look at the waitress. "I've been hoping you'd ask me."

My eyes widened and I swallowed hard to avoid spitting out a mouthful of Labatt Blue. "Really?" I asked.

"Yeah, really," he answered calmly.

"The problem is, Jim, I can't pay you till we get paid from Spalding, which … could be a while."

He emptied the rest of his stein. "Oh, that's not a problem, Tom. I can wait to be paid, but I'm interested in more than just a moonlighting job."

"You are? You want to work for Concord?"

"Well, yeah, but I don't want to just work for Concord. I want to own it."

That shocked me, and I spoke through a smirk. "If you're saying you want to buy my company, pal, it's not for sale."

"I don't want to pay for it, dummy, and I don't want the whole company." He cradled his empty stein in both hands. "Why don't you make me your partner, Tom, and I'll come and bail you out on the Saint Lawrence Project."

"Holy shit!" I said loudly. Just then the waitress sat down two new beers at our table. She gave me an odd look for my outburst but said nothing and walked away. "I'm ... I'm honored, Jim," I continued. "How long have you been thinking like this?"

"Ever since you announced you got the Spalding Order. I've been watching you, and waiting for a chance to move in. I've always wanted to own my own business, you know."

"No, I didn't know that about you, Jim. But if that's so, why don't you just start your own?"

Jim held out the palms of his hands as if he were hefting a couple of bowling balls. "I don't have the coconuts you do, Tom," he said with a smile. "It's not so easy, you know. But you've done it! And I'm jealous. So, if I can weasel my way in, that's what I want to do." He was still smiling, but deadly serious.

"But I can't offer you one iota of security, Jim," I protested. "We only have this one single order. You'd leave APS for that?"

"You bet I would, buddy. I'm not the least bit worried about future work. That'll be easy," he said with a dismissive wave of his hand. "You've already done the hard part. You got the ball rolling."

Holy shit I said again that time to myself. But I knew Jim could read my lips. *This could be the answer to all my problems* I thought. *This could make everything work.*

Looking him carefully in the eyes, I said, "We have a lot to talk about, pardzy. Let's get more beer."

*****

Over the next two weeks Jim and I worked out the details of his partnership, and we hired a business attorney to put things into legal order. An appointment was made for Tuesday afternoon to sign the final papers in the attorney's office.

I had not discussed the matter with my wife – it was easier that way. But since she was half owner of Concord, it was necessary to bring her to the signing.

The kids were already asleep, and Nancy was in the bathroom with the door open getting ready for bed, when I arrived home late Monday night. Standing in the hallway, without even saying hello, I declared. "I need you to come with me to the attorney's office tomorrow, honey, to sign some papers."

She didn't bother to turn around. "What kind of papers?" she asked.

"Stock certificates and stuff. Remember Jim Abbeville?"

"Yeah," she answered, rifling through the junk drawer looking for toothpaste.

"Well," I said proudly, "I'm making him a partner in Concord. Isn't that cool?"

She froze in mid-search. Suddenly, I had her undivided attention. She looked quizzically at me. "What are you talking about, Tom?"

"Jim Abbeville," I said, as if that explained everything. "He's coming to work at Concord to help us with the Saint Lawrence job. The project I'm stuck on. Remember?"

"No, I don't member," she said, shaking her toothbrush at me. "You haven't talked to me about business for two months now, you know."

"Really?" I responded in surprise. "Two months? That's not true, but you've been keeping track?"

"Yeah, I'm keeping track. We've hardly talked about anything since I told you I was pregnant, two months ago."

I felt the heat rising in my face, threw my hands in the air, and said way too loudly, *"You act as if that's my fault, woman!"*

"Shhhhhh, bonehead," she hissed. "You're standing right next to Jamie's bedroom."

213

My arms akimbo, I lowered my voice to a less abusive level. "You haven't exactly been easy to talk to, you know. You've been a real snot. How many times did you tell me to go away?"

"I never told you not to talk business with me."

"Maybe not, but you're pregnant. I haven't wanted to get you riled up, so I avoided business-related conversations with you."

She thrust her head left and right like an Egyptian. "Oh," she sassed, "so you admit purposely not talking business with me?"

"Well ... yeah, I suppose so," I said, calming down as I loosened my tie. "But what do you care about the business anyway? It's not like you're involved in anything." Then I looked both ways down the hallway. "Do you know where my slippers are?"

"I thought I was your partner?" She spoke to my back as I disappeared into our bedroom and flicked on the light.

Turning around, I poked my head back out the doorway and peered down the hallway at my wife poking her head out at me. "You *are* my partner," I said with an almost straight face. "But you're just a woman."

"Ooooooh, you bastard!" she shot back good-naturedly, and ran at me with fists clenched. I dove onto the bed and covered my head to protect myself. She piled on and pummeled me viciously with a pillow. "How dare you patronize me, you condescending moron!"

"Oh! oh! Cut it out!" I begged, struggling to get hold of her arms. Then, with the barrage under control, I took note of the complex sentence she had just used to admonish me. Still holding her at bay, I said smart-alecky, "You use too many big words, woman."

"Ooooooh, you bastard!" she said again, this time using her legs to punish me.

Our first physical contact in two months was more than either of us could contain. Our playing soon gave way to urgently needed passion.

Afterwards, she lay peacefully on my chest and spoke softly to the darkness beside her. "Don't ever do that again," she said softly.

"Do what?"

"Ignore me for two months. Not touch me for two months. That's what."

I agreed, and we fell asleep.

*****

December 3, 1979

Awakening the next morning for work, I was on top of the world. It was my 32nd birthday, the ice had been broken with my wife, and our business affairs were about to change for the better.

Returning from the shower, glancing at my spouse rising peacefully from her sleep, I wished I didn't have to open the shop in 40 minutes. "Oh man," I said, rubbing my hands together. "I can't wait to get home tonight, sexy lady. I'm going to take full advantage of your newly plump body."

She gave me a teasing smile.

Picking my clothes from the closet I said, "I'll run by the house at 1:30 this afternoon to pick you up for the 2 o'clock appointment. I'm sure it's okay for us to bring Jamie, and Dennis will be in school. But please be ready at 1:30 so we won't be late."

The smile never left her face, and her head never lifted from the pillow, when she calmly asked, "What are you talking about, Tom?"

Standing at the side of the bed in my underwear, I put my hands on my hips and said tersely, "I hate it when you act so stupid. You know damn well what I'm talking about. The appointment with the attorney to sign papers."

Nancy raised up on one elbow, not smiling anymore. "Oh, quit acting like such an asshole. I'm not signing any fucking papers."

"But you have to. Jim's already quit his job. It's too late to stop this now."

215

"Too bad for Jim," she said flippantly. "I'm not going to just give him half the company."

"Oh, so that's what you're thinking." Relieved then that I knew what was bothering her, I sat on the edge of the bed with an understanding smile. "No wonder you're so upset, honey. We're not giving Jim your half of the company. We're giving him one-third. You and I will still own two-thirds, together."

She abruptly sat up and narrowed her eyes. "One-third, two-thirds, what's the fucking difference, bonehead? I'm not gonna let you replace me with Blurbyville."

"No, no, no!" I said, jumping up, losing patience. "I'm not trying to replace you with anybody, Nance. You and I are taking on a partner, that's all."

She shook her head. "I'm not giving away the company, Tom."

Angry then, I grabbed a shirt and said through my teeth, "That's not what I'm doing, dumbbell. You're not listening to me. But I don't have time to explain it now. You're just gonna have to trust me." Buttoning my shirt, I tried to speak more calmly. "I'm sure, honey, when you understand what we're doing here ... you'll agree."

"Maybe I will, Tom, after you explain it to me – you buttoned your shirt wrong, bozo. But I'm not gonna sign any papers today just cuz you're saying so."

"No?"

"No!"

"Don't you trust me?"

"I guess not."

~

Chapter 29   *Trust*

Walking into the lobby that wintry day, I could see my attorney through his open door. It was a few minutes before 2; Jim had not yet arrived. The receptionist took my coat and bid me to please have a seat. Having no idea how the meeting was going to play out, I was more than a little embarrassed to be present without my wife.

Dave Traipak and I did not know each other well then, that being only our third or fourth meeting. However, I already had a sense that he would be of great value to me someday. Despite his average appearance, everything about Dave stood out as competent and correct. His eyes had a smile when he spoke – which was often – and his voice was honest and reassuring.

"Will your wife be along soon, Tom?" he asked.

I stood up to greet him and was about to answer his question, when Jim walked in stomping the snow off his feet. "Hi Tom," he said. "Hi Dave. Where's Nancy?"

"She's not going to be here today," I answered to both. "Can we go inside?"

Dave stretched his arms out to corral us toward the hallway. "Sure, sure," he said. "Let's go into the conference room. Right this way fellas. Julie, would you bring us coffee, please?"

I started explaining before we even arranged ourselves around the big walnut table. "Nancy's being stubborn," I said. "I didn't tell her about this until last night – dummy that I am. She's confused about some things. It's going to take me a while to explain it to her."

Irritated, Jim furrowed his brow. "Why didn't you cancel the meeting, Tom? I've got other things I could be doing?"

"Because I need this time with the two of you, Jim. I have some of my own questions."

Dave spoke up then, "What's the problem, Tom?"

"Nancy doesn't want to sign anything, Dave, until she understands exactly what she's signing and approves of it."

"Well, that's reasonable, isn't it?"

"It *is* reasonable for her to want to know what she's signing of course. The approval part is a problem, though. She just doesn't have the capacity to make levelheaded business decisions, and I should *not* have to have her involved in that."

Dave sat up straighter and clasped his hands in front of himself on the well-polished table. "I'm puzzled, then, Thomas. If you don't want her input, why did you make her a partner in the first place?"

Gathering my thoughts, I absently moved the papers around the table in front of me, then answered. "It was meant as a way for her to inherit any wealth that might be there in case of my death, like having both names on the deed to a house. I never expected, though, for her to work for the company, or to be an advisor, or a director. Now, I'm in this spot where I need her permission to do something, and I'm not sure I can get it. And, even if she gives her okay this time, what about the next time? And the next?"

Jim took my words in with great interest, but he only listened. By the time I had finished speaking, however, Dave already had a plan.

"Since we're restructuring Concord Design anyway," he began, "while we're at it, we can get your wife out of a voting position and still protect her interests."

Then it was my turn to sit up straighter in my chair. "You can do that?"

"Of course. We can structure the corporation how it probably should have been in the first place – only this time we'll include Jim."

Dave had Jim's attention then too. "How's that?" he asked.

"One-third of the stock will be issued to you, Jim, and two-thirds will go to you, Tom, not to you and Nancy, just to you. That'll take Nancy out of the *liability position* she's in right now."

"How does she have a liability position, Dave?" I asked.

"She's currently an officer of Concord Design, which means, whether she's active in the business or not, she has certain fiduciary responsibilities, for which she can be held accountable."

"You use too many big words, Dave," I said with a smirk. "What's a fiduciary responsibility?"

"Fiduciary is law involving *trust*. The best example is employee-withholding money. That money belongs to the employees, not the company. Yet the company has an obligation to collect and distribute the funds. The company, therefore, is *trusted* with other people's money. If those funds are somehow mishandled, even if by mistake or by others, all the officers can be charged with an offense."

Julie carried in a tray of coffee and cups and silently poured three servings while Dave continued. "For Nancy's sake, Tom, you should get her out of that position. We can create documents, which will, upon your death, transfer your assets to her, but at the same time leave the liabilities in the corporation for Jim. That'll also end the issue of you needing her signature for company business."

"Wow!" I said with a huge grin. "That sounds perfect." My grin quickly faded, though, as I realized the next impossible task. I stared vacantly at nothing and asked, "How the hell am I ever going to explain this mumbo jumbo to my bubble-headed wife?"

Jim nodded his head as if he had the very same question I had. We both looked at our attorney, praying he had an answer.

Dave sat back with cheerful eyes and took a sip of coffee. "That shouldn't be so difficult," he said. "She may just need to feel that someone is looking out for her too. It may just be a matter of showing her that she's *my* client every bit as much as you two are. I'm bound by my profession to look after all of you equally, you know." He displayed a reassuring smile. "I'll have a talk with her if you like."

*****

219

That same night I took the new plan to my bride. I kissed the back of her neck as she was loading the dishwasher. "Hi honey," I said. "How's it going?"

She looked at me quizzically. "Aren't you mad at me for not signing those papers today?"

I smiled like a Cheshire cat playacting a snake. "You thought I was angry with you?" I spoke. "Why ever would you think that my dear?"

Not taking the bait, she rolled her eyes and asked, "Do you want any of this food before I throw it out?"

"No thank you, sweetheart," I said, nearly choking on my own syrup. "I've already eaten at the club. May I help you with the dishes?"

"Alright, what do you want from me Tom?" she said. "I'm not signing those fucking papers!"

I took a beer out of the fridge and unloaded myself at the kitchen table. "I'm not worried about those papers, honey," I said in my normal voice. "In fact, I think now we should go in a different direction."

She scowled with contempt. "What are you up to, Tom? I really don't trust you."

"Yes, I know," I responded with sadness. "You said that this morning. When did that start?"

Angrily scraping the leftover dinner into the trash, she looked up and said, "I don't know, Tom. After what you did, trying to get me out of the company and all. I don't think I can ever trust you again. I've been talkin' to everybody today, and they all say *not* to trust you."

Certain that the only people she had been *talkin'* to were her family (the Clampetts), I asked as uppity as I could manage, "Really? Whom have you spoken with, darling?"

She stepped back to the kitchen sink and mumbled, "Nevermind."

"Why don't you talk to our attorney, dear?" I said in all seriousness.

She glanced over her shoulder at me and asked, "What attorney?"

"Dave Traipak."

"He's your attorney, bozo," she said, resuming washing the pots in the sink.

"He's your attorney as well," I said to her back.

"No, he's not."

"Yes, he is … just ask him."

"I don't have to ask him. You just told me you weren't worried about me signing those papers."

I got up from the table and grabbed a towel to start drying. "But I want you to understand things, honey," I pleaded. "And Dave can explain it much better than I can. He's looking out for your best interest, you know." I nodded my head vigorously. "You can trust him."

She did her Egyptian head move. "Oh," she said snottily, "so you admit I can't trust you. What makes you think I would trust your fucking attorney then?"

I threw my towel down in frustration. "Because he's your attorney too, that's why."

"No, he's not!" she said again.

I yelled then in her face. *"Get your own fucking attorney then, if that's what you want, but I need you to sign those goddamn papers!"*

Almost ready to cry then, she thrust her chin forward and spat out in defiance, "See, I *knew* you were lying to me." She threw the sponge into the soapy water and stomped away, leaving me alone with the rest of the cleanup.

"Jesus Christ!" I barked to the empty room and paced around the small area with clenched fists. "How much of this can a man take?"

Every night for the next week, I made earnest, urgent attempts to sway my wife to reason, but to no avail.

"We can't just do nothing about this Blurbyville thing, Nancy," I said to her. "We have to sign papers tomorrow to bring him into the corporation. Will you come with me?"

"No."

"Why the hell not?"

"Never mind."

The next night I tried again. "I made an appointment for you, Nancy, to see Dave Traipak, so he can explain this business move to you."

"I'm not going."

"Why not?"

"Never mind."

"Will you at least, then, let me try to explain it to you?"

"No, I won't, Tom. Will you just forget it?"

Meanwhile, deadlines on the Saint Lawrence project were slipping again, my new partner was getting apprehensive, and my own effectiveness at work dwindled to almost nothing. The way things were, Jim wouldn't stick around much longer, I knew, and without him I was sure to crash and burn. So much, it seemed, hinged on my wife's cooperation. At least until I got her out of a voting position, and time was running out.

"I'm going to give it a final push tonight, Jim," I said as I was leaving work for the day. "I'll get this thing fixed one way or the other."

"Okay, buddy," he responded without looking up from his drawing board. "Good luck."

After dinner, after the kids were put to bed, Nancy clicked on the TV and assumed her usual position on the sofa with a cigarette and a beer.

I boldly walked in, switched off the TV, and announced, "We have to talk, Nancy Jean. Are you in the mood?"

She actually smiled. "I'll talk to you, Tom," she said evenly. "Just not about business. I'm pregnant, ya know. I'm not supposed to get upset. Member?"

It was my first chance in what felt like a long time to be near my bride again, and I was grateful. I slipped in beside her and cuddled her arm. "I do remember, sweetheart," I said warmly, "and I'm very worried about getting your blood pressure up. We should be more conscious of that point."

Sitting up straighter then, I looked into her blue eyes and said, "In fact, honey, I'm not going to yell anymore. I promise, no more yelling." I put my head back on her shoulder. "You and the baby are a million times more important to me than any stupid business deal."

"Good Daddy," she said, patting the top of my head.

Then, I added too quickly, "But we can't just do nothing about Concord Design, honey."

Shrugging my head away, she said stiffly, "Why not, Tom? We've been doing just fine. Why do you have to change things now?"

I smiled, happy at the question, and asked in return, "Do you really want to know?"

Nancy knew she had let her guard down but didn't seem to mind. "Yes, I do, Tom," she answered. "I'm sorry I've been such a bitch. I'll listen to you, but don't expect me to change my mind about signing those papers."

"Fair enough," I said. "I'll even rub your feet while we talk."

She gladly rearranged herself on the sofa to deposit her feet onto my lap, with her head deep in a soft pillow. I took a moment to tenderly stroke her slightly rounded stomach, which I hadn't touched in way too long, before I moved my attention to her feet. After three minutes of massage therapy, I began my spiel to the almost dozing queen.

"There are lots of reasons," I began, "why we need to make some changes in the corporate structure of Concord Design. We expanded our business at a time when we probably shouldn't have ... but we did it ... and we're stuck with that now. We have no real choice but to continue. But we need some help. You know that."

I braced myself for the *you should have thought of that beforehand* remark, but it never came. Her breathing was deep, and her eyelids never moved. I progressed my massaging to her ankles.

"I'm sorry to burden you with all this stress," I continued. "That's not what I meant to do when making you my partner. But from a purely business perspective, there really is no stress at all. The company is in exceptional shape, you know. We have money, we have work, and we have this wonderful opportunity to expand now, at no actual cost. Jim's an incredibly talented guy. He'll allow us to get larger and more profitable projects. He'll earn a lot of money for you and me, for years to come."

Not sure if she was still awake and listening, I tickled the soft spot above her knee cap. "Doooon't," she complained, but never opened her eyes.

"It's important for you to not even think of this stuff anymore, though, honey," I continued. "You've got a new baby to be thinking about. Besides, your business affairs are in the hands of a very competent guy, don't you think?"

Her eyes popped open in questioning disbelief, "Are you talking about Toepak?"

"No, goofball. I'm talking about your husband."

"*You?*" she said pointing a finger at me in sincere surprise. "You think you're copitent?"

Perturbed, I jumped up from the sofa, spilling her feet off my lap, and said loudly, *"Yes, I think I'm copitent!* But the problem we have here, Nancy, is that *you don't.* You've lost confidence in me, and I don't know why."

She swung her feet around and sat up. "I have confidence in you, Tom, but how the hell do you know about stock things, and corporations, and all that stuff?"

"You're right Nance, I'm not knowledgeable in those areas, but that's why we have lawyers and accountants. They don't know how to engineer a machine either, but together we get things done correctly."

I paced the floor looking for a way to continue. "Things have worked out well for us so far," I finally said. "We've raised our standard of living considerably these past three years, haven't we? You've never questioned my ability or sincerity before. What has changed Nancy? Why now?"

Rare tears began to form in my wife's eyes as she choked out her thoughts, "I want to stay your partner, Tom. That's what. Why do you have to trade me in?"

I held my hand out in front of me. "You know I'm not trading you in, Nancy. Don't be silly. Where are you getting that idea from? We need some help in the company is all. Please don't cry, honey, you're stressing out. Without Jim, Concord is going to fail. Then we'll have nothing. We're lucky he's still around the way we've treated him. But we can't dilly dally around any longer, or we'll lose him. Then we'll be screwed."

Tears built in her eyes again. I got on my knees and took her hands into mine. "You and I are partners in every way you can think of, sweetheart," I pleaded. "We're husband and wife. We have two and a half kids together. We love each other. We look out for each other. We're partners, but I need you to trust me with business affairs."

She jerked her hands away from mine. "I *don't* trust you, Tom!" she blurted out, tears no longer evident. "I just *don't* trust you."

Shocked, I stood up. "What do you not trust me to do, woman?" I demanded.

She didn't answer, obviously having no answer. Her expression changed from hurt to anger and back to hurt again.

Furious then, I was completely at my wits end. "I don't know what I did to earn your distrust this way, wife," I stated truthfully. "But we have no more time to debate these matters. "Whether you like it or not, we must sign those papers. Will you agree to that?"

Never one to accept an ultimatum from me, she dug her heels in and stated flatly, "No."

"If you agree to nothing then, woman, understand that you're leaving me no choice but to force you entirely out of the picture."

"Ha!" she roared superiorly. "And how do you think you're going to do that, bozo?"

I turned red-faced and thrust a finger in her ugly mug, forgetting completely my promise not to yell. *"I'll give you Concord Design, that's how,"* I shouted. "You can have it *all* since it means so fucking much to you. I'll start up again … *as Bozo Design* … without you. I'll lose nothing, and you'll lose everything! That's how.

~

Chapter 30   *Ghost*

January 1980

I was not proud of myself, the way I had badgered my hapless wife to get what I wanted, but my threats worked. She signed whatever papers I asked her to, and I was then able to move Concord Design along as required. It was a victory of sorts, but at what cost to our marriage? For the most important things in life, my bride trusted me less than ever. Nancy never asked me another business question, and Dave Traipak never explained a thing to her. She didn't want to know.

On the plus side, however, the ending of the paper-signing standoff served to free Nancy to focus her attention on the new baby. The apprehension she had displayed about being pregnant seemed to vanish overnight, and she enrolled us into a new session of birthing classes. It quickly became clear, though, she had taken me along strictly because of the requirement to bring with her a delivery partner.

The drive home down 8 Mile Road that wintry night following our first birthing class found both Nancy and me in good spirits. Life seemed clear again, untroubled, when suddenly the road ahead, like an explosion in a pillow factory, vanished in a flurry of snow. Gripping the steering wheel with white knuckles, I desperately searched the blinding glare for red tail lights to guide us through the glass of milk.

Nancy, oblivious to the horrendous driving conditions, asked, "Tom, did you notice that Dorothy chick in the front row?"

Not daring to look away from the road for even a second, I answered, "You mean that fat redhead with a girlfriend as a partner?"

"Yeah, that one," she pondered. "So, it's okay then, to *not* have the father as a partner?"

I took a quick glance at my wife. "I'm sure it's okay, Nance," I said. "Perhaps she doesn't know who the father is. Or maybe he doesn't want to do it. Or maybe he's married to someone else. Who knows?"

A few silent moments passed between us as traffic continued at turtle speed. She finally spoke up with what I feared she was working up to. "So, I can have someone else as my partner if I want to?"

"I suppose the hospital would let you have whoever you wanted, Nance, if that's what you're asking."

"Yeah, that's what I'm asking. So why don't I bring Sharon, so you won't have to do it?"

"Have to!?" I barked. "You think this is a chore for me?"

"I know you're busy is all, Tom," she said apologetically. "And I'd like to have my sister helping me, if you don't mind."

My heart sank. It had been a long time, but that old familiar hurt of being excluded from my own family was burning its way back in. "You want your sister with you," I whispered. "Not me?"

Nancy saw the pain in my face, and she knew damn well its cause, but that knowledge did not change her course of action one bit. "It's a girl thing, Tom," she said calmly. "She knows better than you do how to help me."

An incredulous gasp escaped my throat. *"Help you!"* I yelped. "You think the *only* reason for a dad to be in the delivery room is to help the mother?"

Her voice was strong and clear, with no hesitation. *"Yes!* That's exactly why. What else could it be for?"

Incensed, I forgot about the snow and the traffic. "That's *not* how you felt two years ago, dammit!" I screeched. "As far as delivering Jaime, I was no help to you whatsoever, but you wouldn't have traded me then for Mother Teresa and Ben Casey put together!"

"Huh?"

I spoke then, slowly, and deliberately. "You did *not* just want me there as a pain coach, Nancy. You wanted me to experience, *with you*, the birth of our child. Or did I misunderstand your intentions?"

"No, you didn't misunderstand my intentions, bozo, but things were different then." She folded her arms and looked straight ahead for the first time into the blowing snow. "Can you see where you're going?"

"Of course, I can't see where I'm going! What was different then, Nance?"

"Huh?"

"What's different now, Nancy Jean, with this child, than two years ago when you so very much wanted me in the delivery room with you? What has changed?"

Her arms still folded, still looking straight ahead, she took a deep breath and answered. "You cared about me then."

*****

Except for the noise of the storm, the rest of the long, slow trek back was completed in silence. The wind was still howling when we finally arrived home, extremely late. I helped old Mrs. Norman, our babysitter, across the snow-covered street to her little, corner house. Nancy was already in bed pretending to be asleep when I got back in. I knew I'd never be able to sleep if I didn't first fix the bad feelings that we both harbored. I turned on the night light and quietly took a seat on the bed.

I spoke softly. "I know you're weary, honey, but can we talk?"

Without opening her eyes, she asked: "Do I have to stay awake?"

"Can you listen while you sleep?"

"Sure, I can," she said with a yawn. "But why now?"

"Cuz I really feel terrible. Don't you?"

"Yes, I do, but why now?"

"Cuz I just had a talk with my mother, and I thought you might like to hear what she had to say."

Nancy showed no surprise from my statement. "Mrs. Norman only lives across the street, Tom. That musta been a short conversation."

"Not really, she took a walk around the block with me."

"Mrs. Norman?"

"No, silly, my mother."

"So, how'd that happen?"

"Well, at her side door, after saying goodbye to Mrs. Norman, I turned around to come home, and I noticed that the wind had stopped blowing. In fact, it was perfectly still, and incredibly quiet. I took a few steps, and I could hear the snow scrunch under my feet. I like that sound. Nobody was around and, without even thinking about it, I just turned right at the gate, and went crunching into the darkness with my head down and my hands in my coat pockets."

I stopped telling my story long enough to study my wife for signs of life. She took a deep breath and said without stirring, "And your mother went with you?"

"Yes, she sure did," I continued. "I was halfway down the block when I heard her footsteps crunching next to mine. And she said, 'Why the long face, Tommy?'"

"Bullshit."

"No really, honey, she did. But she told me not to expect for you to believe that she was there."

Her eyes popped open upon hearing that, and she sat up in bed and said excitedly, "Oh, I believe she was there, Tom, but she wouldna said, '*Why the long face?*'"

I laughed heartily at that. "See?" I spoke. "When I tell you my long-dead mother just now walked around the block with me, scrunching in the snow, you believed every word of it just because I said it. I love that about you, honey. I really do. But when I tell you about the conversation, you doubt what I say, even if I swear to it."

She looked at me curiously. "I don't get it, Tom. Do you want me to just believe everything you say to me?"

I grew serious then, and answered, "Yes, Nancy, I do."

"But you always teach me to be skeptical, don't you? You always say I should question everything."

"I don't mean for you to question *me*, sweetheart. At least not my honesty, or my love for you. I hate it when you do that. *I hate it!*"

Her head drooped and she stared, lost, at her pillow.

"Not you Nancy!" I added quickly. "I don't hate you. I just hate it when you doubt me so much, when you don't trust me."

"Really?" she asked as her eyes brightened.

"Yes, really."

"So, what'd your mom say?"

"Well," I hesitated for suspense, "she said, *'Why the long face, Tommy?'*"

That time I got a chuckle out of my wife, so I continued. "I told her I had a long face because I was sad. I told her about the new baby coming and all, but she already knew all about that. She was just aglow with happiness about the baby, and she reminded me that this was not an appropriate time for me to be sad. 'You have such a lovely wife and such beautiful children,' she said. 'You really don't have a choice, Thomas. They need *all* of you now, not just part of you.' She said, also, that I shouldn't be always judging others and trying to change them. Then I told her that I was upset because you don't want me with you during the delivery, and ..."

"And what did she say to that?" Nancy interrupted.

"She said," I extended my arms theatrically, *"bullshit!"*

Nancy's eyes widened, and a grin the size of Vermont filled her face. *"Ha!"* she laughed deafeningly. *"Bullshit she said bullshit!"*

"Okay, okay!" I threw my hands up in surrender. "I'm kidding about the *bullshit* part. But she did say that you really do want me with you, and that you're probably just upset with me about something else."

She smiled and bit her lower lip. "See, your mother's pretty smart, Tom."

"Really?"

"Yeah, really."

"Does that mean you *do* want me with you in the delivery room?"

"Of course, I do, dummy."

"Then why did you say what you said?"

"Cuz I'm mad at you for something else, just like your mom said."

I reeled back, dismayed. "But you tore my heart out, Nancy, when you said you wanted to trade me in for Sharon!"

She stuck her chin out unyielding. "See what it's like, Tom?"

I furrowed my brows menacingly and burned a stare deep into her persona. I spoke with my most sonorous voice. "What do you mean by that, woman?"

Unphased by my intimidation act, she answered in good cheer.

"You traded me in for Blurbyville, member?"

~

Chapter 31   *Jessica*

March 31, 1980   Tom 32, Nancy 23, Dennis 7, Jamie almost 2

"I should call Mrs. Norman, Nance, to see if everything's okay at home. Would you be alright without me for a while?"

"Sure."

"But don't you need me here, hon?"

"Tom," she said, not in the best of moods, "I've been having contractions for nine hours now, and I could be going through this bullshit for three more fucking days. I need to know what the kids are up to, and I'm sure Mrs. Norman would like to know what's going on here, too. So, go, please."

"But, if I can't get back in 12 minutes, you'll be having another contraction, and I won't be here to help you. I better wait till later."

"Later I may be in the delivery room, bozo." She dabbed the sweat off her own forehead with a towel. "When are they going to give me that goddamn epi-thing? You better go, Tom. I already know what to do here anyway. Don't worry about me."

"Okay, okay, I'll go now," I said, taking her hand into mine. Kiss. Kiss. "I'll be right back." Kiss. Kiss. "Don't go anywhere, honey." Kiss. Kiss. "I love you." Kiss. Kiss. "I won't be long." Kiss. Kiss. "I …"

She jerked her hand away from mine and barked, *"Get the hell outta here! Will ya?"*

"Goodbye my love," I said dramatically, backing out of the labor room door and clumsily bumping into an entering nurse. "Excuse me," I said. Then gave a salute to my wife. "I shall return."

Finding a payphone at Providence Hospital shouldn't be all that difficult, I thought, except that I hadn't paid attention to anything coming in, and I really needed to use the men's room. I glanced at the room number sign and committed to memory 4, 2, 7, before I dared to try to merge into the heavy traffic.

After a quarter mile hike down the hallway, and three or four intersections (no sense asking for directions), I finally found a men's room. It was quite a relief. I was still holding my morning coffee, and it was by then 4 in the afternoon.

Perhaps I should not have gone to work that morning at all. Nancy had been having pains on and off all night long, but she didn't think she was ready to deliver, so off to work I went. I received her panicked phone call about 9 o'clock, telling me that her water had broken. I hadn't had time to go to the bathroom since.

After exiting the men's room, feeling much better, I quickly found an empty payphone inside the Woman's Surgery Waiting Room.

A professional-sounding voice answered my call, "VanBuren's residence."

"Hi Mrs. Norman, it's me."

"Oh, thank God you called!" she gasped.

"Is something wrong?" I asked, alarmed.

"Just that you've been gone so long, and I didn't know why you hadn't called yet."

"Oh, I'm sorry! We've been rather busy, but everything's okay here. She's in a lot of pain, but she's only dilated to 3 centimeters, so they won't give her any numbing medication yet. This is likely going to take a while."

"Oh, that's good," Mrs. Norman said. "I guess. Here, you'd better talk with Dennis."

"Hi, Daddy, do I have a brother yet?"

"Not yet, buddy, but are you going to be disappointed if it's not a boy?"

"Yeah, ain't you?"

"No, I *ain't*, Dennis. I've got you, remember? You're enough boy for me. Besides, chances are rather good that it'll be a girl, so I hope you won't mind too much if it is."

"I won't mind too much, I guess," my boy answered. "But when's it gonna be?"

"It could be any minute now, but probably not for a few more hours. So, don't be giving poor ole' Mrs. Norman a hard time, ya hear? And I'll call back as soon as I know any more."

"Can I talk to Mama?"

"No, she's on the other side of the hospital, Dennis, and I'd better get back to her now, but let me talk to Jamie first."

Then came the little voice and the two words I treasured so much. *"Daddy! Daddy!"*

"Hello, sugarplum," I swooned. "Are you okay?"

"Where Mommy?"

"She's right here with me, my little cherub, and everything is fine. She's gonna have a big surprise for you, though, when she gets home. Are you being a good girl for Mrs. Norman, I hope?"

"Ahhhh … yes … I lub you."

"I love you too, pumpkin. Let me talk to Mrs. Norman again now, okay?"

"Da Da bye bye." Click.

Finding my way back was easy enough. I just asked the first pretty nurse I saw if she would please direct me to Room 472.

She looked at me puzzled for a moment, then said, "I'm sorry, sir, but the room numbers end at 460 on this floor."

I raised an eyebrow and cleverly asked, "Do they go above 460 on some other floor?"

She pursed her lips. "No, sir, 460 is as high as they can go anywhere. What are you trying to find?"

"My wife is in labor someplace in this hospital."

She smiled at me knowingly and pointed down the hall behind herself. "See those red doors *way* down there?"

"Yes. Yes, I do."

"Just before those red doors, turn right, go about 200 feet, and ask at the Maternity Nursing station."

"Thank you so much," I said, and hurried away.

Five minutes later, directly across from the Maternity Waiting Room, I spotted room number 427. I immediately heard my wife's painful wail from within. Rushing through the door, I saw a nurse busy at Nancy's bedside. "What's going on?" I demanded.

The older black lady attending my wife had the kindest face I'd ever seen. She disregarded my curt remark and smiled up at me. "I'm nurse Claudia, Dad," she said. "We're going to get your wife some relief."

*****

"Jesus Christ, Tom!" Nancy cried to me a few minutes later. "Why did they wait so damn long to give me that epi-thing? When's it going to start working? I can't stand it for another minute!" Her lips quivered. "Where have you been? Are the kids okay? Did you call my mother?"

I grabbed her hands and squeezed. Tears ran down my own face, understanding her pain. "Relax, honey," I said, "and it won't hurt so bad. Take deep breaths. Inhale through your nose. Deeeeep breaths and blow out your mouth. Deep breaths now and try not to tense up."

She did as I begged, and slowly, slowly, her shoulders began to relax, her shaking subsided, and some color returned to her face. "It's better now," she whispered, obviously relieved. "Will it stay gone, Tom?"

"I don't know, honey," I said honestly. "I don't know if that numbing stuff takes all the pain away, or just most of it, but it should be better for you from here on."

"Don't leave me again, Tom, *ever* again," she pleaded. "What took you so long?"

"It didn't seem so long to me," I said sincerely. "I'm sorry, sweetheart. I'll never leave your side again as long as I live. I promise." Kiss. Kiss. "I promise."

"You didn't call my mother, did you?"

"No, I didn't. I didn't know I was supposed to."

"Go call her right now!"

"Are you kidding me! I just swore on my life I'd never leave your side again, and now you want me to go call your mother?"

"Well, she's gotta know I'm here, don't she? Just don't take all day. Go. Go!" she said with a dismissive wave of her hand.

That time I used a payphone in the waiting room across the hall, and I was done in five minutes.

Nancy seemed asleep when I returned, but her eyes popped open when I touched her hand. "What are you doing here?" she demanded.

I answered defensively, "I called your mother. I told her everything. She's standing by for my next phone call. I came back to you."

"How'd you do it so fast, when it took so long the first time?"

"It's a long story, honey, I'll tell you all about it someday." Anxious to change the subject, I asked, "How are you now? Are we gonna have a baby anytime soon?"

"I don't know, maybe," she answered wearily. "Right now, I don't care if he ever comes out."

"He?"

"Yeah, he."

"Well, now I hope it *is* a boy, cuz Dennis said he'd be disappointed if it isn't. Did you know he felt that way?"

"Yeah, didn't you?"

"No, not really."

"Don't you want a boy, Tom?"

"It doesn't matter to me, Nance. You know that. I'm going to be happy either way. But really, I don't have enough females in my life yet, so if this one's a boy, we'll just have to try again right away."

"Bullshit! After this experience you'll never touch me again!"

"Ha!" I laughed at my worn-out spouse. "I suppose we can take a break for a week or two."

Nurse Claudia walked in then, still in possession of her kind face, although she looked a bit worn out herself. She stood at the foot of the bed with one hand on her hip and a sheaf of towels in the other. She spoke heartily. "How are you folks doing now?" She looked closely at my wife. "Are you feeling better dear?"

Nancy nodded her head and managed an appreciative smile.

I asked, "Nurse Claudia, can you tell us if the epidural will work all the way to the end?"

"It should, Dad," she answered while taking Nancy's pulse. "We'll keep it coming. Isn't modern medicine wonderful?"

"It sure is," I answered.

"Not that she won't have any more trouble," the nurse continued. "But it should be a lot less painful from now on. Would you like something else to drink sweetie?"

"Yes, I would like a Labatt Blue, please," I answered.

"Not you, bozo," Nancy responded. "Ignore him, nurse. I'm okay, thank you."

The nurse ignored me as she smiled and spoke to Nancy. "Doctor Graybaum said you're dilated to 8 centimeters now, so it won't be too much longer, and everything seems to be in order. So, what are you folks hoping for, a boy or a girl?"

Nancy looked nervously at me, then to nurse Claudia, then back to me, but she did not respond.

"We were just talking about that," I spoke up. "Most of us seem to want a boy, but it really doesn't matter."

"What names do you folks have picked out?"

"Good question," I said. "I forgot all about that issue." I glanced at my wife. "We don't have that sorted out yet, do we, honey? It's going to be Thomas John if it's a boy, but we haven't agreed on a girl's name yet. I want Jessica."

Nancy then spoke up, leaving no doubt as to the answer to the question. "If it's a girl," she said firmly, "she's gonna be Jennifer."

"Oh," Claudia interjected. "I guess we better hope for a boy then." She made a notation on the clipboard. "Is there anything else I can get for you, dear?" She shot me a look with a wry smile. "Not you Dad."

I kept my mouth shut that time. Nancy smiled meekly and shook her head *no*. "Okay then," the nice lady said. "Just press the nurse button if anything changes."

*****

By 9 pm nothing much had changed. Nancy's contractions were then about five minutes apart, but they didn't hurt her badly. "You better go call Mrs. Norman again, Tom," she said during a break. "She'll be worrying. Tell her to be sure Jamie's in bed by 10 o'clock, but Dennis can stay up till 11. And call my mother again. And call Sharon, too. Do you have her number?"

"I guess I could make those calls now. I can get Sharon's number from your mom. But it's gonna take me a while to do all that. Will you be alright? I'd hate to miss any of the action."

"I'm pretty sure nothing is gonna happen anytime soon, Tom, if that's what you mean."

"Alrighty then, I'll go now. I've got to use the little boy's room again anyway. I'll see you in a few."

It took me about half an hour to complete my mission. I made my phone calls, talked to the family, and used the men's room. Then I strolled casually across the hallway to rejoin my wife in her labor. Entering the room, however, I was stopped in my tracks with puzzlement as I encountered a missing bed. After a few seconds of blinking, I smiled at myself, knowingly, and backed out the doorway to check the room number. Surprisingly, it read 427.

"Hey!" I shouted to no one and spun in circles with my arms flying. "Where is my wife?"

"There you are Mr. VanBuren!" exclaimed Claudia running down the hallway. "I've been looking all over for you. We've taken your wife to the delivery room. Hurry, come with me!"

Nurse Claudia dressed me and herself in blue hospital garb. We scrubbed our hands and our arms, and each slipped into a pair of latex gloves. She backed through the swinging doors, careful not to touch anything with her hands. "Come this way Mr. VanBuren."

I went directly to the head of the bed and looked for the magical overhead mirror that I had remembered from the last time.

"Come over here, Dad," Claudia said. "You get a front row seat."

Oh my God, I thought, as I roosted atop the stool next to the doctor, my face only inches away from the incredible action. *I was just in time. How could things have moved along so quickly?*

"Push!" the doctor pleaded. "Push!"

The wet, wrinkled orb was already straining to escape. The head slipped out with a squirt – a scrunched up, bruised, masculine face with no hair.

I inhaled a short gasp.

"What? What's wrong?" Nancy howled.

Claudia cheered with obvious joy and clasped her hands together in praise. "Oh, you have your boy!"

Swiftly, the rest of the sopping figure wiggled out, proudly exposing its very unmasculine trait.

Chagrined at her error, Claudia's voice fell as she quickly corrected herself. "No ... it's a girl!"

"It's a girl!" I cried triumphantly, not understanding until that very moment how deeply I really did want another daughter – *needed* another daughter. And how magnificent she was! Squawking. Squirming. Splashing. Loving me already – forever, I knew. Trembling with awe I reached with both hands to touch her, to behold her, to love her in return – forever, I knew.

*****

Some hours later, in a guest chair in a private recovery room, I was awakened from a sound sleep by a gentle tap on my shoulder. In the soft light, Claudia flopped down in the next chair with the clipboard in her hand and a sigh.

"What are you still doing here?" I mumbled.

"I'm almost done with my shift," she said quietly, not wanting to wake my wife. "Just got to complete these papers. Have you two decided what to name your baby yet?"

I studied for a moment my exhausted, gently snoring spouse, then looked at Claudia with a smile beginning to break on my face. "Yes," I whispered as my smile broadened. "Yes, we have ... her name is *Jessica,"* I beamed. *"Jessica Jean."*

~

Chapter 32   *Ice*

April 1980

With no complications of any sort, three days after Jessica's glorious birth, we brought the newest member of our family home from the hospital. Dennis didn't seem to mind one bit not having a brother, and Jamie just wanted to hug her new little sister to bits. I was bursting with pride at my entire fabulous family, perhaps like never before. Nancy, for her part, bounced back easily enough from her birthing ordeal, but she was slow to recover from her other perceived wounds.

Some days later, upon returning from a busy day at work, as was often the case, the entire family was gathered in the blue living room anxiously awaiting my arrival. Dennis jumped up from his trucks and army men on the floor to greet me. "Hi Daddy! Can we go fishing?"

Having never spoken previously of fishing with my son, I wondered where he had gotten that idea. "What do you know about fishing, buddy?"

"I know how to fish, Daddy. I saw it on TV. I'll show you."

I removed my tie and tossed it on an empty chair. "Okay, Dennis, show me."

"You just need a pole, some wire, and a hook. Throw it like this." He cast an imaginary line that would have flown to Kalamazoo. He then asked proudly, "Can we go now?"

"Nooooo," I said playfully. "We can't go now. I crossed my arms and stood like Mr. Clean. "I've got to cook up some grub for us to eat. Remember?"

I looked down at Jamie then, who was standing on top of my right foot. "But after we eat, Dennis, we can play some catch in the front yard if you want." I pounded my fist into my palm as if it were a catcher's mitt. "You think you can still catch a hard slider?"

Dennis ran circles around me as Jamie climbed up my right leg as if it were a flagpole. "Yeah, Daddy," he said. "I can catch a hard slider, but when can we go fishing?"

"I don't know, Dennis," I responded. "Someday when we have more time, I suppose we can go fishing. I'd like that."

I reached down and peeled Jamie off the flagpole, held her high to the ceiling with both hands, and pumped her up and down, planting kisses on her face, one after another.

"Ha ha, da da, ha ha ha!" the little cherub screamed and giggled in delight.

I sat my daughter on top of my head and bounced around the room. I thought more about the fishing idea. "Maybe we can rent a boat, Dennis, or a canoe on the river. That'd be great!"

Through all the commotion, Nancy sat stiffly at the end of the blue velour sofa silently feeding the baby a bottle of formula. I took Jamie down from the top of my head and placed her onto Dennis's back as he continued to run in circles.

"Giddy-up horsey!" Jamie demanded.

With a giant grin on my face, I got down on my knees in front of the mother and slobber kissed the baby in her arms six or eight times about her sweet face and bald head. The infant rudely ignored me as she patiently tried to enjoy her evening meal. "Oooooh, I love you," I cooed. Kiss. Kiss. Kiss. "My tender little butterball." Kiss. Kiss.

"Will you cut that out, bozo!" the irritated, obviously overworked mother barked at me. "Can't you ever just act normal around the kids?"

Somewhat used to this type of unpleasant greeting from my cranky wife, I sat down wearily on the sofa next to her without bothering to say hello. "How many years do you have to know me, Nancy Jean, until you understand what *my normal* is?"

Her lips puckered, not in preparation for a kiss from me, but in a sneer. "Do you always have to act like a clown? Can't you ever just have a normal conversation with the kids?"

243

I looked carefully at my wife, not really understanding what her point was, and said, "With a 2-year-old?"

She didn't respond to my question, and she didn't notice that the bottle the baby was sucking was empty. Her foot, with a dangling flip flop, bounced incessantly on her knee.

I was concerned then that I was irritating my wife, but I needed to know why. Putting my foot up onto my knee to match hers, I probed. "Does this mean you're still mad at me for naming the baby Jessica?"

Her foot stopped bouncing, and she looked sharply at me. "Of course, I'm still mad at you. You went behind my back like an asshole. But I forgot all about that until you just now reminded me."

"But you don't dislike the name, do you?"

"That's true, Tom," she said as if she'd been saving up the remark for some time. "I don't dislike the name Jessica. It's *you* I dislike."

I heaved a sigh and sat back heavily on the sofa. *Here we go again*, I thought. Joining my hands behind my head I spoke sadly. "That's really a wonderful thing for a man to hear from his wife, in front of his children. I love you too, Nance."

Totally missing my sarcasm, and still not noticing the empty bottle, she responded. "I know you don't love me, Tom! I wish you'd quit saying that."

This type of remark coming from my wife was becoming familiar. I knew I needed to get off the subject quickly, especially with the kids around. I had no desire to hear again what would certainly be coming next – just how inconsiderate and self-centered she thought I was.

I sat up straighter and spoke sincerely to my wife. "You are mistaken about that, Nance. I *do* love you. But if you keep asking me to quit saying it, eventually I'll grant your wish. But I'll never quit displaying my affection for the kids, no matter how abnormal you may think I am."

I stood up then and glared down at my spouse who was staring intently at the sucking empty bottle, not really seeing it. A happy family moment had just been ruined.

"I'm going into the kitchen now," I continued sternly, "to prepare a meal for this family of mine, which I love so much."

I took a couple of steps towards the kitchen, stopped then, and turned back to face the mother and child. Shaking my finger at the empty bottle I said, "Why don't you quit trying to feed the baby air? You're going to make her sick."

*****

May 1980

I did not understand what my wife was so damn unhappy about. I didn't believe she truly felt left behind by me concerning the business. I didn't believe she felt overwhelmed being tied down by three kids, and I didn't believe she really felt unloved by me either. Perhaps, though, her unhappiness was caused by a little of each of those things, all muddled together. But really, I just didn't know.

Following the birth of Jessica, Nancy treated me coolly every day of our lives. She offered no sensible explanation for her icy behavior, just sarcasm and criticism. After a while, after many attempts by me to restore friendly relations between us, I mostly gave up trying to placate my bride. Instead, I poured myself deeper into my work and the other aspects of living.

Both Nancy and I continued our highly active lives. Three kids at home under the age of 8 demanded vast amounts of time. Home maintenance chores never ceased. Concord Design was experiencing phenomenal growth. Nancy did not slow down partying with her family, and I never reduced sports and activities with my friends. Through all this life, though, Nancy and I spoke less and less to each other each day. Differences between us were no longer explored, and no longer resolved. The intimacy and physical contact

245

that had been so automatic before also faded as we drifted unceasingly apart.

*****

June 1980

Jim Abbeville and I moved into new, much larger office space on Middlebelt and 12 Mile Roads, across the street from our favorite lunch spot, Ginopolis's. In addition to engineering work, we expanded into the contract labor business. This meant the hiring of skilled workers such as electricians, machine builders, and pipefitters. After only a couple of months at our new location we were already feeling cramped and wishing we had some shop space.

Work was plentiful and money flowed nicely. New cars, trucks, tools, furniture, and a bigger, better blueprint machine were all bought and put to effective use. We leased a dark gray Buick Riviera for Jim and a bright silver Toronado for me.

Late one sweltering summer evening, after the mosquitoes had driven me indoors before I had finished cutting the grass, I sat alone at the kitchen table reading the newspaper, nursing my third cold beer. The kids had been bathed and put to bed. Nancy grabbed a beer of her own and took a seat next to mine.

"I wanna go back to school, Tom," she said after taking her first swig.

I put my paper down in genuine surprise. "Really?" I said smiling. "That's great!"

"But don't you want me to stay home with the kids?" she asked.

"Of course, I do, but you're not talking about going off to college full time, are you?"

She rolled her eyes. "No, dummy. I'm just talking about GED classes two nights a week at Riley Middle School."

I slowly nodded my head in approval. "That'd be really nice, Nancy," I said in complete sincerity. "Really nice."

"But you'd have to babysit," she protested.

"Babysit?" I responded, annoyed. "I don't consider caring for my own children as babysitting."

"But the classes are on Tuesdays and Thursdays. And you golf on Tuesdays."

I gave the matter thought for about three seconds, then said affably, "Then I'll have to golf on Wednesdays instead, Nance. If you want to go to school, I'll stay home with the kids ... no problem."

She seemed surprised and almost disappointed by my take on the issue. "Really?" she asked.

"Yeah, really."

~

Chapter 33   *Lessons*

September 1980

I dropped out of my Tuesday night golf league so I could be home with the kids two nights a week when Nancy went to GED classes at Riley Middle School. Those evenings soon became my favorites. The tension that had grown between Nancy and me was absent those nights, of course, and I got a chance to do some parenting things that were usually handled by the mother. Things such as bottle feeding and changing diapers.

Even though dealing with an infant at a restaurant was difficult, the four of us often went someplace nice for dinner. Dennis, Jamie, and I enjoyed the meals we never got to have at home. It was relaxing family time for all of us, with lots of enjoyable conversation.

Afterwards, Dennis and I usually hit the second-grade books to study arithmetic and phonics. By the time Mom arrived home, around 9:30, all three kids had been bathed and tucked snugly into bed for the night.

*****

October 1980

One Sunday afternoon, when I arrived home after playing a round of fall golf with my dad, I found Nancy studying English grammar at the kitchen table.

"Hey," I said, "I know that stuff well. Want some help?"

"No, I'm okay," she said without lifting her eyes from the book.

I pulled a beer out of the fridge for each of us and took a seat beside her. "Do you remember that stuff from high school, or is it new to you, honey?"

She looked up at me then. "I don't member one bit of it, Tom, but I'm getting help from another student."

"Another student? What's her name?"

"It's not a *her*, Tom," she answered snidely. "It's William, a really smart, older guy."

I scratched my head, trying to decide how to reply to that. "How smart can a GED student be Nance?" I asked.

"You're not the only person in the world who knows things, Tom," she said, miffed.

"I didn't mean it that way, Nance."

"Yes, you did."

"No, I didn't," I insisted. "But how old of a guy is William?"

"He's 30." She took a swig of her beer. "But why do you ask?"

"It's just that you mentioned he was an older guy. Thirty doesn't seem that old to me."

"Well, he's the oldest guy in the class, is all I'm sayin'."

"And he knows the subject matter well enough that he can be of help to you?"

She stuck her chin out defiantly. "Yes, he does, and he doesn't make fun of me like you do."

I blinked in disbelief. I'd never heard that accusation before. "Make fun of you?" I stammered. "You think I make fun of you?"

She stood firm, as usual. "Yes. Yes, you do, Tom. You laugh at me all the time, and you correct me."

I felt instantly like an ass. "Oh my, honey," I said sincerely. "I'm so sorry." I inhaled slowly. "I never meant, sweetheart, to make fun of you. I always thought we were laughing together. I love the way you handle the English language. I always have. It makes me smile, and I thought you wanted to be corrected."

"Well," she said with pride, "William corrects me just fine, and I feel better round him than I do round you."

My irritation building at hearing my wife speak fondly of another man, I could feel the heat as my face reddened like a ripe tomato. I slammed my beer down on the table, splashing some onto her books. "It sounds like there's more going on here, woman, than just English grammar!"

Her face broke into a giant grin. "Whoooa!" she said with immense pleasure. "Tom's jealous."

"You think this is funny?" I said incredulously.

"Ha!" she bellowed with an even bigger grin. "Yes! This *is* funny! Ha, ha, ha! You're jealous," she sang like a playground snot. "Jeaaaaalous. Jeaaaaalous."

For the first time in my life, I felt like choking my wife. Instead, I took my beer, stomped out of the house, and sat alone on a lawn chair in the backyard. My anger slowly subsided, but my unhappiness remained.

Sometime later, I was rescued from my misery by a delightful, endearing little pipsqueak. Jamie crawled up on my lap, wrapped her tiny arms tightly around my sad neck, and made everything better all at once. "I lub you Daddy," she said.

*****

November 1980

It was an early winter storm. Not a lot of snow was on the ground yet, but the roads were very slick. It would take a while for the salt trucks to get out and do their work. I was worried about my wife being out at night in her rear-wheel drive Camaro. At 10 pm she was already half an hour late getting home from school.

The last few weeks – ever since she announced her friendship with William – we hadn't spoken much. She had made no attempt to ease my mind about the situation, nor did I pursue the issue with her again. But life continued.

Sitting on the blue sofa, as the snow began to accumulate on the street, I looked through the picture window and wondered where my wife might be. With the house darkened, and the porch lights and streetlights on, one could see the neighborhood clearly at night. The kids were quietly in their beds. The minutes ticked slowly away.

I wondered if I should go out and shovel the drive so Nancy wouldn't have trouble getting into the garage. That seemed silly, though, since the snow would probably all melt the next day anyway. I wondered if I should call her sister or her mother to see if maybe she went over there after school, but certainly she would phone me if that were the case. I wondered, also, if she was with William. The green monster began to rise in me again, but I pushed that idea out of my head the best I could. *Don't be so stupid*, I thought.

For four more hours I paced the dark house wondering and worrying. I strolled between the picture window in the living room and the view of the side street from the kitchen. *Maybe I should call the police*, I mused.

I sat at the kitchen table with the phone in my hand, ready to call someone, I didn't know who, when I heard a car door slam. I hung up the phone and stepped to the side window in time to see an old black pickup truck backing out of our driveway.

With books in her arms, Nancy staggered, zig zagging, through the snow to the side door. White fluff already dusted her golden hair. The pickup spun all four of its wheels as it disappeared quickly around the corner.

As she fumbled with her books and her keys, I observed the scene from the still darkened kitchen. Although I was happy to see my wife in one piece, the anger was building rapidly inside me again.

The side door crashed open as she stumbled onto the landing. Loudly stomping the snow off her feet, she dropped her books, and closed and latched the door behind her. With hands on opposite walls to steady herself, she made her way up the two steps into the kitchen. Unnoticed by the interloper, I leaned against the counter with arms folded, as she teetered past me towards the bedrooms.

"Nancy!" I shouted.

"Aaaaah!" She jumped out of her socks and spun around in fright. "Jezhush Chrish, Tom!" she said with a hand on her heart. "What'd you do thafor? The fuck you doin in the dark?"

"I've been looking out that window the last four and a half hours, Nance," I said passionately, pointing outdoors. "I've been worried sick about you! Do you know it's 2:30 in the morning? Where have you been?"

"I washz ach school," she slurred. She clumsily switched on the overhead light, blinked in its brightness, then switched it off again.

"Where's your car, Nancy?" I asked.

She didn't seem to know the answer to my question. She stood silent, wobbling in circles, wringing her hands. The hallway light silhouetted her dizzy motion. The alcohol stench and stale smoke were sickening from 10 feet away.

"Where is your car, Nancy?" I demanded, louder.

She turned quickly, then stumbled, and without answering, disappeared around the corner, the same as I had seen the black truck do just minutes before.

At that moment, my jealousy and rage reshaped itself into hopelessness. Whatever zeal still resided in my soul departed when I heard the slamming of the bedroom door. I was totally alone then, like a foreigner in my own life.

*****

I called into work the next morning and gave directions to a few key employees. Something was always lost at Concord Design whenever I was unexpectedly absent, but I had no choice.

While Nancy slept it off, I got Dennis fed, dressed, and off to school in his galoshes. Jamie and Jessica both required diaper

252

changes, of course, dressing into play clothes, and each their individual breakfast items.

By 10 o'clock, as I had predicted, the snow had begun to melt. I sat reading the morning paper and drinking my fourth cup of coffee, when Nancy shuffled into the living room clutching her blanket tightly around herself.

She smelled like a tavern toilet. Her hair was a tangled mass of barnyard straw. She squinted through one eye of her puffy face and struggled to clear the fur off her tongue as she rasped, "What are you doing here?"

I folded the paper onto my lap but did not respond. Jamie, sitting at my side with Winnie the Pooh, held out her arms and called out, "Mommy! Mommy!"

Nancy snatched Jamie and Winnie up and engulfed them in her blanket, as if she had just rescued them both from peril. "Where's Jessica?" she demanded.

I spoke up then. "Gee, Nancy, I don't know. I haven't seen her yet today. Why don't you check her crib, maybe she's in there?"

"Asshole!" she said and stomped away.

From my seat on the sofa, I heard the commotion in the girls' bedroom. "Oh, my little precious baby! Are you okay? Did you think Mommy forgot about you? When was the last time you ate, baby child? Your diaper needs changed, of course. Don't you worry little one, Mommy will take care of you now."

The heroine returned a few minutes later with Jamie, Winnie, and Jessica all comfy in her blanket. "Where's Dennis, asshole?" she demanded.

My calmness broke at that. I jumped up from the sofa and threw my arms out in anger. *"He's at school, fool!"* I shouted. "Properly dressed and fed, as are Jamie and Jessica, no thanks to you!" I thrust a finger towards her nose and yelled, "Don't you dare call me names, and act as if *I'm* the villain here, after the stunt you pulled last night!"

Hearing my booming voice, both Jamie and Jessica began to cry.

"Now look what you've done," Nancy said as she turned away from me and left the room. "Asshole!"

I followed the crying blanket down the hallway and asked, "Where's your car, Nancy?"

She stopped in her tracks, glanced over her shoulder at me for a moment, puzzled, then took off again.

I followed closer. "Where is your car, Nancy?" I asked again, louder.

"Would you shut up, bozo. My head is splitting."

"Where is your car, Nancy?" I repeated in a sarcastic whisper.

She peeked nervously at me then, and finally yielded. "Ain't it in the garage?"

"No, it ain't in the fucking garage!" I roared.

Nancy, the blanket, and the bawling babies all collapsed then into a heap on the bed. Nancy joined the wailing chorus.

I knew then that further yelling wasn't going to get us anywhere, but I had to continue questioning. I asked in a more placid voice, "What did you do last night, Nancy?"

Nancy wiped her nose on the blanket. "I went to school, Tom," she said between sniffs. "Then, some of us went to a bar. Then," she flashed guilty eyes at me for one second, "We might a smoked some pot." Her sniffling then began in earnest. "Then ... then. I don't member!" She broke out in sobs.

I watched pitifully as my wife, a child in each arm, turned an even more sickly shade of pale and began to shake. "Take the babies, Tom," she said as she thrust them out to me. "I gotta puke!"

~

Chapter 34   *Get Out*

By 2 pm my wife had recovered sufficiently for us to go out and search for her car. Dennis wouldn't be home from school till about 3:30, so we had more than an hour. It didn't take long. We found the white Camaro sitting next to an abandoned mechanical bull in the corner of the parking lot of Charley Bob's Horseshoe Bar. While the babies and I watched quietly from the warmth of the Toronado, Nancy cleared the snow off her car and carefully drove it over the mound of snow that had been plowed around the Camaro and the bull.

The details of the infamous *GED Snowstorm Caper* were never fully revealed. For sure, Nancy could not recall some of what took place, and she felt no obligation to share with me what little she did recall.

Partying hard was nothing new to my wife, of course, but she had never blacked out before that I knew of. Totally ignoring her parenting duties was new too, and the possibility of her involvement with another man was certainly new. I couldn't just let the matters drop, but my concerns, my questions, and my pleas fell upon deaf ears. Nancy, in fact, thought the whole thing was rather funny. I was being jealous and stupid; she said many times.

"I didn't black out, Tom!" she insisted. "I just don't member."

She denied any dereliction of duty concerning the kids. They were, after all, my kids too. "If the kids are being cared for by their father, then they ain't being neglected, now, are they?" And I could just shut up about her drinking and smoking, she said. If I couldn't accept her for what she was, then I might as well just get out.

She would not confirm or deny that she had been fooling around with William. That was for her to know and for me to find out, she said. "Ha. Ha."

"If you've been cheating on me, you ought to at least tell me," I said with some desperation. "If you say you haven't and you don't intend to, I'll believe you. But you need to tell me!"

"I guess I just don't feel that I need to tell you anything, Tom. It's not your business."

Nancy and I had been arguing this point for hours. The kids had been put to bed, and I stood in the middle of the bedroom with hands on my hips, while my spouse was trying to go to sleep. "I can't see how you can conclude that it's not my business, Nancy Jean. Would you say what *I* do is not *your* business?"

"I don't care what you do, Tom. I just want to be left alone."

"I see."

My arms dropped to my sides in dejection, but I quickly gained back my animation and spoke louder than I had intended. "I'm not leaving you alone, woman. You're still my wife, and I'll continue to concern myself with your behavior."

"Knock yourself out, Tom," she said sleepily.

"But I'll tell you something," I continued speaking to the lump in the bed. "I'm not going to suffer like this anymore. I cried hard for you last night … for many hours. I will not cry for you again."

*****

Nancy had no desire to discuss the three issues that were threatening our marriage: alcohol, neglect, and infidelity. I, however, was relentless in the pursuit of some answers and some resolution.

One evening near bedtime, while in the play area of the basement, I harped away. "You've got to talk to me, Nancy." All three kids, waiting for their baths, watched intently as their mother and I picked up their toys. "We can't just ignore the issues we have here, Nance. It's bad. I hate what we have going on."

"Then get out!" she screamed in frustration. "Just get out of here if you hate it so damn much!"

I looked at the kids looking at me, and then pleaded in a quieter tone. "I don't hate it here, Nancy. I just want us to have a better life together. Don't you?"

"Not if it means you telling me what to do all the time," she spilled out quickly as she bent over to pick up the baby. She held Jessica in her arms, then seemed to pause for a moment to gain the attention of Dennis and Jamie before she calmly stated, "Living with you, bozo, is bringing me down."

"Is that so?" I responded. "You think life with your mister cowboy would be more exciting?"

"He's not a cowboy, Tom," she said with self-satisfied delight. "He's a mountain climber."

I looked away from her eyes at that shot, tossed the last Lego into the toy box, and took a deep breath. "I see," I said then. "So, you think life with Mr. Kilimanjaro would be more exciting, Nancy?"

"Ha!" she laughed loudly. "Killer man, anybody would be more exciting than you, asshole! Ha! Ha!"

Feeling considerable pride in her wit, she looked to Dennis for approval. The boy giggled.

I didn't find her comment the least bit funny, particularly in front of the kids. I spat through gritted teeth, "I'm not going to take your name calling or your ridicule any longer, woman."

With Jessica on her hip, she sang like a schoolyard bully, "Oh yeah? What you gonna do 'bout it aaaaasshole?" She turned then, laughing to herself and disappeared up the staircase.

*****

I didn't know what I was *gonna do 'bout it*, but for me to just *get out* was not a viable option. We needed a different solution. We needed a way to live together without wanting to tear each other apart.

257

Nancy and I began, then, living separately in the same house. She lived her life as she pleased, without comment from me, and I lived mine. We each did our share of the household duties. We sat at the same dinner table without speaking to each other, and we slept in the same bed without touching each other.

Somehow, through it all, the kids were cared for by the two of us and they did not seem to suffer. I detested what we had, but to avoid breaking up our family, I was prepared to live that way forever. Nancy, however, didn't want me in the same house as her any longer.

As I was getting dressed for work one morning, she folded clothes on the bed next to me, and said casually, "Why don't you just leave Tom? You'd be happier."

"I'm not going anywhere, Nancy," I answered. "I've told you that often enough."

"Why not, though?" she asked sincerely, rolling tiny socks together.

I pointed to the pile of children's clothing in front of her. "We have three kids. Haven't you noticed?"

"So what? People with kids divorce all the time."

"Divorce?" I stopped buttoning my shirt. "Is that what you want?"

She turned to me and said with a smile, "Sure, why don't you divorce me?"

"Honestly, I can't tell when you're serious or not." I finished buttoning my shirt and picked out a textured blue tie from the closet.

"Course I'm serious," she said, still smiling. "And I know you'd like to be rid of me."

"I don't want to be rid of you, dammit," I said, anger rising. Then, wagging a finger at her, I added, "But even if I did, I'd never divorce you, Nancy … never."

Not fazed in the least by my ire, she said without malice, "But why on Earth not, Tom, since we don't like each other anymore?" She then turned back to her laundry.

I hated her cavalier attitude, but I tried to remain calm and to answer her question the best I could. "Because we have three children, Nancy," I said once again. "That's why. Three very young children, I might add. It's not just you and me anymore. We can't stay married or get divorced based solely on whether we like each other or not. We must consider the kids first – you and I come second."

"But you said yourself a long time ago that it's better for kids to be *from* a broken home than to *live* in one. Member?"

I froze in position, reaching for my coat in the closet. I couldn't believe she remembered I had said such a thing so many years before. Visions of Kristen and Amy flooded my mind. My knees weakened as I understood that I could lose three more kids, the very same way I lost my first two. I slowly finished removing the coat from its hanger, put it on, and absently adjusted my tie in the mirror, not really seeing my reflection. I tried hard not to show how Nancy's comment had affected me, not knowing if I succeeded.

I stood then, before my spouse, who was folding a pair of Jamie's little cotton coveralls and said with a tear, "Our home is not broken, Nancy. Not beyond redemption, anyway. At any rate, what I said years ago doesn't apply here. We may not like each other much, we may not agree on much, but we don't hate each other. If you can tolerate me, and I can tolerate you, then we have an obligation to keep our family together – for the kids' sake – even if it means us living together simply like roommates. There's no way we can pretend our children would be better off without all of us living together in the same house."

Nancy continued folding clothes, intent on the chore. To be sure I had her complete attention, I bent at the waist, positioned my face in front of hers, and looked into her eyes. She stopped her work, straightened up, surprised, and listened. "No, Nancy," I said adamantly. "No matter what we do, no matter how much we dislike each other, you and I can *never* let the kids grow up without both of their parents ... *never.*"

*****

For the most part – following my *children first* speech – the hostilities between Nancy and me subsided. The indifference that we both felt toward our marriage, however, increased many times.

Nancy knew I'd never leave her or the kids, and she seemed to accept that idea – she may even have embraced it. For my part, I gave up trying to understand or to control her behavior. Eventually, I quit even caring about what she did. She certainly did not care what I did. But I did not *get out*.

If I paid the bills and gave her money, *Nancy* would be happy. As long as my daily life with our precious children continued unabated, I would be happy. If the kids were growing up with both of their parents in the same house with them, they seemed to be untroubled. It was the best we could do.

*****

January 1981

Nancy and I did not celebrate our fourth wedding anniversary. We didn't even acknowledge it to each other. We hardly even recognized each other's existence. Except to be sure that my wife was at home and sober when I needed to leave the house, I quit paying attention to her life. She paid even less attention to mine.

Although my life at home was missing adult companionship, it was, in many ways, simple and satisfying. The kids needed me, I needed them, and it was good to be needed.

Away from home, however, the next few months were anything but simple. Concord Design was exploding with work, and as predicted, in less than a year, the company had outgrown the offices at Middlebelt and 12 Mile roads. Jim and I sought out a new and larger location – this time with shop space – so we could begin to build some of the products we had been designing. We found an 18,000-square-foot building under construction on Freeway Park Drive in Farmington Hills. It was in the same industrial park as my former employer, APS. The building was big, beautiful, and expensive. It was perfect.

Jim and I stuck our necks out and signed a five-year lease. Our new landlords were willing to finish the inside of the building to our specifications, which included a large open engineering room and deluxe front offices. The high-ceilinged shop came complete with provisions for a crane, a double truck well, and an overhead surface door with automatic opener.

~

Chapter 35   *Fishing*

April 1981

"It's almost the opening of trout season, Tommy boy," my good friend Donny Braye mentioned to me one afternoon over a cold beer. A group of guys from the industrial park often met at the Interchange Bar after work. Donny was an installation manager at APS, and he was the recipient of much of Concord's work.

"Yeah, so what?" I asked.

"So, I'm heading up north this weekend to my brother's place in Gaylord, along with half the state of Michigan. Why don't you come with me?"

"I don't know how to trout fish, Don," I responded.

"I can teach you how to fish easily enough, Tom, but you already know how to drink – that's the main thing."

"Don't you have to work on Saturday?"

"They let us take the weekend off every year at the start of trout season, then again at the start of deer season. It's tradition, man!" Donny said with a giant grin. "No women, no kids ... we have a riot."

I signaled for two more cold ones from the bartender. "Does your brother have room for me?"

"Yeah, all kinds of room. You remember Gary from us going to the Tiger game last year – all you need is a sleeping bag in a corner somewhere, anyway. Will your wife let you go?"

"She doesn't much care what I do anymore, if it doesn't interfere with her partying. And as far as I know she doesn't have anything planned for this weekend. I haven't taken two days in a row off from work or from home in at least four years. I'd love to go, Donny, even if we don't go fishing."

"Oh, we'll go fishing, Tom. Don't worry 'bout that."

At about 6 pm the next Friday evening, following a full day at work, overpacked with fishing gear, beer, clothing, and food, we headed out of town in the Toronado. Donny was correct – it seemed as if half the state of Michigan was on northbound US 23. The excursion, normally about four hours and six beers long, soon found us in riveting conversation and a million laughs.

It was after 11 o'clock by the time we found our way to the cabin deep in a white pine forest. The air was cool and incredibly fresh. Through the treetops, a brilliant stellar blanket contrasted with the pitch-black sky. Gary's place turned out to be a small two-room affair – a toilet and a shower in one room and everything else in the other.

Four guys, playing cards and smoking cigars, were already there when we arrived. A cast-iron stove – the sole source of heat – stood beneath a dusty deer head, beside it a small, neat pile of birch and oak firewood. A matched, duct-taped, leatherette sofa and chair, arranged around an oval braided rug, completed the living area. Hanging from the vaulted ceiling, a rough-timber chandelier shown above a round maple table with six armchairs. An ancient white electric range and Frigidaire filled most of the kitchen. Hunting pictures, fishing gear, and multi-paned windows covered the knotty pine walls. I was welcomed aboard, introduced around, and handed a beer. I was then instructed about the three-step rule.

"We use the toilet in here, Tom, only for shitting," Gary informed me. "When you have to piss, just go outside, but take three steps away from the building first, so nobody's gotta step in it later."

Gary was a high school teacher, I was told. He was a decade older than Donny and me, stood about 5 foot 5, and weighed maybe 110 pounds. I assumed he behaved with decorum while at school, but anytime I'd ever seen him, he always, always had a beer in his hand, and he almost always had something witty to say with a hardy laugh. The Braye brothers laughed better than anyone else on Earth.

Gary finished his beer with a flourish and grabbed another. "We'll be leaving here by 6 tomorrow morning, Tom. We gotta be sure to get a good spot on the river. By 7 o'clock the place will be swarming with weekend fisherdopes."

"Sounds good to me, man," I said. "I'll be ready." I opened another beer for myself.

Donny and I took positions around the poker table then and began a long night of drinking, cigars, and smoking beer. The beers went down easily enough, but eventually they gave way to 10-year-old bourbon and homemade peach brandy.

Some hours later, I don't remember when, I fell asleep in a pile of hay underneath a pine tree about three steps from the cabin. I think I was trying to conform to the toilet rule, when I decided the hay looked like a mighty fine spot to bed down for the night.

I was awakened too soon, however, by sunlight in my eyes, chirping birds, and an extremely foul barnyard odor. Stiffly and quietly, I moved then to retrieve my duffel bag from the Toronado and went indoors to use the toilet and shower before anyone else even stirred. It was 10 am.

The aroma of fresh coffee and stale donuts filled the cabin when I got out of the shower. By noon, three others were awake and seemed to be ready to go fishing. Gary, who seldom ate more than a cracker, announced, "If we hurry up guys, we'll still be okay." Then he looked at me. "Do you have a fishing license, Tom?"

"No sir," I answered. "Do I need one?"

"If you wanna drop a hook in the water you need one, but don't worry ..."

"Don't worry is right," Donny interrupted. "We're not going fishing till we've had some breakfast. I need bacon and eggs!"

"We don't have time for that, Don," insisted the older brother. "The day's half over. Eat some of those donuts I bought last month."

"Fuck the donuts," said Old Fat Joe. "Let's go to the Riverside Tavern for some real breakfast."

"The Riverside already put breakfast away, Joe. It's lunch time."

"We gotta have bacon and eggs," Donny maintained. "It's tradition."

Disgusted, Gary took off his fishing cap and slammed it onto the table. "Oh man!" he complained loudly. "We might as well give up fishing for today then."

The last two near-comatose forms, Gary's son Matt and Matt's buddy Richie, still wrapped in their sleeping bags on the worn wooden floor, stirred from the commotion.

"At least nobody seems to be dead," Gary said with a snicker.

*****

The four of us old guys drove into town in Matt's Jeep. We bought bacon, eggs, butter, orange juice, beer, and ice at Glen's Market; bread and fresh donuts at Aunt Bea's Bakery; and a fishing license for me at the Mobile. By the time we arrived back at the campsite the young guns were cleaned up, playing horseshoes, and mighty hungry.

By 4 that afternoon we finished cleaning up the breakfast dishes. "Let's go dusk fishing," Matt said.

"Duck fishing?" I asked.

"No, dummy, D-U-S-K! You know ... at the sun setting. The trout come to the surface looking for bugs."

"There's four million morons on the river by now, Matt," Gary said in his sardonic style. "We're better off getting up early tomorrow morning." Gary then popped open another beer and said with a grin, "All we have to do is get to bed by midnight."

*****

By midnight, however, we were having our 14th pitcher of Budweiser delivered to our small round table by a harried middle-aged waitress. The Riverside Tavern, overpacked and smoke-filled, rocked with a loud four-piece band playing country music and golden oldies. The young guns and Old Fat Joe were doing line dances with some of the local talent. Donny and Gary were telling fish stories, which seldom included actual fishing.

In the middle of a story about the time he had passed out in the bottom of his homemade wooden canoe while floating down the Rifle River, Gary stopped talking in mid-sentence. He gawked open-mouthed at the space behind my back as if he had just seen an apparition. I turned around in my chair to witness the sight of two young gals, a fat one and a skinny one, making their way through the crowd.

"Lori!" shouted Gary.

The 6-foot-tall, 300-pound female clad in a brightly flowered granny dress and white sandals looked across the crowded room and smiled broadly at her former high school teacher. "Hi, Mr. Braye!" she bubbled. "How are you doin?"

The skinny one (skinny by comparison, anyway), bouncing in her red minidress, waved at our table also. "Hi Uncle Gary. Hi Uncle Donny."

"Holy shit, Tommy Boy," Donny whispered in my ear. "Today's your lucky day."

With raised eyebrows, I gaped at Don. "Oh, how's that?"

"That's our cousin Connie," Donny said excitedly. "You'll see."

Connie and Lori sashayed up to our table and Connie asked in a sweet voice, "Can we join you guys?"

"You betcha," Donny replied as he stood up and pulled out a couple of chairs for the welcomed guests. "This is my good friend, Tommy VanBuren from down below," he said proudly pointing at me. "He owns his own business, he's independently wealthy, and he's single."

266

Before I even had a chance to blush, Connie held out her hand to me, seemed to check her ample cleavage to see if it was still there, and said brightly, "How you doin', Tommy V? Pleased to meet you. Would you like to dance?"

Trying hard not to appear drunk, I stood up, took her hand in mine, and said as seductively as I could, "Sure, let's go."

I swear the band played that old Beatles tune at that very exact moment.

Well, my heart went boom.

As I crossed that room.

And I held her hand in mine.

Two songs later the band slowed the music way down as it did Elvis's *"I Can't Help Falling in Love with You."* Connie wrapped her arms sensuously around my neck and pulled me close. As we swayed around the room, I noticed the back of the billowing, flowered granny dress on the other side of the dance floor. Slowly, Lori turned to reveal the little man leading her around in bliss. *Gary!*

At 2 am they kicked us out of the tavern. Gary and I stood together leaving a final deposit at the urinal trough. "Well," Gary said with an ear-to-ear grin. "I've got my swamp angel for the night, Tom. How are you doing with Connie?"

"I'm not doin' nothing with Connie," I responded. "We gotta get to bed early tonight, member?"

"Well, I'm not passing up this opportunity just to go fishing tomorrow," he said, zipping up his pants. "I'll catch up with you guys later."

Connie and I soon said our goodbyes in the parking lot next to the back door. We watched Gary's old red pickup truck clank down the street, listing to the right.

*****

267

Gary got back to the cabin about noon the next day, tired but smiling. We never learned exactly what took place with Gary and Lori, but neither did we press him for details. "You and Connie should have come with us, Tom," is all he said before curling up to sleep on the sofa.

With three of the guys having already left for home, and Gary sawing logs, Don and I decided to pack our bags for the trip home as well. Carrying our stuff out to the Toronado, Donny said to me, "I'm sorry you didn't get to go fishing, Tom."

"That's alright," I said. "I don't mind, really. I'm just glad to be able to get away like this."

"Yeah, I hear ya, Tom, but I really wanted to get you out fishing, man."

We then heard a horn beep and looked up to see a blue Plymouth Horizon driving up the long dusty driveway.

Donny grinned and poked me in the ribs. "There's your swamp angel, Tommy Boy."

"My what?"

"That's Connie, dummy. Our cousin, Connie!"

"Cousin?" I questioned. "She called you and Gary *uncle* last night. That'd make her your niece, wouldn't it?"

"Well, she's really our cousin, but because she's so much younger than us, she's always called us uncle. I used to change her diapers, man."

I looked at my friend with some suspicion. "I won't ask you about that one, pal."

Connie got out of the Horizon wearing jeans and a sweatshirt, her fresh auburn hair bouncing on her shoulders. She looked much younger then than she had the night before. "Hi guys," she said as she gave her uncle and me hello kisses. "Are you going somewhere?"

"Yeah, sweetie," Don said. "We're going home. What are you doing?"

"I just thought I'd come out here and have a beer with you guys. I didn't know you'd be leaving so soon, though."

"Well," Don scratched head. "I'm sure we have time for a beer. Don't we, Tom?"

"Sure, we do," I said smiling at Connie, "or two."

"Alrighty, then," Don said, rubbing his hands together. "Have a seat on that picnic table, and I'll be right back."

We did as Donny bid us, but on opposite sides of the table. In a minute, Don came out of the cabin, and planted four long-neck Stroh's on the table between us.

"Here's two beers for each of you," he said. "I'm gonna go inside and take a shower now while the bathroom's empty." He winked at me. "And we should be leaving, Tom, as soon as I get done."

"Okay," I agreed.

"Thanks Uncle Donny," Connie said.

"Yeah, thanks, *Uncle Donny*," I repeated.

Don turned to leave and said over his shoulder, "No problem, children."

I took a long swig of my beer. "Ahhhhh, that's good, isn't it?"

"I don't really need any more beer after last night," Connie said. "But I'll drink one."

"It seems as though your uncle is trying to drive the two of us together, Connie. Don't you think so?"

"Yeah," she said knowingly. "He is. Do you mind?"

"Mind?" I replied. "Of course not. You're a pretty young female, and I'm a lonely old fart. How could I possibly mind?"

She held her hands around her beer and smiled slightly. "You're not so old," she said shyly, trying to hide her blush.

"It's just," I continued, "that I'm not single, like Don said I was."

"I know."

269

"You do?"

"Yeah, he told me last night when I was dancing with him. But he said your marriage is in awfully bad shape, though, and that you could use a friend like me."

Wow ... I didn't know how to respond to that. I sat speechless for a moment staring into her brown eyes, then said sincerely, "Thank you, friend. It's nice to be around you."

We sat awkwardly silent for a few moments, then I finally asked, "Where do you live, Connie?"

"In Novi with my parents. We used to live up here, though. I went to high school in Gaylord with Lori. I visit her on the weekends a lot."

"When are you going back *down below?*"

"First thing in the morning," she said. "There'll be a lot less traffic than tonight."

"So, you'll be in Novi sometime tomorrow?"

"Yes, I sure will."

"Would you like to have dinner with me tomorrow night?"

Her eyes lit up, and a broad smile broke across her full red lips. "Why yes, Tommy V," she said. "I would very much like that."

I thought for a second as I opened my second beer. "Would you mind meeting me someplace? I wouldn't feel all that comfortable picking you up at your parents' home."

"Sure," Connie said sweetly. "I don't mind. Just tell me where and when."

"Well, let's see," I said, ruminating while tapping my beer bottle. "Do you know the Mustang Grill on Grand River?"

"Yeah, that'd be a good spot for me."

"Okay," I said. "I have to work all day, then go home and clean up, so how about 8:30?"

"Eight thirty it is, Tommy, at the Mustang Grill." She held out her hand to me across the table.

I took her hand into mine and glanced at the cabin window. "I can see your Uncle Donny moving around in there," I lied. "It looks like he's getting ready to come out. Can I get a goodbye kiss before he gets here?"

*****

Arriving home from my fishing trip Nancy ignored me as usual. The kids, however, were extremely glad to see me, and I was happy to be home with them. It wasn't easy, though, admitting to my son that I hadn't caught any fish. I didn't bother to tell him that for the entire weekend I never even got close to water. I just said, "Maybe next time, Dennis, you can show me how to do it better."

At work the next day, the weekend's activities were heavy on my mind. I wasn't thinking about fishing, or the lack of it, but of Connie. And I wasn't thinking so much about the girl herself, but more about what my behavior with her meant to my marriage.

I had by then no illusions that my marriage to Nancy could be salvaged. After all, Nancy had all but admitted to an affair with Kilimanjaro, and she had asked me to *get out of her life* a hundred times. Still, it had been my first time near another woman, and I had plenty to feel guilty about. It may have been nothing more than a goodbye kiss on a picnic table, but I knew what it meant. It meant I could never complain about my wife's behavior again. *I was just as bad as her.*

Guilty feelings aside, however, I was excited about the upcoming evening. The little time I had spent with Connie reminded me of what I had been missing for many months – *the touch of a woman* – and it felt very nice.

~

271

Chapter 36   *His View*

It was not a school night for Nancy, so sometimes on Mondays she would actually attempt to prepare dinner for the family. Nevertheless, I was surprised to see my wife slicing boiled potatoes when I arrived home at about 7 o'clock that night. "What are you doing?" I asked, with hands on my hips.

"What do you think I'm doing, dummy?"

I pointed to the butcher knife in her hand. "Be careful with that thing, would you? I don't want anyone to get hurt."

She hefted the big tool for show. "I'm sure you'd like me to cut my own throat with this thing, wouldn't ya?"

"Not really," I answered truthfully. "I rather like your neck the way it is, but I'm wondering what you're gonna do with all those potatoes."

"Don't worry 'bout it, bozo, you're not invited to dinner anyway."

I knew a slam when I heard one, but I was glad to have a return volley ready. I smiled and said, "That's fine with me Nance, since I have other dinner plans for tonight myself."

"Oh?" her eyebrows shot up. "And just what plans do you think you have for tonight?"

I tried to wobble my head like she had just done. "Never mind," I said. "Your plans don't include me, and mine don't include you."

She bared her teeth like an angry dog and shook the knife in my face. "If you're up to no good, asshole, you're gonna be sorry!"

I backed away from the big knife just to be on the safe side, and said laughing, "Whoooa there, pardner! If I didn't know better, I'd say you're jealous!"

"Don't count on that, asshole!" she said with a snarl and turned back to her potatoes. "I don't give a shit what you do."

Just then all three kids ran into the kitchen and attacked me, breaking up the tension. "Daddy, Daddy, Daddy!"

I flung Jamie up with one arm onto my right shoulder and Jessica onto my left. Dennis hopped on my back. With the kids giggling, I trudged toward the living room. Stopping in the doorway, I turned with the kids hanging on and spoke to their mother's back. "I'm going into the torture room now for some fun, then I'm heading into the shower. I'll be leaving the house in about an hour. Good evening, my dear."

8:10 pm

Dressed in what was rare for me (something other than a business suit or golf clothing), I left the house, whistling. The Toronado was clean and ready to go. I didn't know whether the Mustang Grill was a suitable spot for dinner, having never been inside before, but certainly it would be good for at least a cocktail and some conversation.

8:30 pm

Turning into the asphalt parking lot from Grand River Avenue, I spotted the blue Horizon right away. It was backed into a space a few places past the front door. I was relieved. I half expected Connie not to show up. But there she was, sitting in the driver's seat.

I pulled straight into the spot next to her so that our windows lined up. We exchanged smiles and I quickly got out of my car and opened her door for her, but she didn't move from behind the wheel. My eyes glanced involuntarily down at her long, tanned legs extending from a dark blue, quite short summer dress, then up to a concerned look on her face. "Is something wrong, sweetie?" I asked.

"Yes, there is," she said hesitantly with her hands still on the steering wheel. "I can't go in there with you, I'm … I'm not 21."

"Really?" I asked, genuinely surprised. "How'd you do it up north?"

"Oh, they don't check IDs at the Riverside," she said. "But I'm afraid to try it here."

Not about to let those legs get away from me, I said, "No big deal. We can go somewhere else, okay?"

"Okay," she said, looking hopeful. "Should I leave my car here and come with you?"

"You betcha," I said, extending a hand for hers.

Helping her get out of her car was worth the price of admission all by itself. She gave me a smile and a short kiss, then I walked her around to the other side of my car and loaded her up. I ran back to the driver's seat and hopped in.

"Any idea where we can go?" I asked without bothering to start the car. "I'm sure you're allowed into any place they serve food, whether they serve alcohol or not. I take my kids all the time."

"Yeah, I know I can get in," she said. "But I really feel like having a drink tonight."

"Well," I said after giving it some thought. "I'm not going to try to prevent that. Maybe we can take a six pack to the park along Bell Creek and watch the submarine races. Then we can go later to Denny's for breakfast."

She brightened up. "That'd be great!" she said. "It's warm enough."

"Alrighty then. We have a plan, but can I get a real hello kiss before we get going?"

8:45 pm

Ten minutes later we were heading happily down Grand River Avenue. Connie made herself at home tuning the radio to her liking. "This is a great car, Tommy V," she said. "I love it!"

I smiled in agreement. "I must admit, it looks very nice around you.

She's Got Bette Davis Eyes blared from 12 speakers as I turned onto Meadowbrook Road toward a party store I was familiar with. "What would you like to drink?" I asked Connie when we arrived at the Novi One-Stop.

"I'll drink whatever beer you like, Tom, and maybe a little peach brandy?"

"Really? You like peach brandy?"

"Yeah," she answered. "My Uncle Gary's got a giant jug of it up north. It's terrific."

I laughed, remembering that we drank half of it last Friday night. "Peach brandy it is then," I said. "And beer and munchies. I'll be right out."

I came back to the car with two six packs of Stroh's Signature, a fifth of Mohawk peach brandy, some cheese combos, and two bags of jalapeno crunchers. *Very sophisticated.* After putting the groceries into the back seat, I hopped in, stole a quick kiss, and said, "Hey, I just had an idea. I've got a new building under construction close to here. I'd like to check on a couple of things. I could show the place to you, and we could hang out there for a while if you want."

"Okay, Tommy, whatever you like. Is there a ladies' room there?"

"Sure, there is, sweetie, and it's completely stocked."

9:30 pm

Don't It Make My Brown Eyes Blue? played on the radio as I pressed the clicker to open the garage door on the side of the building. I drove the Toronado into the spacious, nearly empty shop, then closed the door behind us.

"Look!" I said excitedly. "There's our new hi-low. Well, it's not exactly new, but it's cool, no?"

Not as excited as I was, the pretty girl responded, "As far as hi-lows go, Tom, I guess it's nice. But do you know how to work it?"

275

"Of course, I do," I bragged. "I was a certified hi-low driver in the military. Would you like to go for a ride?"

"Okay," she answered hesitantly. "But there's only one seat."

I smiled wickedly and twisted my mustache like Snidely Whiplash. "Heh. Heh," I spoke. "That's what makes it so fine, my dear. You'll have to sit on my lap."

Jumping out of the Toronado, I left the girl and the brandy behind. After a few minutes of fooling around, the diesel engine roared to life. Connie was standing next to me then, looking neglected. "Ha! Ha!" I announced. "Nothing to it. Hop on up, sweetie."

Getting Connie onto my lap was even more fun than helping her out of her car. When she was in position, I lifted the forks, put the beast into forward gear, and let out the clutch. *"Yee-ha!"* I shouted with glee and drove around the shop in circles while Connie played with all the levers.

10 pm

Following the thrilling hi-low ride, I proudly showed my date around the place. The lower ceilinged front area was still just one large room – the frame walls to divide the space into offices had not yet been installed. Much of the electrical work was not completed, either. The future office area was dark except for the outdoor security lighting showing pleasantly through the two full walls of picture windows.

Connie used the ladies' room while I set up a picnic area for us on a convenient 4-foot-high stack of oak paneling which had been delivered to the shop floor. Delighted with the opportunity, I lifted the lovely gal onto the platform and took advantage of my position to secure a long, gratifying kiss. I reluctantly pulled away to open a bag of chips and a beer for each of us.

After 40 minutes, a few beers, and a quarter bottle of peach brandy, things were steaming up. We both had forgotten all about our dinner plans. Our 4-foot by 8-foot bed of wood paneling stacked in the fringe of an empty factory seemed, at that moment, like a perfectly natural location for first-time lovers.

10:45 pm

Few words were spoken as we began to kiss. The temperature seemed to have risen a hundred degrees. A bouquet of French perfume, fresh-cut lumber, and perspiration filled the air. Rod Stewart sang passionately from the Toronado's stereo.

> *"Tonight's the night.*
>
> *It's gonna be alright.*
>
> *Cuz, I love you, girl.*
>
> *Ain't nobody gonna stop us now."*

Bam! Bam! Bam!

"What's that?"

Bam! Bam! Bam!

"What's what?"

"That pounding. You'd better go see what it is, Tom," she begged.

"Fuck!" I cried. "I don't care what it is," and continued with my kiss.

She tugged at her dress and pushed me out of the way.

Bam! Bam! Bam!

"Godammit!" I said, climbing down from the altar. "Don't go away, sweetie, I'll be right back." I turned the car radio off and listened closely to hear the direction of the pounding.

Bam! Bam! Bam!

It came from the front of the building. I carefully opened the shop entrance to the front area and peeked in. Nothing!

Bam! Bam! Bam!

The sound was louder then, and it came from my left. I entered the dark room, letting the door close slowly behind me. I saw then – in the glow of the outdoor lighting – the source of the incessant pounding.

My heart sank.

~

Chapter 37   *Her View*

"I'm slicing potatoes when Tom walks in like a smart-ass and tells me to be careful with the butcher knife. He don't want me to hurt myself, he says. Then he asked me what I'm doing with all those fucking potatoes, as if he never saw me in the kitchen before," I said to my sister.

"'They're for dinner, dumbass,' I told him, 'but don't worry 'bout it, cuz you're not invited to dinner anyway.' He says, 'That's good, cuz I've got other plans for dinner, and they don't include you.' Then he laughs at me like I'm some kind of piece of shit. I coulda cut his balls off, right then and there. I shook the knife in his face and told him, 'If you're up to no good, asshole, you're gonna be sorry!' *Ha!* You should have seen the look on his face."

"Well, Nancy," Sharon said sarcastically from the other end of the phone line. "That is a very interesting story. What do you suppose the little sneak is up to?"

Watching through the kitchen windows as the kids played in the backyard, I considered my sister's question. "I don't know Sharon," I answered, "and I really don't give a shit."

Sharon huffed. "But if he's cheating on you, Nancy, don't you wanna know?"

"Cheating?" I was surprised to hear Sharon say that. I lost focus on the backyard events for a moment. "You think he's cheating on me?"

"Sure, he is," she insisted. "He said he has dinner plans, didn't he? What else could that possibly mean?"

"Oh, it's prob'ly just his stupid golfing buddies, or maybe he's going to see his dad."

"Yeah right, maybe he's going to meet some girl with big tits."

"Oh, c'mon Sharon. Tom's got it too good here to do something that stupid."

"Are you kidding me? That horndog? You cut him off months ago, didn't you? When was the last time you gave him any?"

"Well, it's been a long time," I admitted, beginning to see Sharon's point. "But still, I don't think he'd ever cheat on me."

Sharon sighed. "Oh boy, you sure don't know men very well, little sister. I'd say he's got himself a hot date tonight. You ought to follow him and find out."

"Follow him? Yeah, right … me and three kids in the Camaro. Like that'd really work."

"Okay then, I'll trail'm for ya. *Sharon Mannix Private Eye*, at your service."

"Really?" I asked. I got up from my seat and turned the heat off from the boiling water. "You'd do that?"

"Sure," Sharon answered. "What else are sisters for? Where is that bastard now, anyway?"

I glanced at the kids in the glow of the porch light, then at the kitchen clock. "He's in the shower right now, but he said he'd be leaving the house around 8 o'clock."

"Perfect, I have enough time, then. I'll park in the shadows with my lights off. He'll never notice my car. He's too stupid. Then I'll follow him. No problem."

"What if he drives all the way to Royal Oak to see his dad?"

"He won't … I guarantee it."

*****

I hung up the phone and went back to my potatoes. Dennis would be pestering me soon to eat. It was, after all, sort of late for supper. Sharon had planted the seed of doubt in me, and questions began running through my mind. *Could she be right? Tom wouldn't just throw me and the kids away like that, would he? Maybe me, but not the kids. He would never be so careless with the kids' lives; I was almost certain*. I heard the bathroom door opening and Tom came out singing like he didn't have a care in the world. It was then that I seriously began to wonder what my husband was up to.

Dennis appeared suddenly next to me. I hadn't even noticed him come into the house. "What you doin' with all those 'tatoes, Mommy?" he asked, just like he had heard his stupid father say.

I scooped up a handful of *tatoes* and plopped them into the steaming water. "I don't know, Dennis," I responded, tired of hearing the question. "Do you want butter on 'em?"

"Yeah, but what else we havin'?"

"Mrs. Paul's fish sticks and applesauce."

Dennis made a face like I was gonna poison him. "Yuck!" he said. "But can you hurry up? I'm starv'n'!" I made a face back at him and sent him off to wash his hands. I then went into the backyard to fetch Jamie and Jessica.

In the middle of our nice family meal, asshole came out of the bedroom all dressed up in clothes I'd never even seen before and smelling like English Leather, which he hadn't worn in years. Right then and there I knew Sharon might be right about him having a hot date. But still, I just couldn't believe it.

Tom, as usual, made a big dramatic show about kissing the kids goodbye. "Where ya goin' Daddy?" Dennis asked while wiping his kiss away.

"Just out with some friends," his father answered. He didn't bother to kiss me goodbye, though. Not that I gave a shit.

8:10 pm

After he left the house, I got up to spy out the kitchen window. I watched as he turned left onto Vermont Street, and sure enough a few seconds later there went Sharon, hot on his trail. *Damn,* I thought, *that woman's got balls.*

8:45 pm

It didn't take long. I didn't even have the kitchen cleaned up yet when the phone rang.

"Hi Nancy. It's private eye Mannix checking in. I've zeroed in on that bastard husband of yours."

"Really?" I asked. "Where you at?"

"I'm in a bank parking lot – in Novi, I think – at a drive-up phone on Grand River, across the street from the Mustang Grill. That's where he's at."

I had no idea where the Mustang Grill was, but it didn't really matter to me. "Who's he with, is all I wanna know?"

"I don't know, Nance. I'd have to go inside the restaurant to find out. Then he'd see me. Do you want me to do that?"

"Hell no! If he's not doin' nothin' wrong, I don't want him to know you followed him."

"Oh, I know he's doing something wrong, but I'm with you. I don't want him to see me, either."

Not knowing what else to do, I asked, "Are you coming back, then?"

"Yeah, I guess so."

"Are you hungry? I've got lots of food leftover."

"No thanks. I already ate."

"What am I gonna do with five pounds of potatoes?"

"Geez, I don't know. Cut'm up for potato salad or throw 'em out."

"I guess I'm throwing 'em out, then."

"Oooooh!" Sharon gassed.

"What? What? What?"

Sharon sounded all excited. "It's him!" she said in a loud whisper. "His car is coming out of the Mustang Grill, and he's got a girl with 'm." Louder then, *"I told you he was a cheating bastard!"*

I felt instantly sick to my stomach and angry as a hornet, but I couldn't believe it yet. "Are you sure it's him?"

"It's him alright," Sharon said quickly. "I gotta go before I lose this guy. Call you back later." Click.

*****

I sat alone in the living room trying to make sense of what seemed to be happening. *Maybe Sharon made a mistake*, I thought. *Maybe it was just one of his sisters. Maybe it was not even him…. No, it was him; Sharon wouldn't have made that kind of mistake. But why would he have done that to me? Did I deserve that, after giving him three babies? How dare he?*

I'm gonna kill him! I finally decided.

10 pm

The phone rang. "It's me," Sharon said.

"What took so fucking long?" I barked.

"Oh man. I've been traipsing all over town following your stupid-ass husband."

"Then it *was* him!" I almost choked, but I managed to ask, "Does he really have a girl with him?"

"He sure does, and she's young, and she's got big tits, and I saw him kissing her."

I squeezed the phone with all my might. I felt the veins bulge in my forehead. No sound came from my mouth as I tried to speak.

Sharon continued. "They went to a party store. He kissed her, then went in and bought a grocery bag full of booze. Then I followed him across town to his new shop … I think. Is his building behind the Holiday Inn?"

"Yeah, next to the hockey rink," I said haltingly, my voice beginning to work again.

"Yeah, that's where he drove into the building. I waited outside for 10 minutes, but they never came out. Right now, I'm at the Holiday Inn."

"Are they still inside the building?"

"I don't know, Nance. I can't see it from here, but I bet they are."

I felt a wave of panic come over me. I whispered, mostly to myself, "What do I do now?"

Sharon heard me but didn't answer for a moment. Then she said in a steely voice, "Cut his balls off, Nance, just like you said!"

I inhaled deeply through my nose, trying to gain the strength I needed to make a move, "Okay," I said, determined. "I'm coming over there right now. The kids are in bed and Mrs. Norman will babysit. I'll be there in half an hour."

Sharon seemed electrified. *"Alright,"* she said. "I'll go over to the dark spot in his parking lot and wait. If I'm not there when you arrive, it is cuz I had to follow him again."

On the drive over there, I got madder by the minute. I ranted out loud. "How can he do this to me? I haven't been the best wife, but I don't deserve this. He says repeatedly that he wants to keep our family together. *Bullshit!* And that bitch he's with … I'll kill her, too!"

10:45 pm

It was almost 11 by the time I got there. I found Sharon in her car in the shadows. "Are they still inside?" I demanded.

"I don't know, Nance, but I did *not* see them come out."

"I'm going in!" I screeched, "I'll break the fucking windows if I have to!" I turned and stomped towards the building.

"Wait for me!" Sharon said, scrambling to get out of her car.

I was stopped a few steps short of the building by music I heard. Rod Stewart, no less:

> *"You'd be a fool to stop this tide.*
>
> *Spread your wings and let me come inside."*

Running to the entrance door, I shook it hard. "Damn, it's locked!" I pounded on the door glass. *Bam! Bam! Bam!* I peered through the windows then pounded again. *Bam! Bam! Bam!* I looked around and picked up a cement block I spotted in the dirt and lifted it over my head.

"Nooooo, Nancy!" Sharon screamed.

I looked over my shoulder at my panicked sister and slammed the block to the ground. I pounded on the glass again with both fists. *Bam! Bam! Bam!* I then went to the front of the building, shaded my eyes from the lights, and tried to see through the picture windows. *Nothing!* The room was empty and dark. I pounded again. *Bam! Bam! Bam!*

The radio stopped playing and I shouted, *"They must have heard me, Sharon!"* I went back to the entrance door and pounded again. *Bam! Bam! Bam!*

A sliver of light shot into the empty room from a slowly opening door. There the little creep was, peeking in like a scaredy-cat. I pounded again, harder. *Bam! Bam! Bam!*

He stepped into the room, and I knew he could see me clearly; I was flooded with light and only 20 feet away. Before the door shut behind him, I saw the asinine look on his face.

It was priceless.

~

Chapter 38   *Mist on a River*

His View

The raging wild woman on the other side of the glass was madder than a wet cat.

Bam! Bam! Bam! she pounded. *"Open up, dammit! I saw you!"*

Oh my God, I thought, *it's my wife! What's she doing here? How the hell did she know where to find me? Does she know I have a girl here? How could she possibly know that? I must be dreaming. No ... it's a nightmare.* In the dark room I stood with hands on my head in disbelief.

Bam! Bam! Bam! The maniacal beast pounded with both fists. "Open up, Tom! I know you're in there!"

I was afraid to approach the plate glass, sure it was going to break at any minute. Slowly though, I moved into the narrow strip of outdoor lighting which was showing through the window into the building.

She dropped her fists when she first saw me and glared into my eyes. It seemed for a moment as if she were about to cry, but she caught herself quickly, and raised her fists in anger. *"Open the door!"* she shouted. *"I know you have a girl in there!"*

I responded as calmly as I could, but in a raised voice to be heard through the glass. "You don't know any such thing, Nancy. What's wrong with you?"

"Nothing's wrong with me, asshole!" she howled. "I just wanna talk to you. Now open that fucking door!"

Still calm, I answered. "No Nancy. You're going to have to leave."

She put her fists on her hips. "I'm not leaving anywhere." Then, jabbing a pointing finger on the glass, she snarled, *"Do you have a girl in there, Tom?"*

I recoiled in surprise; afraid her finger would come through the glass. I didn't speak right away – I couldn't bring myself to admit I had a girl with me. Finally, I cried, *"Why do you care, Nancy? You said you don't give a shit what I do."*

She stomped her feet in the dirt. "I *don't* give a shit what you do, asshole, *but that don't mean you can cheat on me!"*

I stretched my arms out in question and said like a lamebrain, "But it's not cheating, honey, if I have your permission."

"You don't have my fucking permission *godammit!"* she shouted. *"Now open the door!"* She lifted her fists about to attack the glass again right in my face.

"No, Nancy!" I shouted, holding up both hands.

She froze.

"If you break the glass, honey, we're gonna both get hurt, and you're gonna be in trouble. You better calm down."

She did calm down and stood silent, fidgeting and suffering, staring deeply into my soul. Her chin quivered uncontrollably.

Sick to my stomach, but not knowing what else to do, I said sadly to the mother of my children, "I gotta leave now, honey, please go home. We can talk about this later."

I backed slowly out of the light, hesitating in the darkness to survey the painful scene that I had created. She looked so very alone. Feeling like a putrid bag of shit, I retreated back into the shop.

*****

Her View

I watched him drift slowly into the darkness. Standing then alone in the light, I wiped away my tears. *"Damn!"* I said, astonished at finding my hands wet. "He saw me crying!" Right then and there I swore he'd never see me cry again.

From out of nowhere Sharon appeared and put her arm around me. "C'mon, Nancy," she said calmly. "Let's go home."

Roughly shrugging her off and stepping away, I blared, *"Go? I ain't going nowhere, dammit! There must be a back door to this fucking place somewhere. I'm gonna get in there and cut his balls off!"*

Rushing around the corner of the structure I charged through the dirt towards what looked to me like an entrance door next to the truck wells at the back of the building. "Wait for me, Nance!" Sharon called as she scampered from behind.

By the time I got to the door, I had intended to rip it off its hinges. I turned the knob and yanked with all my might. To my surprise the door was *not locked*. It flew wildly open, just missing Sharon as it slammed against the side of the building. *Bam!* The enormous sound echoed through the canyon.

A hundred feet away I saw my asshole husband jump out of his shoes. Breathing fire with clenched fists, I stormed in. The bitch on a pile of paneling tried to hide behind the little creep, but they couldn't hide from me anymore.

The chickenshit just stood there looking stupid as I barreled full steam ahead while looking for something heavy to kill him with. Finding nothing, my fists went flying as he moved at the last second to cut me off. I got a few solid hits in before he grabbed my wrists and kept me from swinging anymore.

"Let go of me, dammit!" I screamed, biting, and kicking.

"Stop it, Nance! Stop it!" he yelled as he wrapped me up and turned me around.

I struggled in his grip. "How can you do this to me, asshole? I trusted you."

"You said you didn't care about me anymore, honey. How am I supposed to know?"

"You're my husband, godammit! You're supposed to know you can't cheat on me." I stomped on his foot as hard as I could.

"Jesus Christ, Nance! What's wrong with you? *Stop it! Stop it!"*

But I wouldn't stop it; I wanted to hurt him badly. He pushed and dragged me through the shop to the open door, knocking my dumbfounded sister out of the way. With Sharon and me both outside, clear of the building, the weasel shoved me away further and ran back inside. The door slammed shut and I heard it lock.

Midnight

A half-hour later Sharon convinced me to give up and go home. It had started to rain. She loaded me into her car, leaving the Camaro behind. As we drove away, I was so filled with hate for my husband, I couldn't even look at his building.

*****

His View

7 am

The rain continued as I drove by the empty parking lot of the Mustang Grill. Traffic was very light, and because of the clouds, it was still dark. My body was bruised, and my head hurt from lack of sleep, but I was going home.

The events of the previous night were running through my mind for the hundredth time. Even though some awful things had taken place, in an odd way, I felt some encouragement.

On the cold and wet morning, for the first time in what seemed like forever, I thought that my wife cared about me. She had a damn strange way of showing it, perhaps, but nevertheless, it had come out.

She had stopped me from going too far. *Thank God, she had stopped me. Given a chance now, I was sure I could convince her it was not too late for us to save our marriage. Yes, I could convince her.*

I raced down the slick roads, torturing myself with ideas, not wanting to waste another minute. I couldn't wait to get home and make things right again. I wanted my wife back. I should have gone home last night, dammit! But I was afraid. I got myself a room and tried to sleep, but that was a hopeless endeavor.

After Nancy and Sharon had left my parking lot, I took Connie back to her car and apologized for the terrible experience she had just gone through. She gave me an understanding peck on the cheek and wished me well. "Good luck, Tommy V."

7:30 am

Driving into the neighborhood the rain was still falling, and the skies were beginning to brighten, as were my spirits. Turning from Vermont Street onto Montana, and then quickly into my driveway. I was stunned by an awful sight.

On the lawn in jumbled piles in the rain were all my belongings. I could see from the driver's seat vantage my wool suits and cotton shirts still on their hangers, obviously sopping wet. Silk ties, leather shoes, underwear – *everything* – littered the yard.

There were things I used every day, and things I had forgotten about. I saw golf clubs, gym bags, cameras, and baseball mitts. Everything was there from my closet, my dresser, my workshops in the basement and the garage. There were winter coats, summer shorts, boxes of documents, tools, and car parts. It was an enormous, waterlogged mess. I went numb, not from seeing my stuff ruined in the rain but feeling my life ending in disgrace.

The rain fell harder, as I sat with my head on the steering wheel trying to decide what to do next. The hope I had felt just one minute before had escaped me like air rushing from a released balloon. "I must have been a fool to think she still cared about me," I muttered. "She'll never, never, *never* believe a word I say."

As I pondered my fate, the windows of the Toronado steamed up to where I could no longer see what I then accepted was my former life. Finally, resigned to the chore at hand, I slowly opened the car door and stepped into the unforgiving downpour. I surveyed the disarray – my house, the yard, and the neighborhood. I saw Mrs. Norman looking from her kitchen window. A school bus passed down Vermont Street, spraying water and grinding gears.

I opened the trunk of the car and began to load the sodden remnants of my existence. When the trunk was full, I packed the back seat. Twenty minutes later, drenched and very cold, I went to retrieve the final item – a cardboard produce box that I knew to hold 30 years of my life.

Bending down with two hands to heft the soggy box, I noticed not 3 feet away, behind the sliding glass door, three pairs of undersized bare feet. My darling children intently watched their dad as I prepared to leave them. I slowly straightened up to their level, ashamed to be found out.

There they were – Dennis, Jamie, and Jessica, in perfect formation, the tallest to the shortest, from left to right. Dennis was in his too-short Spiderman pajamas with his palms and face pressed to the glass. Jamie, in a light blue nightgown and uncombed hair, wore a big, bright smile. "Hi, Daddy," she mouthed cheerfully. Jessica, having recently taken her first step, sporting nothing but a diaper and a pot belly, sucked her thumb and waved a tiny paw. As my gaze went from one child to the next, then back again, the agony in my heart grew to its bursting point.

Suddenly, Dennis stepped back from the glass, never taking his eyes off his father. In one pull, an unseen hand closed the curtain on my son. The next quick tug covered Jamie. The third devoured the baby and, like mist on a river dissipated by the heat of the sun, all that had meaning in my life receded from view.

~

About the Author

Who is Thomas Doll?

Thomas Doll is not my father's name. However, my father's mother was indeed known as Mildred Marie Doll ... at least for a short while. In March of 1922, at two years old, Mildred was adopted from the *House of Providence* in Detroit by Alfred T and Hersel Maskill. Cuddled in her loving arms, on a bus, Hersel brought Mildred home to a small frame house in Lincoln Park.

But that's another story. Perhaps my father will bring his mother's story to life someday – we'll see. Dad has always been a wonderful storyteller, but he is an exceedingly slow writer. He has been working on *Best Interest of the Children* for more than fifteen years. Instead of typing, Dad insists on hand-lettering in pencil. Then someone, namely me, must put his writings into the computer.

Also, he cannot dictate or even speak well anymore because he stammers and stutters from Parkinson's Disease, and he is getting slower and clumsier in his movements every day. Despite the challenges, he has already accumulated more than 1500 hand-lettered pages of manuscript, which he hopes someday will turn into three published books. You are holding book number one.

Best Interest of the Children aptly demonstrates the shortcomings of family courts in the 1970s and 80s and a father's struggle to stay relevant in his children's lives following divorce. It is based on real events although names have been changed to maintain anonymity. I believe you will find this story to be enlightening, heartwarming, and heartbreaking all at the same time.

Jamie Jean Doll

This sketch of my father was drawn by his art teacher at Oakland Community College in 1965.

Made in the USA
Middletown, DE
25 July 2024